Lewis Hamilton

Lewis Hamilton
A Dream Comes True

Brian Belton

First published in hardback 2007
by Pennant Books

Text copyright © Brian Belton 2007

The moral right of the author has been asserted.

British Library Cataloguing-in-Publication Data:
A catalogue record for this book is available from
The British Library

ISBN 978-1-906015-07-7

Printed and bound in Great Britain by
Clays Ltd, St Ives plc

Pictures reproduced with kind permission of PA Photos.

Pennant Books
A division of Pennant Publishing Ltd
PO Box 5675
London W1A 3FB
www.pennantbooks.com

CONTENTS

Dedication

To Adelle Scarr (nee Adriaenssens – 'Sons of the Sea')

A noble woman with a strong, kind heart and the
spirit of a Lioness.
With awesome human dignity,
In the face of cruel illness,
She remains a mother and wife
with towering care and inspiring, powerful devotion.
Our shining silver sibling still
Adored by they for whom she has always been a comforting,
welcoming,
Golden presence,
From the start.

Men driving terrorisingly fast in cars may be brave
But I have not experienced,
A soul with courage like hers.
Never beaten,
Not even retreating,
At no point has she given up ownership of her life.
She is ours,
But she belongs to herself.
Her integrity is as big as the sky,
Her smile alone lights up the darkest of nights,
Dark eyes full of passion and warmth,
Have never faded.
Depart with our deepest love our sister.
No death, no end, only life.

Author's note

Throughout this book, I have used the masculine pronoun when referring to 'drivers' purely because the main subject of the book (Lewis Hamilton) competes, as a driver, only against men and the fact that Formula One racing is exclusively a male sport in terms of competitors. This is not meant to detract from the part women play in motorsport and it is the author's sincere hope that Formula One might one day in the not too distant future give women their rightful place on the grid.

INTRODUCTION

H! young Lochinvar is come out of the west,
Through all the wide Border his steed was the best;
And save his good broadsword he weapons had none.
He rode all unarmed and he rode all alone.
So faithful in love and so dauntless in war,
There never was knight like the young Lochinvar.

From 'Lochinvar', Sir Walter Scott

The feelings of the English rookie waiting for the start of his first experience of a full Grand Prix event were pretty similar to those he had felt during all the tests he had carried out in preparation for this moment. However, at the same time it was extremely special because it was his 'baptism of speed' and the time when the veil between his dreams and reality would be drawn back; he had been in this position many times before – strapped into the great hornet of a car, with a wisp of metal separating him from the track beneath. But, oddly, the familiarity of his situation was overlaid with a powerfully stirring novelty. Not least because the ethos of the great crowd created a heady ambience as it intermingled with the floods of adrenaline that pumped through his being and the gaseous fumes of oil and fuel that hung in the strangely claustrophobic atmosphere.

The capital city of the State of Victoria provided a beautiful autumn day for the running of the 2007 Australian Grand Prix at Albert Park. It was 18 March and the gathered Formula One teams couldn't have asked for better conditions as the track was bathed in sunshine tempered by a light breeze filtering across the 5.3030km (3.3-mile) 58-lap circuit that would be hit at 68 per cent full throttle.

In 2006 the then Renault Wolf Fernando Alonso had won the event, but the lap record had been set in 2004 (1:24.125) by Michael Schumacher, who, although defeated in the previous two years by Alonso, was the ghost that haunted all those taking part and whose achievements cast a great, seemingly permanent shadow over the future. It was generally and sincerely thought that his like would not be seen again; the 'Schu' had been deified as the zenith of the sport and, as such, for many, it was all downhill from now on. The absence of the 'Cyclone from Cologne' draped a shroud of inferiority over those he had left to fight over the crown he had thrown back to them like the bones of a kill he had finished with. His greatness was hard to deny but seemingly impossible to match.

The huge Italian community in Melbourne almost guarantees a good turnout for the Grand Prix, and petrolheads, together with other sports fans, began to arrive early for the 11th running of the race since Melbourne purloined the event from South Australia.

Around 40 minutes before the competitors were called to the grid, the entertainment began in the main straight. For those who protest when Formula One is called a circus, the goings-on in front of the Fangio Stand might have been a tad embarrassing, including as they did gaudily erotic dancing girls, giant artificial bouncing kangaroos that 'kangered' around, starey-eyed with great voluminous grins, a huge banner extolling the virtues of the race's main sponsor and an ear-splitting flyover by the RAAF F/A-18s.

Before that weekend, the young McLaren-Mercedes freshman had only ever driven the circuit on his PlayStation. But, by the race day in Melbourne, he had been the fastest non-Ferrari driver in practice, despite carrying more fuel than the double World Champion Alonso, and, as such, had put himself on the second row of the grid. British Formula One Knights Jackie Stewart and Stirling Moss congratulated the 22-year-old. Moss said of his young compatriot, 'I think he's really what we need and he's shown it. I think what he did was absolutely terrific. First non-Ferrari is fairly important, let's face it. He's certainly stamped his position.'

Triple World Champion Stewart hailed the youngster as 'the best-prepared first-year Formula One driver that I've ever seen'.

Fernando Alonso, perceived by the public and media as the senior McLaren driver at the start of the 2007 season, had been second fastest overall and shared the front row of the grid with Ferrari's Kimi Räikkönen, the driver he replaced at McLaren.

The lights flashed and suddenly everything ignited into movement. The younger of the McLaren men noted that the BMWs seemed to be extremely quick off the grid. Robert Kubica switched across in front of his car and got past him. He knew there was no way he could stay on the inside, he just didn't have any room to manoeuvre, so he jinked the wheel to the left and swooped around the outside in an elegant arc, diving back to the left, to out-brake the Pole and the slow-starting Alonso, putting himself into third place. It was a bold and stunning start for the rookie, whose front wing had come very close to Nick Heidfeld's rear wing; Alonso had been watching, and had seemingly been distracted by the German on the inside. Hamilton had just gone round the reigning World Champion on the outside, an act of consummate impudence.

Alonso had not been happy in testing, and the fact that he had been obliged to follow the man regarded as his number two, who had been slightly faster than him over the winter testing, did little to alleviate his mood.

The fresh-faced newcomer had gone the long way round in what looked like an instinctive rush for the front, but he had been preparing throughout the off season for that moment. He had a steering wheel at home and had taught himself about the starts.

When he got to the grid he didn't even have to think what sequence he was going to adopt. He knew exactly what to do, when and how to do it; it was in him and of him, and the confidence that came with this knowing abolished the threat of nervousness. His audacious first corner manoeuvre had catapulted him into immediate notoriety. He had known that if he had stayed on the inside he would have come out in fifth; so he needed to go for it. He had been fortunate that Alonso was held up by Heidfeld, but fortune always plays a big part in Formula One.

The Finn on pole made an excellent start, maintaining his position at the front of the pack. Running light on fuel, he quickly pulled away from those in pursuit; the reigning World Champion found himself in fourth place.

Räikkönen got some fast laps under his belt, and went into his initial pit stop on lap 19 with a 15-second lead. Despite having hit the kerb earlier, when the force of the impact had lifted the car into the air, Hamilton had somehow managed to literally stay on track, and, at this point, he took the lead. It was an historic moment and he held on to P1 until lap 23, when he came in for his own pit stop. Räikkönen rejoined in third but soon reclaimed the front spot and opened the gap between himself and the young Brit while notching up a few fastest lap times.

On lap 42, Räikkönen moved into the pit lane for his second and final pit stop; he emerged just behind both McLarens, but within four laps he regained the lead after his Woking-based rivals took their second pit stops.

Ferocious Fernando came out of a lightning stop in the pits. But Hamilton, a few corners before his second stop, had been held behind Takuma Sato's Super Aguri; his inexperience at lapping backmarkers (although they were being blue-flagged extremely late) cost him time as did following the Japanese driver down the pit lane. Alonso took advantage and second place.

For all that, the novice made it home in third place, 18.5 seconds behind the leader – a podium in his first race. Swift, fluent and fan-friendly, this new prince of the track delighted the Melbourne crowd as the youngest winner of a podium place in Formula One history.

Niki Lauda, three-time World Champion, claimed that the youthful Briton was simply the best rookie driver he had ever seen. He eulogised, 'It was the best. I've never seen anything like this!'

McLaren CEO Martin Whitmarsh was full of praise for the manner in which the beginner had remained calm at the wheel of the great beast of a car and managed the pressure of the race, saying that no one in the McLaren set-up had any doubts about whether he could 'get the job done'. 'You start listening to him on the radio and you just think, "This is incredible"; how articulate, intelligent, insightful, the gravitas that he was commanding from the driver's seat was truly amazing.'

He went on to say that great drivers always find a little bit more and, during the weekend at Albert Park, McLaren's new young racer had been truly remarkable. According to Whitmarsh, 'We know he had absolute greatness ... it is the most impressive debut that I have ever witnessed ... I think sometimes we felt more pressure than him.'

Alonso finished in second place, crossing the line 7.2 seconds after Räikkönen, but the world's media were much more interested in the Formula One newcomer who after the race had expressed his pleasure, but his demeanour betrayed an unspoken disappointment at missing out on second place. The Japanese driver had cost him a couple of seconds but the reality was that he had lost the place because Alonso's strategy was better. The youngster had pitted earlier than the Iberian. Usually, in such a situation the engineers working with the racer stopping second would add a splash more fuel to ensure that he stayed ahead at the second stops. This didn't happen. Alonso stopped two laps later at the end of the second stint and it was those two laps that won him the place.

But the debutant had matched the two-time World Champ in a race that ranked as one of the most impressive in Formula One history. In the eight seconds that took him into the first corner, he had shown himself to be a daring and skilful, and therefore dangerous, marauder and he had made a great start. Schumacher, driving for Jordan in the 1991 Belgian Grand Prix, opened his Formula One career with a clutch problem and Alonso began his days in the top flight of racing in a Minardi with a 12th-place finish at the 2001 Australian Grand Prix. As such, the youthful Brit had every reason for being 'overwhelmed' and 'ecstatic'; smiling into the television cameras, he confessed, 'I am living the dream.'

The Nature of the Beast

There are few sporting subjects so deeply set in the human psyche as Grand Prix racing. To write about this, and Formula One in particular, is to write about the modern condition. That begs questions about personal motivation, courage and sometimes foolishness, which most people can identify with. But this focus at the same time involves both the reader and the writer in an attempt to come to terms with the most primal of our instincts and drives, albeit in a subconscious and/or approximate way.

The attempt to transfer motor racing on to the page is to be obliged to explore not only the context and the nature of a sport, but also the borders of culture, that which makes us human or better or worse people.

The process of writing this book has involved my being grasped by a puzzling, mysterious obsession, at a time when Formula One in Britain was riding on the cusp of exhilaration. Without most people being fully aware of it, interest was soaring, as a new, glorious epoch seemed to be dawning in this tumultuous and perennially precarious sport. The phenomenal and unique Michael Schumacher had just retired, but Fernando Alonso was a worthy and resolute double World Champion, a brilliant tactician with tremendous technical know-how. The ingenious Felipe Massa was rising in the firmament of the track with surprisingly dramatic consequences. There was Kimi Räikkönen, Nick Heidfeld, the super-smooth and dangerous Giancarlo Fisichella. There was the apparently immortal David Coulthard, the popular Pole Robert Kubica and Honda's talented Rubens Barrichello.

Like the legendary Schumacher, Alonso appeared to educate himself in his racing and drove with persistence of spirit, but as he started his career with McLaren he was joined by a new force. Although more than a decade in preparation, Lewis Hamilton seemed to arrive in a rush of glory: starting his Formula One journey in public triumph and carrying a golden thread of success throughout the first half of his initial season at the summit of motorsport.

Much has changed in Formula One since the time British drivers and cars could match the best the world had to offer, and the idea of a British World Champion was as faded as racing green. The rewards for just getting to Formula One standard and dipping a toe in are now enormous. The sport has gone through crises; its best practitioners no less than its more mediocre participants have been questioned in terms of talent and honour. Threats to the very existence of the category have been whispered, resentment has been stimulated, analytical editorials have been published in their shoals, compromises continue to be made, drivers bend and resist the will of manufacturers and both seem to be involved in rebellious variance under the gaze of the sports authorities.

Over the last decade or so, that special race that manifests skill, courage, intelligence and hope, seeming to redeem the whole extravaganza, had become something of a rarity. But there was a shift in 2007. It was more than a response to technical tinkerings and had little to do with the likes of Bernie Ecclestone and Max Mosley. Without reservation, humanity's most vividly primitive yet technologically advanced sport, one which has huge potential for self-destruction while demanding the most of what we are, rediscovered itself. This is not the first time this has happened and, for some of us, the enduring fascination of Formula One emanates from its ability to do this. Lewis Hamilton is the personification of this latest resurrection. He epitomises the future of the sport, both challenging and praising its history by his charisma and physical capacity simply to win.

At the start of the 2007 Formula One season, Hamilton was

thought of as the 'boy racer' of the Grand Prix circuit; a rookie with potential and a record to make him a 'name for the future'. But in the space of a few months in 2007 he had become almost legendary even before there was a myth to define him. With his virtuous looks and in his predominantly white racing attire, he was reminiscent of a saviour angel that has zoomed out of the clouds to rescue the sport from itself. And never has the collective will of a packed 95,000 crowd, the tangible desire of a sporting audience, been more powerfully expressed than it was on 8 July 2007 at Silverstone. The overwhelming wish for Lewis to fulfil the collective dream was something that had to be felt to be understood and there are no words to paint that exuberant momentum. With his much-publicised brief but glorious CV as a Grand Prix driver preceding him, a great avalanche of expectation hovered above the young rising star as the 'new hope' of motorsport in Britain and the world; everything about this man was new and never was newness more needed.

Those who really understand the depth and breadth of the commitment and strength of character that Formula One demands are a very small circle, but most have some idea of the incredible self-belief and sacrifice it takes to push to the top of the Grand Prix elite. This being the case, in today's wannabe culture there are precious few role models like Lewis Hamilton. Yet you would have been hard pressed to find his name outside specialist journals before, authoritatively, from the front, he triumphed in the first GP2 race at Silverstone. He also won the second heat in that event with a remarkable drive from eighth on the grid (including a dramatic and enthralling double pass for second in the Becketts complex). Now it seems his name and handsome face are everywhere. The mainstream press appear to have guaranteed him a place alongside the likes of Wayne Rooney and Andy Murray as sportsmen most likely to succeed, and have been touting him as a possible champion from as early as the conclusion of his first Grand Prix. For British involvement in Formula One, his achievements seem to have more than made up for Jenson Button's failure to live up to expectation and David Coulthard's seeming demise.

But the truth is that, while we certainly have strong evidence of Hamilton's ability, he has had a number of advantages – for instance, his association with the mighty ART team – that will not, however, be relevant on the battlegrounds of Formula One. But Sir Stirling Moss describes Hamilton, an articulate and charismatic young man, as 'the most impressive upcoming driver I've seen in a long while. He has the car control and he has the calmness when he is driving but he is also a fighter and has a great manner about him.'

It's not just Lewis's driving ability that causes him to stand out; his bright-yellow helmet also makes him hard to miss. He explained how this goes back to his days racing karts: 'Dad wanted me to have a bright-coloured helmet because he was so nervous when I was on the track. When there's 30 guys going round, you don't know who's who. With yellow, he was able to spot me half a mile away!'

Lewis reminds those of us with long enough memories or familiarity with Formula One history of the young Sterling Moss. But, although he took part in some spectacular races, the man who tore up the tracks with the likes of Juan Manuel Fangio, Mike Hawthorn, Jack Brabham and Phil Hill never became World Champion. However, like Moss in the upward trajectory of his career, Lewis suggests a rare type of disciplined belligerence only symbolically contained within the track environment, with its pits, its mechanics and technicians, its meticulously observed rules, regulations, customs, rites and rituals. Like Moss, Hamilton has the power to electrify crowds, causing them to express the impulse and appetite not merely for raw daring and the mysterious will to pass the other man that burns, for better or worse, in the human soul, but also for suggesting the incontrovertible honesty of such an instinct.

But there is also a nurturing side to the man; Lewis displays a deep understanding of where he has come from and empathy for those about to start out on the path he has trodden. As patron of the British Racing Drivers' Club (BRDC) 'Stars of Tomorrow'

Championship, at its launch in March 2006, he said it was great for him to be part of the scheme and see young kids coming through as he once did. He recalled that when he was involved in karting he and his peers looked up to people that had moved on from karts. However, he saw his involvement with the BRDC and his sponsoring of one of the series as a way of putting something back into karting. He told his audience that he was conscious of the expensive nature of the sport and the fact there were so many people trying to get involved. He saw the BRDC giving these young drivers an opportunity and said that he hoped the series would inspire them to work hard and follow him into bigger things.

Lewis's presence at the launch, and his support of young karters, not only shows how he values his sporting roots and commitment to those who will follow him, but, without really meaning to, it is also evidence of a new spirit he has brought to the realm of Formula One, which draws a different constituency of followers to the sport that has the potential to change the character of motorsport in Britain and beyond.

This is just one of a number of gifts Hamilton has brought to Formula One; others include a way of driving that brings all the intricate skills of karting into a different dimension, a sense of fearlessness and daring that uniquely among his contemporaries is mediated by a cool, self-confident calculated intelligence.

Then there is his colour. Although as he prepared for his Formula One debut Lewis said, 'It will be good for the sport to have a black driver, because it will make people realise you don't have to be white and affluent to make it,' he and his backers in McLaren seem to have consistently sought not to emphasise Lewis's ethnic or racial background. However, it cannot be denied that he has broken a barrier in motorsport, the existence of which has been more a subject of avoidance than analysis. While there have been numerous books written about the advances of black people in other sports, most predominantly football and boxing, and endless dissertations, papers, theses and studies about prejudice and discrimination, including masses of work on baseball, athletics and cricket, motorsport in general and Formula One in particular have to a great extent escaped scrutiny, even though black competitors are noticeable mostly by their absence.

Throughout the world, black people are associated with sporting excellence; the top performers in gridiron football, soccer, boxing and athletics are so often men and women of African descent. But, in sports which require expensive equipment or investment such as equestrian events, winter sports or sailing, the same success is not replicated. There are exceptions in the British context, for example, Oliver Skeete in show jumping and Tony Nash in bobsleigh, but these individuals prove the rule rather than break the mould.

Like hockey, gymnastics and swimming, motorsport is an arena of competition not traditionally indulged in by black people. There have been as many excuses as reasons offered for this, but those least convincing refer to 'physical types'.

Motor racing has not identified a reason or an excuse why so few black people have been involved in the sport. It has been said that the answer to the begged-for question has not been given because the enquiry has not been made with any real force, but it is more likely that past queries have just not been heard. It has been claimed that Formula One is evidently the most non-racial of sports, but this assertion doesn't really convince when one looks for confirmation. Of course, what complicates the issue is that there is no evidence of *active* racism in the organisation of competition or participation, but that could be said of many institutions in Europe and America wherein the participation of black people is uncommon. As always, a lack of evidence does not prove innocence, it just fails to demonstrate guilt.

Whatever one's conclusions, although he looks completely at home in the gleaming boardroom at McLaren's Surrey headquarters, leaning on one of the pillars of Norman Foster's floating white masterpiece, in 2007 Lewis Hamilton was the first black driver to take a seat in Formula One for some time. There were many other 'firsts' he would claim that season. However, he is not the first person of colour to compete in the World Championship. Narain Karthikeyan, who in 2005 became the first Indian to race in Formula One (with Jordan) and who is currently a test driver for the Williams team, has that distinction. Indeed, there has been Asian representation in the sport since the Championship started in 1950. But Africa is not represented in Formula One and the Arab World has only one race (Bahrain).

This said, it has been some time since the first (and last before Lewis) driver of African descent took the wheel of a Formula One car. Willy T Ribbs tested for Brabham at Estoril in January 1986. He was once asked how he felt turning up at a NASCAR event as the only black driver. The Californian replied, 'This is about racing, not race.'

Willy went on to be the first black driver to start the Indianapolis 500. Years later, he said, 'I never considered myself a black race driver. I considered myself a race driver. Period.'

Looking at Hamilton's attitude to his colour and his sport, it is a good bet that he would wholeheartedly endorse the attitude Ribbs expressed two decades ago. For him the tone of his skin is 'clearly not why I'm in this position'. Given his record, there is no arguing with that.

For all this, historically Formula One has not provided much in the way of opportunity for participation outside a comparatively small section of relatively wealthy Europeans and the odd rich Brazilian. Although in the current generation some drivers have come from relatively humble roots, for those with ambitions to become a participant in the world of Formula One being born outside European heritage is a disadvantage. Even the inclusion of Australians and Americans has been relatively recent. To make the breakthrough as a driver in Formula One, it has been a covert but concrete requirement to know about racing in Europe. If evidence of this is needed, one only needs to look back to as recently as May 2006 and the case of the fast Japanese driver Yuji Ide; his various shunts demonstrated that he was just not able to learn what he needed to in the short time a driver is given to prove himself.

Formula One has traditionally been an inward-looking environment and people involved have often become closed, enveloped in what can be a world of its own. This can limit perspectives to the confines of the paddock. To break into this domain, a driver has to produce something extraordinary; Lewis Hamilton did this and as such didn't wait to be noticed but insisted on the attention of participants – fans, constructors, fellow drivers, the media and organisers – by the exertion of his ability. But to a certain extent it was something he could not do anything but express. He has admitted that he doesn't know what it is that makes him so good at what he does and that he just believes that, if there's one thing he's meant to do really well, it's racing. He has claimed that he is motivated by a desire to be the best at whatever he decides to put his mind to and that, once he has decided to take up a challenge, his inner self will not let him give up unless he achieves his goal. He went on, 'I love motor racing and I have done so since I first watched it on TV when I was about five. The key element in all of this is that I am not here to take part, I am here to win, and I will do whatever mentally and physically it takes to achieve that in due course. I do not plan to waste this opportunity.'

It is an inescapable fact of the globalisation of sport that Formula One must feature black, white, Chinese and Asian drivers as a matter of course if it is to be recognised as a truly major phenomenon on a planetary level. As such, it is hard to avoid the conclusion, albeit by accident or default, that Lewis is a pioneer of such inclusion that might allow Formula One to enter a new dimension. For so many young people around the world, Hamilton standing on the podium at the apex of motorsport makes him more than a role-model or a breaker of stereotypes; he towers above the track as an archetype, paradigmatic of the claim 'it is possible'. In 1968, Tommie Smith and John Carlos did much the same thing via an emotive outburst of righteous anger. Although a brave, open attack on the system, the clenched fists they raised on the Olympic stage caused them to be banished from the world view and as such made them anonymous to most of those they looked to influence and inform. This meant that their noble, justified and courageous contribution took generations to incubate, but even today their names only resonate among scholars of black sporting and social history. The impact Lewis has made, and will make, is likely to be of a different order and provoke unprecedented change at a rate that is likely to match the speed he has achieved on the great racing circuits of the world.

All this might not convince you that Lewis Hamilton is a one-man revolution, but his impact on Formula One racing and its community has been profound and it is clear that his success means that the spectacle that is Grand Prix racing can never be the same. His part in his sport's transformation has been achieved with the same calm and focused energy that first brought him into the heady universe of motorsport.

Hamilton remains the youngest driver ever to be signed by a Formula One team. But he is very mature for his age and comes across as a thoughtful and insightful person. Looking at his own demeanour, he has said that, since he was 10 he has been at the race track every weekend. He wasn't hanging out and doing stuff with his friends. He was with his dad and so he had to be best friends with his father. For Lewis, 'You want to fit in and mix with the grown-ups … you have to learn at a faster pace than other kids. It is tough growing up and missing your childhood, because you never get it back, but if I make it I can have all the toys that I want!'

Above all, Lewis comes across as a genuinely pleasant person. When he was questioned about his respect for other drivers shortly before his first race in Formula One, he told how he and Nico Rosberg had been team-mates for two years and that they had and still have a fantastic relationship; going everywhere together, they were like brothers. For Hamilton, that type of rapport generates respect. He also reflected on his admiration for Robert Kubica: 'I did not have too many wheel-to-wheel races with Nico but I have had some extremely exciting races with Kubica. He is one of the best drivers and I think one day he will be a World Champion.'

Lewis recognised that his style and technique was different from Kubica's and Rosberg's, but that Kubica seemed to be able to pull out extremely quick laps. 'But then he used to blow his engines all the time! Nico and I would be up the front and consistent. I think we all have the potential to race in Formula One and to be World Champions.'

But, after being pressed about his ability in comparison to his racing colleagues, he replied, 'I am not the sort of driver to answer that question.'

That response shows his wisdom and modesty: the driving will speak for itself.

A cursory sweep of the present sporting landscape fails to throw up a figure who might be usefully compared with Lewis. Even Wayne Rooney started on the bench. World champion swimmer Michael Phelps is a year younger than Hamilton, but many seasons more experienced. The same applies to Rafael Nadal, who burst into tennis with the physical persona of a muscular man-boy.

Hamilton is still just 22; he looks to the future with the same calmness and focus that have made him the most talked-about figure certainly in motorsport and probably across the horizon of sport in general.

At the BRDC 'Stars of Tomorrow' Championship launch in 2006, talking about the young drivers taking part in the round of the Championship in Belgium, Lewis was conscious of the importance of young people experiencing different and foreign environments, and warned of what a 'big culture shock' it can be for them to travel and race overseas 'going to a different track, different climate and possibly racing against some new, different drivers. It's just a great experience. Kids, when they are at a young age, need to experience as much as possible and it helps them become a better person ... a better driver in the future.'

The emphasis Hamilton puts on confronting difference and

accommodating it, becoming part of it and thus overcoming it, seeing this as making us 'better' people, is poignant. Lewis has had a powerful hand in making his own world for himself. In the process he has changed and is changing the world, smashing through and effectively destroying barriers that he regards with the most forceful form of disdain possible; he all but ignores them, seeing them as just a part of what makes him stronger. His most potent weapon in this cause has been his focus on what he wants and his belief in himself.

A Society of Speed

Human groups evolve into a society. A nation might be seen as a big group, while the local kart track is generally populated by one or more small groups. But all groups, to remain in a grouping, need structure and they will evolve hierarchies, rules, rites, rituals, customs, traditions and regulations. Motor racing, and specifically Grand Prix racing, which started in 1906, has all these elements. Its hierarchy emanates from the governing body, the Fédération Internationale de l'Automobile (FIA), which regulates the sport, and Bernie Ecclestone's Formula One Constructors Association (FOCA), which was founded to foster the continued commercialisation of the sport. It is within this 'society' that the drivers operate and to a certain extent it makes them what they are, but in many ways they are sportspeople like any others.

Drivers are not as different from other sportspeople as their demeanour and conduct might make them seem. They are just the same as a golfer or a swimmer in many ways. However, Formula One racing is immersed in profuse quantities and a unique variety of hype and imbued with massive financial interests. In the history of the sport, not a few drivers have succumbed to the glamour and publicity that makes them appear to be something between a Greek god and any one of a plethora of cinema super-heroes. In this process they can lose their own identity and integrity and become Frankenstein-type creations, as they take on the persona that the media has generated for them, at the cost of the qualities that took them to the highest echelons of motorsport in the first place.

But there are those that remain comparatively untouched by the sensational organised chaos that surrounds them. They develop a veneer of detachment and concentration that is founded on the aim to get themselves as far up the field as their nerve, talent and luck can take them. But, whatever a driver's situation or disposition, as the minutes tick down to the next race, the racer sits alone in his car – it comes down to just him and his equipment; whatever happens is going to happen to him and him alone. Aspects of this condition might equally apply to the shot putter or tennis player at that moment when they begin a performance, looking to achieve a feat, a result. But the tool used by the tribe that has included Fangio, Moss and Lauda, a massively complex and in many ways monstrous apparatus, place the rawness of the human frame in a machine that has the potential to totally destroy that relatively frail structure; to leave nothing but vapour. It is this inescapable vulnerability that makes Grand Prix drivers become different from everybody else, infected as they are by their environment and purpose.

The milieu of Formula One is subject to strict control, precision measurement and dense scientific endeavour but this at the same time is the canvas on which cavalcades of pure fantasy are laid; a world that is guided by facts, statistics and real naked danger is engulfed in clouds of wishes, desires and dreams.

This is now the habitat that Lewis Hamilton occupies and what follows might be understood as his journey to and through this place where the ephemeral reveries of the mind meet the iron-hard realism on the very periphery of life and death.

Although now being hailed as a saviour of British motor racing and of Formula One in general, no one can say what will become of Hamilton over the next few years. Julian Bailey, who with Lotus and Tyrrell in Formula One between 1988 and 1991 mustered just seven races and only one point, like Hamilton, came from a working-class background. But Bailey, unlike his class and competitive contemporary Romford boy Johnny Herbert, hit a psychological wall. Coming from a council house in Woolwich, Bailey felt inferior and/or out of place practically from the start. Almost anything can kill you in Formula One: your own mind, the car, the track, your competitors. Everything is a test of who you are and what you are and it is only the strength of your own direction that will take you through in the end.

What follows tracks the path Hamilton has trodden and his burning philosophy that is etched on the world by his faith in his own ability. It is hoped that the reader will learn their own lessons from the tale of a person who is in the process of becoming a legend. Lewis Hamilton races to win, plain and simple, but in that and all that surrounds that fact are the reasons and purpose for taking part in and watching sport; we can become more than what we were by it and through it – unless this happens, Formula One racing – in fact, any sport – has no lasting purpose.

Lewis may well have his bad times to come, and in 2007 at the British and then the European Grand Prix he had a taste of what those feel like in the Formula One milieu; as a society we like to see our heroes humbled or at least proved to be human. In Formula One, a failure of one sort or another is as inevitable as death and taxes. Then again, in his case, maybe not.

BLACK PLATES

The hearts of his enemies were struck with terror at the
  news of his advent.
He never ceased to encounter them at every battle.
Always taken care of by an affectionate father
The hearts of the enemies flew into terror (due to their) prowess.
Even if a lion meets him in its den it begins to fear.
From Qasidah Burdah

Sepang

In Australia, Lewis Hamilton had achieved the best Formula One
debut since Jacques Joseph Charles Villeneuve in 1996, but Lewis's
achievement was much more impressive as the Québécois had acres of
experience with big powerful cars when he took the Williams to
second place in Melbourne's first Formula One Grand Prix. The third
place at Albert Park was certainly the best British debut performance
in a Grand Prix since Mike Parkes, the tall, aristocratic-looking
automotive consultant, was runner-up driving a Ferrari in the French
Grand Prix at Reims in 1966, after John Surtees had left the Scuderia.
Reims had seen the most successful Formula One debut in history
achieved by the Italian Giancarlo Baghetti in a shark-nosed Ferrari. He
had won his first race in the same event five years previously. Parkes's

Formula One career was cut short by an accident at Spa in 1967 but his prowess as a racer was the stuff of myth, as was his career as a car designer and engineer before he was tragically killed in a crash during a storm on an Italian autoroute in 1977.

Of the other British Grand Prix first-timers Lewis had matched Peter Arundell's third place in a Lotus at Monaco in 1964 and outshone Innes Ireland and Vic Elford who both finished fourth on their initial races.

However, in Australia, Hamilton had stated, 'To me, as a driver, finishing third has not really made much difference.'

Following Lewis's triumphant start to his Formula One career, his father smiled as he told the world, 'Formula One had better watch out … All those years in karting paid off in that first corner.'

It was true that his son had thrown down the gauntlet and indeed Lewis had manoeuvred his car as if it had been a kart and he again just a kid on the grid at Playscape, the SW16 kindergarten of karting.

On the Monday after his first Grand Prix, Lewis set out on one of the great journeys of his life: a road trip around Australia with his fellow rookie, the Spyker Formula One driver (and accomplished pianist, who goes to bed listening to Beethoven) Adrian Sutil, still buzzing from the extraordinary third-place finish in Melbourne 24 hours earlier. Before leaving, he told how it was his dream to win the World Championship: 'That's my target, whether it takes me two or three or four years. It's my goal.'

Vodafone, his McLaren-Mercedes team's title sponsors, were already in advanced talks over a private deal which had the potential to make Lewis one of the world's highest-paid sportspersons, vying with Tiger Woods and David Beckham.

But, moments after that historic Sunday race, Hamilton's first concern was to telephone his half-brother Nicholas.

McLaren's Martin Whitmarsh had nothing but praise for the way Lewis had managed the race and the maturity he had shown in the process: 'This was the first appearance in the 57-year history of the Formula One World Championship of a black racing driver, a young man who was coming on to the grid with a huge reputation from the junior ranks. The scrutiny was immense. He dealt with all the issues.'

After his tour down-under, Hamilton moved on to Thailand with Sutil for some rest and recreation before the start of testing at Sepang, the venue for the Malaysian Grand Prix. He certainly would have needed a break. It is hard to tell anyone who hasn't experienced it what it is like to manage the forces the mind and body cope with during an extended period of time spent in a Formula One car under race conditions. In Lewis's own words, 'I finish every race with a black ...' He paused and, with a little smile, went on, '... a *darker* line down my side where I've been pushed against the seat.'

But he was as optimistic and confident as ever looking forward to his next challenge. However, ITV Formula One pundit Martin Brundle warned, 'It's going to be a long haul for Lewis and there are a number of things he has yet to face – his first big shunt, for instance, and all the travel, which can be pretty wearying.'

However, the former McLaren driver was more than hopeful for the young British racer: 'All the ingredients are there. He excites me. Will he be up there one day with the likes of Prost, Senna and Schumacher? He's got a chance, definitely.'

The International Circuit, Sepang, hosted its ninth Malaysian Grand Prix on Sunday, 8 April 2007. Recognised as the toughest race of the year with the oppressive humidity and 60°C temperatures, it is the supreme test of fitness for those taking part and drivers really feel the full impact of the ordeal when they get out of the car. During the race, a driver can take on fresh water supplies every five or six laps, but this is hardly sufficient; as Fernando Alonso put it, 'After 10 laps it's like tea ... It's 60-degree water! I didn't want to drink it! Drinking it was not a pleasure.'

But, even before the race, the drivers and crew were dripping with sweat. Track temperatures were above 135°F.

Sepang, however, is a real racer's circuit, where qualifying is always difficult, but it was particularly tough that second weekend in

April because a soft tyre wasn't lasting a whole lap for everybody, although it did for Felipe Massa and he took pole for the fourth time in seven races.

In the Grand Prix, drivers would race at 70 per cent full throttle round the 5.543km (3.4-mile) 56-lap circuit. The lap record of 1:34.223 was set in 2004 by Juan Pablo Montoya and the event was won in 2006 by Giancarlo Fisichella for Renault.

Sepang features a number of slow corners, two lengthy high-speed straights and a right-hander that feels like it goes on for an age, generating G-forces that can cause a driver's neck to ache just contemplating it.

Turn four is a testing, uphill, bumpy braking zone. Hamilton would hit it at 190mph but plummet down to 70mph by the apex. If most racers survived turns one, two and three, they would be tightly packed going into that fourth and made to deal with all the incidents that might entail. Kimi Räikkönen certainly found out about these in 2006 when he was tagged on the apex and crashed in turn five with suspension failure; most drivers believe they can really attack turn four, but, if they get it even slightly wrong on the top of the bend, they can drift wide and lose time on the grass.

The race day began with a clear track; after heavy rain the night before, the entire surface had been cleaned and any rubber that had been laid down following the practice and qualifying was gone. This meant that in the early stages of the race there would be a little less grip.

Most of the front runners chose to start with the softer tyre, and this seemed to be the choice for most of the race. Although the striped tyres wear faster, something that was soon to be noted on Hamilton's McLaren, which handled hard before his first pit stop, they laid down rubber and provided much-needed grip.

Alonso was alongside Massa on the front row while Räikkönen and Hamilton made up row two; two Ferraris on the right, two McLarens on the left – the perfect positioning for the neutral spectator.

The start saw Fernando Alonso overtake Felipe Massa and grab the lead before the first corner, putting two Ferraris between him and

Hamilton, something Lewis was not going to settle for. From the off he had tucked in behind Räikkönen and, although he had started at the same pace as all the cars around him, after feigning an overtake on Räikkönen, he passed the fast Finn on the opposite side.

Now with the scent of blood in his nostrils Hamilton looked at Massa and immediately took him on the inside of the first corner and held the position; at that point McLaren had captured the front two places. The Brit had taken a big risk going round on the outside, but the previous night he had studied half a dozen starts on video and had learned well; he had pulled his start off beautifully and bravely, although not getting away as well as he might.

This said, dealing with two Ferraris in two corners showed Lewis's qualities and set the standard for the race. Massa had been focusing so closely on Alonso he hadn't noticed Hamilton, but for all that the Brazilian should have kept Lewis at bay; the young man had embarrassed the São Paulo pulsar and would cause him to become over-anxious to the point of making a string of mistakes.

This opening performance by the British driver was even more impressive when it was understood that he was carrying difficulties right up to his first pit stop; he needed front-wing changes to allow him to step up his pace. At that stage, though, he was going slowly compared to Alonso, yet he continued to keep the two Ferraris behind him.

Massa tried to overtake Lewis twice; on one occasion he was almost past him on the outside but Hamilton made good his reclaim of the place. On Massa's second attempt, the Brit handled the Ferrari man with massive poise. He *knew* the Brazilian would be slip-streaming him to turn four (the strong overtaking corner). Lewis moved over, but not too far to compromise his exit. Massa dived but Hamilton had anticipated that and tried to brake as late as possible, looking to out-brake his pursuer, but Massa braked even later than Lewis and the 'Herts Hero' was able to get his car into the corner while Massa was still travelling in a straight line.

Massa had managed to move beyond the Englishman, but had

braked too late and ended up off the track, losing five seconds and dropping a couple of places, at the same time allowing Räikkönen to take over the battle. After the race Lewis commented on the battle between himself and the Brazilian: 'Felipe had a couple of moves to try and pass me, but, unfortunately, I was able to trick him into out-braking himself and then I was very fortunate to cut across and get in front of him again.' He smiled. 'And then he went off and I apologise for that.'

Hamilton's driving had been supreme; he seemed totally immune to Massa's and Räikkönen's attempts to pressurise him and managed to hold them both off. Alonso claimed his first victory since leaving Renault for McLaren. The Spaniard crossed the line more than 17 seconds ahead of Hamilton, but it had been Lewis who had won the race for the team, acting as a dam against the combined assault of the two Ferraris throughout the race. After the race, Lewis told how 'defending is 10 times harder than trying to pass someone ... Seeing two Ferraris behind you, knowing they are slightly lighter and quicker than you ... it was very difficult to keep them behind ... To have two Ferraris behind you is definitely what we want but I probably don't want them to be that close to me next time, because, I'm telling you, it was so hard to keep them behind ... but eventually once they pitted I could relax a little bit, but I still had to push. I'm really happy I got the fastest lap of the race so I couldn't be happier.'

Shortly after crossing the line, Lewis announced on his radio, 'I wanna win ... doesn't matter if it's not the next race, but sometime this year I'm gonna have one!'

But Lewis had driven like a veteran and now had the distinction of leading both Grands Prix he had raced in. All the drivers were pushed to their physical limits by the sweltering conditions but the heat had really taken its toll on Hamilton in the closing stages of the race when he was coming under severe pressure from Räikkönen. He declared the race the most difficult he had ever contested, telling how it had been 'incredibly hard in the car ... I had to dig deep and preserve what energy I had left ... I ran out of water and it was so tricky and it got hotter and hotter. I just kept pushing and concentrating on making no mistakes.'

Hamilton had worked like a Trojan to make sure he was fit enough for this race and had taken on liquids all day to fend off dehydration. But in the last stage of the race he had been obliged to cope with raging thirst as the whole of his being fought to keep the Ferraris back.

It was McLaren's first race victory since October 2005 and, as the drivers walked away from their cars, Ron Dennis, the Vodafone McLaren-Mercedes team principal, embraced both his racers but there was a slightly longer, closer hug for Hamilton.

For Lewis's father, Anthony, his son had given him an 'absolutely proud moment – he felt good this morning again [he smiles] and I knew we were going to be in trouble ... It was all a matter of just getting round the first couple of bends and keeping the car on the circuit and, to be quite honest, had he finished fourth today I'd have been absolutely happy. He believes in himself totally and is just so determined. It was absolutely cool the way he got round the Ferrari and held them off – that's the thing with Lewis, he is not easy to fluster; in fact, I don't think you can fluster him at all, because he mentally prepares himself and I think what he was thinking about was how to get first place. Lewis is still a feet-on-the-ground kind and when he gets back home he just won't believe what's going on, but for now he's happy, missing his brother Nicholas and missing some home cooking, and he's looking forward to getting back after Bahrain.'

Lewis had got under the Ferrari at the start. He had destroyed their tactics and well-laid plans, working his tyres overtime. In the process he had frustrated Massa to the point of provoking the Brazilian into effectively throwing the race. At the same time Lewis had manufactured events to produce McLaren's first one-two since Brazil 2005. On top of all that on the 22nd lap he had claimed the fastest circuit of the race: 1:36.701 (128.249mph).

Lewis admitted, 'I didn't really expect to be on the podium in the first two races.'

However, in doing so, he equalled the achievement of Ilford's Peter Arundell, who was the last Briton to achieve two podiums in his first two races, but Arundell had the advantage of some competitive experience at Formula One before his Championship exploits. In 1963, he competed in non-Championship Formula One races with Team Lotus after Trevor Taylor was injured in a spectacular crash in the non-Championship Mediterranean Grand Prix at Enna. Arundell had made his Championship Grand Prix debut the following year after Taylor was dropped. Life as Jim Clark's team-mate was not easy, but, having finished third on his debut at Monaco, he repeated the performance at the Dutch Grand Prix two weeks later. He overheated his car in his next race at the Belgian Grand Prix and came in ninth. So, in fact, Lewis's performance in his first two Grands Prix had actually bettered the Essex racer's 43-year record, having achieved third- and second-place finishes.

Hamilton's preparation had stood him in good stead and, while he might have been modest in much of his summing up of his weekend, he said of Sepang, 'I have not found myself coming here and going, "Wow, I was not expecting that." Everything went to plan.'

Herts Heartlands

In 1999, in a television interview, Lewis Hamilton represented the future of British motor racing alongside the sport's then current British hope David Coulthard. The interviewer asked Coulthard, 'So this is a lad with promise, do you think?'

The Scot responded immediately, 'Oh, definitely. Lewis has a better record in karting than I ever achieved and I expect we'll be seeing him in Formula One in the future.'

The interviewer then turned to the 14-year-old. 'So, 21st century, you've got hopes, have you?'

Lewis answered, in clear confident tones, with the broad smile of self-assurance on his face, 'Yes, yes, hopefully coming to take David's place.'

Coulthard's uncomfortable half-smile and fixed gaze on the middle distance told its own story. Even then it was pretty obvious Hamilton meant what he said and was building a reputation to back his words.

Named after the famed American Olympic sprinter and long jumper Carl Lewis, Lewis Carl Hamilton was born on 7 January 1985 in Stevenage, where he started life in a council house. About six years ago, along with his father Anthony, stepmother Linda, 43, and younger (by seven years) half-brother Nicholas (Anthony and Linda's son), he moved to Tewin (aka Tewin Wood), a small Hertfordshire village between Welwyn Garden City and Stevenage. Before the Hamiltons moved in, the most exciting weekly event in Tewin was the guided walk around the village. The Hamiltons' £1 million mansion does not appear on the itinerary (at the time of writing anyway).

Tewin has most of the features typical of English country villages: a church, a village green, a couple of pubs, a red telephone box, a shop and a post office serve the population of about 2,500. Some of its inhabitants work locally, but many commute to London each day. The village has a history that dates back to at least Anglo-Saxon times (its name has its origins in Anglo-Saxon English) and is set in a superb rural landscape that retains many features characteristic of ancient countryside and supports a rich variety of wildlife.

Lewis's paternal grandparents came to Britain from Grenada with their three-year-old son Anthony. Lewis's grandfather found work with British Rail and the family settled in West London.

Anthony is a focused, intelligent, resourceful and ambitious individual (qualities it seems his son has inherited) and a devoted father. As a young man, he followed his father and became a British Rail employee, working as a clerk. But he sought to advance himself by studying at night school before establishing his own IT consultancy in London and was successful enough to move his family out to the leafy, prosperous suburbs of Hertfordshire (when he sold the company late in 2006, it had a workforce of 25 people and achieved a multi-million-pound turnover). This demonstrated the intense work ethic and self-discipline that seems to have been passed on to Lewis. Anthony's maxims have always been 'preparation' and 'diligence' and he leaves nothing to chance.

Anthony's only experience of motorsport before his son's success was watching Keke Rosberg winning the Formula One Championship in 1982, but he has long been the engine of Lewis's ambition: 'You soon get to learn that it isn't just about arriving and driving. There wasn't that much money around at that time [when Lewis first started kart racing] so I had to go out and try and get sponsors or try to get people interested.'

While Lewis understands that he has inherited a lot of his father's qualities, he is also conscious of his mother's contribution to his character: 'A lot of my personality comes from my mum. It's a real half and half.'

Lewis's mother, Carmen Lockhart, 51, a healthcare worker, split from 47-year-old Anthony when Lewis was two years old. He was her third child (Lewis has two older half-sisters, Nicola Hewitt, 31, and Samantha Shickle). After the separation, Lewis lived with his mother in an end-of-terrace house on the Shephall estate.

Carmen has told how she believed Anthony's all-embracing ambition for their son had been the factor that ended their marriage. Although the couple broke up when Lewis was just two, well before he developed any kind of interest in racing, she told of how her ex-husband's drive to help Lewis make the most of his abilities and the hectic lifestyle this involved was not for her.

Carmen is sure that Lewis has not been damaged by the experience of his parents' separation and that the break-up was probably better for him in the long run than having to endure his parents' unhappy marriage. However, she feels that maybe during his school years he might have wished he had a mum and dad who were together. But she sees Lewis as the best thing to come out of her marriage to Anthony and emphasises that her son was very special to her because she and Anthony had tried for a long time to have him.

Carmen saw that Anthony wanted to 'be somebody' but all she desired was a quiet life and that put a barrier between them, although she chose not to be an obstacle to her husband's efforts to make sure Lewis got what he wanted. She recognised how hard Anthony had worked to raise the money for Lewis's career and that, without his constant effort, her son would not have been able to continue in what was and is a very expensive sport. Looking back on his family and the role his father took in his life, Lewis reflected that, from where he grew up and having a child at such a young age, it would have been easy for Anthony to pack up and leave following the divorce: 'That's what happened to the parents of most of my close friends. Most people from our area were broke and they didn't want the responsibility. He was a real man and stuck by us.'

Carmen knew early on that her son's passion was so big that nothing would stop him. She reflected on how some of the kids who Lewis grew up with on the track had parents who were millionaires. However, Carmen saw that these wealthier families often were not able to understand why their sons didn't win while Lewis did. In Carmen's opinion, they could not grasp that success is not all about money and that talent is a crucial element.

Lewis's mother made what was the heartbreaking decision to allow her son to live with his father when Lewis was between 10 and 12 (as is not unusual in such situations there seems to have been a period of overlap/transition with Lewis finally spending the majority of his time with his father after he had started secondary school). She saw that Anthony could do things for their son with regard to his racing career that she was not able to do. Carmen confessed she had to allow Lewis to live with his father 'for him to be a star'.

Now living in a modest semi-detached house in Sandy, Bedfordshire, with her second husband Ray, 55, Carmen still recalls Lewis's love for speed even as a very small child and how on his first birthday a gift of a big plastic toy steering wheel for his baby buggy delighted him. He drove it along and has hardly looked back since – except in his rear-view mirrors.

Throughout his rise to fame Lewis has remained in contact with his mother who sees the excitement now surrounding her son as 'surreal'.

According to Carmen, Lewis has a racing life with his dad and his normal life when he stays with her. They often go out for a meal or 10-pin bowling. She says that she is her son's 'biggest fan' and is immensely proud of him.

Like most successful sportsmen, Lewis is ultra-competitive, even in the 10-pin bowling sessions with his mother: 'I don't ever let anyone win if I'm honest ... I should let my brother win at some things, but it's very hard for me to do that.'

Looking at this propensity, Lewis admits that at a young age everything he did competitively he wanted to win. He hated not being the best at any sport he was involved in. When he competed against anyone he recalled thinking, 'I've got to win.' But now he plays golf, does lose, and is proud to say that he is able to manage his response: 'It's not a negative energy, I can control that energy.'

Carmen and Anthony remain friends, have attended races and even holiday together with their current partners. The two couples celebrated together at a London nightclub when Lewis signed his first Formula One contract. Carmen has made the point that most people in car racing think the family are an 'unusual bunch' and are quite amazed when they see them come down the pit lane.

Reflecting on the early challenges for the Hamilton family, John Booth, of the Manor Motorsport team that Lewis drove for until 2004, feels that 'things could have gone wrong for them, but Lewis's father has always been totally dedicated to the boys ... The whole family was very supportive: his mum and his stepmum always came to races all over Europe.'

From Carmen's point of view, Lewis has got everything: personality, looks, physique and charisma, all it takes to become a massive star. She recognises his magnetism and how he has a gift for making people get on together and has no doubts that he will become World Champion one day. But she insists that everything he has is the product of hard work and that he wasn't born with a silver spoon in his mouth.

Just prior to stepping into the Formula One limelight, Lewis was living in a style compatible to his elevated status. The family garage housed his Mercedes 4x4, a Saab and a Mini. His affection for the latter has a history. Rachel Butterfield was Hamilton's first serious girlfriend. They both attended the John Henry Newman School in Stevenage. Two years Lewis's junior, she started dating the racer when she was 16. At the time Lewis owned the Mini Cooper. In a recent 'kiss-and-tell' interview, Butterfield shared fond and erotic memories of that particular vehicle. But the salesgirl from Biggleswade, Bedfordshire, recalled that, although he might have been fast, safety was always a priority for Lewis: 'He loved that car … He was always a very careful, safe driver. I don't remember him taking many risks on the road.'

However, Lewis's dedication to his sport meant he was only able to see Rachel twice a week in the four months they dated. She recollected times when he would be racing or in the factory on consecutive weekends and the relationship 'fizzled out'. But what took precedence in Lewis's life was always clear. It seems that, whenever he talked about his career, it was always: '*When* I'm Champion', not: '*If* I'm Champion'.

School Days

It seems that, despite any difficulties that might have occurred between Anthony and Carmen, they kept their son at the centre of their concerns and he began to grow into a balanced and intelligent person. John Seal, the head of Lewis's junior school, Peartree, 200 yards from their home on the Shephall estate in Stevenage, recalled that the young Hamilton stood out at school, and not just because he was winning numerous karting trophies. Seal remembered that Lewis was popular and a composed public speaker. He was also exceptionally focused for his age. But Seal was most impressed by the extent of the support Lewis got from his father and the fact that they were just an ordinary family from a hard-working background. As such, it was good to see that things have turned out the way they have.

The deputy head Carol Hopkins was passing an electrical store in Welwyn Garden City at the start of Hamilton's first Formula One season, and a crowd had formed in front of the shop window. Lewis had just taken the chequered flag in Melbourne and immediately Carol told her husband, 'That's my Lewis ... He was at our school!' She had instantly recognised him by 'his sweet, beaming smile'. Now Hamilton is a hero to all her pupils and they made a card for him and hoped he would come to the school so it could be presented to him. Carol told how the school has 'a strong sports side ... with the children being encouraged to be as active as possible. The children now watch Lewis intently and bring in cuttings for our "Lewis Hamilton corner". He is someone for our pupils to aspire to.'

But, for Carol, Lewis was not a competitive person at Peartree and her memories of him are dominated by 'his bright, smiley face and lovely manners'. But it seems he enjoyed school and was 'just very happy', a 'bright little button, but normal, very normal'.

Lewis moved on to the John Henry Newman Roman Catholic Secondary School. To his credit, Lewis made school what he wanted it to be, a place where he did as much as he had to, while using it as an environment to be young and as a background to his greater dream. But he was not the only pupil at Henry Newman with this attitude. Another was Ashley Young, who was a member of the England under-21 squad that were recently narrowly beaten in the European Championship semi-finals by the eventual champions (Holland, 13–12 on penalties on their home turf). Midfielder Young joined Premiership Aston Villa from Watford in January 2007 in a deal that would eventually cost the Birmingham club close to £10 million.

By the time Young started at secondary school, he was with the Watford Academy, and as he and Lewis shared a passion for sport it is perhaps not surprising that the two got on. They were also both black, and a friend of mine who grew up in Stevenage once told me that, if he was standing outside his home with a black friend, that 'constituted a "posse" in Peartree Way'.

Although the Villa player doesn't follow Formula One closely, he is happy for Lewis. Because of Lewis's constant and all-embracing commitment to racing, he would often attend school for three days and then be away for the rest of the week. Even the weekends were usually taken up, so it was hard for the pair to socialise outside of school and become close friends. After a while, they rarely saw each other.

However, the two budding sports stars were members of the same school football team and Ashley recalled how Lewis played in central midfield and, although he 'wasn't too bad', Young claimed, 'I was a better player: that's why he's doing his driving.'

Lewis offered a slightly different and protracted analysis of his soccer career claiming he was quicker and stronger than Young, but admitted that the Villa man was very skilled and would dribble the ball round people 'very nicely'. Hamilton told how he was very powerful and the 'fittest by far' because of his racing and the training he did in connection with the same. Regularly playing midfielder Hamilton recalled 'running up and down and up and down and if someone tackled me I'd get them back. I'd always get them back because I never gave up; whereas a lot of people would get tackled then just leave it for the next stage of the game. I'd never let that happen.'

According to Lewis's former coach at Bedwell Rangers FC, Ken Headington, he was a leader on the pitch: 'He'd always rally the other players when things were looking grim. If he'd had the time and the commitment to his football, he was talented enough to have done anything.'

It seems Ashley and Lewis were also 'brothers at arms' on the cricket pitch. Young remembered that they were 'the worst ones on the team; I think we were just making the numbers up ... We both said at one point we both wanted to do well, me in my football, him with his driving. We said we both wanted to be at the highest level.'

Like Lewis, Ashley benefited from parental support and guidance. But, although he drives a BMW X5, he has no inclination to break the speed limits.

Girls, Girls, Girls

Hamilton has been dating his current girlfriend and former college sweetheart, Jodia Ma, a stunning brunette, for over four years (they met well before he shot into the ranks of the rich and famous while they were both studying at Cambridge Arts and Sciences College as teenagers). Carmen sees her son's devotion to his 21-year-old Hong Kong-born girlfriend as a very positive relationship that saves him from being distracted by other girls. She describes Jodia as 'a gentle, lovely girl – the sort who will help keep his feet on the ground' and insists that Lewis isn't interested in 'the fake life and people who are just money-grabbers'. For Lewis's mum, Jodia is not 'after the high life' and she believes he would prefer a stable relationship than have 'all these dolly birds in Formula One. You never know what they're after. Jenson Button had a lovely girlfriend and all that finished. Maybe now he wished he had hung on to her.'

Lewis is at his most content spending time listening to his favourite music – R&B, reggae, funky house and has confessed to loving hip hop and 'have it belting out of my own car' – and relaxing with Jodia; however, the couple have found it tough since Jodia, who studied event management and worked in London for a time, moved back to Hong Kong in January 2007. But the pair did find time to take a luxury break in Bali during March.

For Lewis, the only problem with his chosen profession is that he doesn't get to see Jodia as often as he would like. He has said that Jodia is his best friend and they speak every day. But she has experienced the down side of his driving skills. When he picked her up in Paris with the aim of driving to London, in spite of satellite navigation, he got lost. But it is a trait of Hamilton's to turn negatives into positives and, according to Jodia, they spent a lovely couple of hours in Paris and then drove back to London. However, Lewis and the satnav took an extra seven hours to get him and his passenger home. For all this, Jodia said she had a great experience because she had spent that time with Lewis. But after September 2007 Hamilton had little time to see Jodia.

In July 2007, model Danielle Lloyd talked of the six months of romance she had shared with Lewis five years before. The 23-year-old told how Hamilton was 'a lovely person to be with and it was very sweet … But we were both very young. I was 18 … He's a special person, but there's no more romance.'

Lloyd claimed to have sent Lewis a special message before his Formula One race at Silverstone and said, 'We're great mates … We've supported each other in our careers since we first met, so I texted him "All the best".'

Disgraced by allegations of bullying and racism and subsequently dumped by the then West Ham United senior citizen and poker ace Teddy Sheringham, the former *Celebrity Big Brother* housemate was said to have met at Lewis at celeb hangout 10 Rooms. She said that they were both out with friends and 'there was a bit of a spark'. The Scouser swapped numbers with Lewis and 'after that I went back to Liverpool and he lived in London but we stayed in touch'.

Alas, the relationship crumbled, according to Lloyd because of the distance between herself and Lewis, coupled with the fact that they were both teenagers at the time. But it seems that Lewis turned up to see her crowned Miss England in 2004.

Home Life

Anthony has described Lewis's home life and the background he grew up in as 'middle of the road'. His family has always been a significant part of his world. Before 2007, when he was at home in Hertfordshire he'd spend his spare time cleaning the family runabouts. Steve Pocock, the owner of the local garage, describes the kind of person Lewis is – a nice individual, very much the same as he shows himself to be on television. Pocock recalled that when Lewis returned home after testing in Spain he was soon 'out washing and hoovering the family cars'.

A current neighbour of the family had much the same impression, telling how the Hamiltons were 'a lovely family', and that they were proud to have them as neighbours. Having described Lewis as extremely talented, the neighbour declared, 'It amazes me how calm he is despite being so young. He has really inspired me.'

Another neighbour said they set their alarm for 3am to watch Lewis make his Formula One debut live and believed other villagers did likewise. This local went on to say that, although many people had no history of interest in Formula One before the Hamiltons had moved in five years earlier, everybody was behind Lewis now.

Lewis spends significant amount of time caring for his half-brother Nicholas who, although suffering from cerebral palsy, accompanies Lewis to every race, along with Anthony, who now acts as his son's manager, and Anthony's second wife Linda (Nicholas's mother). This strong family unit provides Hamilton with robust emotional support.

Louise Goodman, a member of ITV's Formula One coverage team, has been impressed by Lewis's relationship with his half-brother. She has made the point that most racing drivers go through a phase when they turn into 'a bit of an arsehole'. She sees this as being an occupational hazard of constant exposure in the media spotlight and has some fears that this might happen to Hamilton but on balance thinks he might avoid this, feeling that his family circumstances enable him to realise there are more important things in life than all the glamour and attention that surrounds Formula One.

Reflecting on this bond, Lewis said, 'I have a fantastic family that's been behind me all the way. Nicholas and I get on really well and he's a great kid. I always wanted a brother and I remember when my parents [as he always refers to his father and stepmother] first told me they were going to have a boy, I was well excited. It's quite a cool feeling to watch someone grow up, to see the difficulties and troubles he's had, the experience he's had. To go through them with him and see how he pulls out of them.'

Lewis has said, 'When you have a natural ability, you have to nurture it,' and Nicholas has been a constant source of motivation for his older brother and by his very presence reminds him not to take his gift for granted: 'I look up to him even though I'm the older one ... I've learned a lot from him. As you know, disabled people are looked down upon the majority of time. He's a very strong-spirited person. But at least now I can look after him if anything were to happen.'

But the younger sibling is also an inspiration to other people both in and outside of the family. According to John Booth, Lewis is very close to his brother and spends a lot of time with him when he isn't racing. 'Everyone who meets Nick is won over by him. They are a special family.'

Nicholas has an unfailing smile and positive attitude, which, together with his lack of complaint about his situation, provides Lewis with a strong example of courage and the power of a positive outlook. Whenever he thinks he has problems, he reflects on the difficulties that Nicholas faces in life: 'He might have cerebral palsy but he definitely wants to do something special with his life … maybe in the wheelchair Olympics or even something around Formula One. I wouldn't put it past him trying to be a commentator.'

The time Lewis spends with Nicholas gives him 'real perspective' and keeps his 'feet on the ground'.

The passion Lewis has for motor racing has been with him most of his life, having first watched the sport on TV as a five-year-old. But his 'hands-on' experience began while on holiday in Spain with his family. He took the wheel of a little electric car and something kicked in. He showed immediate talent and recalled, 'There was this really, really small track with three corners … It was so, so short it was incredible, but I loved it. I just had this feeling getting the car back up to power and everything, that it just felt natural.'

On returning to England, he pursued his new found passion.

But Lewis's first brush with fame did not come by way of karting. In 1991, his father bought him a radio-controlled car, an electric off-roader. Anthony noticed that his son had good eye-to-hand co-ordination and encouraged Lewis to try out his skills in competition. Looking back, he recollected, 'When I was five … I was racing these remote-controlled cars and winning club championships against adults.'

This pursuit had started on the balcony of his father's flat in

Stevenage, where he slept over at weekends. The boy went from strength to strength and, at the age of six, in his first competitive season in remote racing competition, he was runner-up in the national championships.

Not long after that, little Lewis appeared on the BBC children's television programme *Blue Peter* and found himself racing his machine around the famous *Blue Peter* garden. He has fond memories of the experience: 'It was a big day out. I think I was at least 20 years younger than the other contestants, but I won.'

After a year in remote-controlled racing, Anthony, thinking that his son's skills might translate from the micro to the macro, took Lewis to Rye House kart track (Hoddesdon, a few miles south of Stevenage) on a whim, 'just to see what was going on'. Lewis had a trial run in one of the practice karts and proved to be a natural, lapping his father with some ease. The lad enjoyed the experience and soon had his first shunt, coming out of it with a bloodied nose. At that point, Anthony thought that his son's track career had ended prematurely. But the boy enthusiastically jumped straight back into the kart. Reflecting on his feelings about his son's safety as a child, Anthony had to be realistic: 'When your kid is driving a little mini go-kart that does 60mph, you're gonna feel fear, a lot of apprehension – are they going to come out of that corner safe? And karting is quite safe, but, you know, accidents do happen.'

So, the Christmas before his eighth birthday, Lewis was gifted with a second-hand kart as well as all the kit – a helmet and suit. Carmen, his mother, admitted to thinking, 'Good grief,' but little Lewis was quick into the gear and driving down the street with gusto. Initially this was part of a carrot-and-stick plan to motivate Lewis to focus on his school work, but, according to Anthony, 'He got way better at karting than he was at school.'

At that juncture, the family had no plans to get involved in organised motorsport but Lewis recalled, 'I went from there to racing karts. That's when I knew I wanted to be a Formula One driver.'

Anthony recollected Lewis's move to the track: 'I was green and

Lewis was green and all we thought we'd do is just go and buy a go-kart and go on the circuit and race.'

Lewis won his first half-dozen novice cadet kart races and, as soon as he lost his novice plates, he was victorious in his first full-plate race. At that point, Anthony began to speculate that his son might have far greater capacities than anyone had anticipated.

Lewis demonstrated, from that very early age, uncompromising driving skills and an ability to win races. According to Anthony, 'So from that point I suppose he was bitten by the bug of wanting to beat everybody. If he doesn't win, it really grates on him.'

But Anthony knew that this is something a champion needs, feeling that, if you are not prepared to give 100 per cent, you might as well do something else. But as he and his son have often reiterated in many ways, Lewis likes to win, even if, as Anthony says, 'He doesn't mind losing now, because he's learned to lose, but winning is his soul objective.'

From the outset Lewis loved the thrill of being on the edge with his heart pounding racing round Rye House or Streatham Kart Raceway (another venue where he learned his trade). The weekend enthusiasm transformed into a committed pursuit, and towards the end of 1993 Lewis was seriously involved in racing karts. Martin Hines ('Mr Karting'/'the karting guru') who owns the kart-manufacturing company Zipkart, which is based round the corner from the Rye House track, remembers 'the little black driver with that lovely smile … You can see the kids who are different and he was one, along with Gary Paffett, who's now a test driver with McLaren.'

Hines, who signed Hamilton and Paffett, recalled that 'Lewis ticked all the boxes. His family were so supportive … he was bright, willing to learn and, above all, talented … An exceptional kid from an exceptional family.'

John Huff, the events co-ordinator at Rye House, recalled Lewis began his karting when the venue was little more than a humble track serviced by a small collection of prefabs and, during the mid-1990s, Huff served Lewis and Anthony in the track's spares shop and prepared them burgers in the cafe. He makes the point that many people are now claiming to have known him from his very beginnings. While Huff does not claim to be a 'personal friend' of the Hamiltons, he has asserted, 'They were nice, normal people, no airs and graces ... we found Lewis as a child. He's not from a ghetto; he has come from a normal working-class environment. The area he grew up in is no squalid council estate.'

The 'vrooms' of the tough little engines that drive the karts round the Rye House track echo off the nearby walls of the Sainsbury's distribution centre in Hoddesdon. If you visit there, especially soon after attending a Grand Prix in say Monaco or Bahrain, it is probably quite hard to imagine that this not altogether inviting part of Hertfordshire was where someone leading the Formula One World Championship started his career in the speed business. Martin Hines recollected how he would visit Rye House to watch the kart racing. Novice racers are obliged to carry a black number plate for their initial half-dozen races and usually you see the greenhorns tugging relatively nervously at the back of the grid as they don't have the experience to weave their way through the pack. But one day Hines spotted Lewis, with his black plate, fighting for the lead in a testing session. An uneducated spectator might not have seen the significance of this, but the Zipkart man immediately saw that Hamilton was 'something a bit special' as he cut 'his way through the field ... he was bang up there so I watched the race'.

Hines introduced himself to the young man and to his father at the end of the session and asked, 'How many races have you done?'

He was told that the event he had just witnessed was Lewis's first race. Hines, more than slightly taken aback, told the boy and man, 'Best you come and see me tomorrow morning to see if we can help because obviously this young man here has got enormous talent.'

That occasion might be taken as the beginning of Hamilton's life in serious racing. Hines was to supply Lewis with kart chassis and other assistance right through his time in karting. In motorsport, it is taken as given that your speed is in direct correlation with the funding you

have available and, as Hines remembered, 'The Hamilton's weren't
rich,' and he wanted to help. As his son was taking all before him in
the karting world, Anthony was once advised not to risk going into
debt investing in parts and told 'just to go karting'. However, after the
initial meeting with Hines, Lewis's ability attracted a lot of attention
and equipment suppliers were soon knocking on the Hamiltons' door
offering sponsorship and support in return for the placement of a
sticker on Lewis's kart. As such, Anthony was able to manage a
financial path through Lewis's initial racing years without too much
of a direct pecuniary burden. But the coming together of Hines and
the Hamiltons in Hoddesdon was the start of a five-year association
between Lewis, Anthony and Hines – the latter was never less than
aware that, in this father and son partnership, he was always working
with a team: 'His dad is absolutely 150 per cent dedicated to Lewis
and you'd have to say there's been a return; they just support each
other unbelievably.'

Hines's son Luke was also an achiever at Rye House. Although
Luke was in an older age group than Lewis, they became friends.
Luke remembered Lewis as a 'brilliant' kart driver and, 'as a bloke,
he was great fun. We'd go to under-18 discos, that kind of stuff. He
was just like the rest of us, an ordinary young lad who liked to have
a good time.'

By the time he was 10, Lewis was fearlessly batting around a track
on a 60cc go-kart. In just his second year of karting, Lewis won the
British Cadet Championship. Looking back, he reflected, 'I don't
think my parents truly understood how dangerous it could be. I had
one big crash where I went off and ploughed into a wall. I bashed my
head and had a nosebleed.'

But Lewis was unperturbed. His response was to ask his dad to fix
the kart and he raced the next day and won. Although concerned about
his son's welfare, Anthony always understood Lewis's drive and the
attitude young boys develop in the racing environment: 'All of those
kids, they actually don't care anyway. All they want to do is they want
to win, and you can feel that tension when they're all sitting on the grid.

When there's 32 karts on the grid and they go round to the first bend all you see is smoke and the occasional white helmet.'

The means Anthony found to allay some of his anxieties about his son's safety was typical of the man's tremendous practical intelligence. Security about the safety of an individual starts with being able to have a good idea, at any given moment, of the location of the person one is concerned about: 'I just thought it would be a good idea to have a yellow helmet which would stand out among everybody else's. At least then you know you can put your mind at rest and your heart at rest and spot your driver all the way round the circuit.'

That yellow helmet has become a Hamilton trade mark but quickly also became a warning signal to others. When Lewis raced at Monte Carlo in 2007, the helmet had some new accoutrement: the words 'MONACO 07' written on the side of it in diamonds, added as a publicity stunt by the Steinmetz diamond company, which brought a new dimension to 'bling'.

Lewis named Buckmore Park, near Chatham in Kent, as his favourite kart circuit in the UK: 'Great track – I really did enjoy racing there.'

At Buckmore, he stood out first and foremost because he was quick, but also because he was black, a characteristic not consistently seen on the kart tracks of Kent in the early 1990s. Bill Sisley, boss of the Buckmore Park track, recalling the first time he saw Lewis in a kart, remembered how within two laps he knew the young lad had real potential to go all the way. He did everything right. He was quick, braked at the right times, overtook at the right times and took the right lines into the corners almost instinctively. Also, quite importantly, he didn't crash. For Sisley, Lewis, even as an eight-year-old, had a palpable abundance of skill and the will to win. He reflected, 'There have been other drivers as naturally talented but lacking that aggression and passion to get to the flag first.'

Sisley saw that Lewis possessed the tripartite talents that would constitute a great racing driver: profusion of physical and mental gifts, financial support and a sense of professionalism that included a steely determination. In Sisley's opinion, together with Lewis's 'very nice, supportive family', this had produced an 'extremely likeable and totally focused young man'.

But the 'nice' tag that Lewis still carries is not a totally adequate label for him. It was in his early karting days that he told TV viewers, 'I've got Ron Dennis's phone number and I'm going to phone him in nine years and he might give me a free drive in a McLaren.'

Later, he remarked, 'When I'm on the track, I'm enemies with everybody ... Coulthard, Häkkinen are probably my main heroes ... right now and hopefully I'd like to be racing against them in a few years.'

As written words, these statements could be viewed as arrogance and aggression, but, although they tell the reader more about Hamilton than the noun 'nice', when he stated these views and perceptions, he did so in a very matter-of-fact way that showed his steely confidence more than shallow arrogance.

Anthony had taken his son to Buckmore because he had heard of Sisley's unparalleled reputation for being able to discern driving talent at an early stage. For the Buckmore boss, the young Hamilton represented a 'once-in-a-generation talent' and who few, if any, would replicate. This view was to be confirmed in 2007 shortly after Lewis achieved his eighth straight podium in Formula One by no lesser light than triple World Champion Sir Jackie Stewart. Lewis's legacy to karting is massive and success has created a huge and unprecedented upsurge in interest in the sport in an amazingly short time.

Although the youthful Hamilton was able to push himself forward and make his presence felt, it was something that didn't come naturally to him. However, at the same time, he seems to always have had an ability to deal with trepidation. As a youngster Lewis was shy but at the same time he has 'never been scared of doing anything exciting'. He says he is 'pretty relaxed by nature' but seems to have an appetite for danger, but, of course, even he has his fears: 'I haven't jumped out of aeroplanes and stuff like that but I will do that at some point … but I hate spiders.'

By 1995, Hamilton, equipped with an assured racing style that belied his years, was the youngest British cadet-class champ and the STP (Scientifically Treated Petroleum) karting champion. In 1996, he repeated the feat and also won the prestigious McLaren-Mercedes Champions of the Future award, the Sky TV KartMasters and the Five Nations Karting series. The following season, he raced in Junior Yamaha and won the Champions of the Future series again, plus the Super One series, and was, once more, British Champion.

Martin Hines put in a word for the Hamiltons with the Topkart Comer organisation in Italy, and when Lewis went to test there he proved himself to be the quickest racer on show. This led to two years as a works driver in the highly competitive European arena.

It was while in Italy that Anthony and Lewis met the 1982 Formula One World Champion Keke Rosberg. He created Team MBM to allow his son Nico to develop his skill and, impressed by Lewis, included the Hertfordshire lad in his plans, with the support of McLaren tsar Ron Dennis. But Lewis was not exactly treading the purple path. While other kids drove top-of-the-range karts and stayed in motor homes for weekend races, Lewis's family scrimped and saved to keep him on the track and lived out of a Trojan-esque but rusting coupé. Lewis's first kart was bought second-hand for £1,000, at a time when Anthony was working as an IT manager. He and Linda were earning just £1,300 a month and living in a flat in West London worth less than their mortgage. Years later Lewis considered those early days in his racing career: 'I don't think anyone came from the same background as us. Most people [in karting] had wealthy parents.'

This was certainly the case at the time. As a youth worker I was able to introduce many young people to karting in places like Streatham. Many of them loved the challenge and thrill of racing, and not a few were very good at it, while being enchanted by the whole atmosphere of the track. But looking back it must have been a frustrating experience for many, because to compete seriously at least one personal kart was needed. On top of this, a successful competitor is going to have to find the entire race and practice expenses as well as meet the costs of transport to and from tracks. All this was way beyond the financial capacity of the kids I took to the tracks. It is a sad fact that much of youth work is like this and in the long run probably does more to undermine the esteem of young people than it does to build it, merely confirming their social position. But Anthony and Lewis did show that barriers are there to be overcome; no youth or social worker was involved; their effort was one that needed the much firmer familial bond than the necessarily time-restricted and relatively emotionally tepid ties that exist between professional and client.

As the young racer became more successful, the bonuses of free engines and tyres were helpful to his cause. But Anthony began to find that getting time off work to take Lewis to races was becoming difficult and he understood that, to give his son any chance of getting to where he wanted to go, more of his own time was needed. Looking back, Anthony said, 'People on the outside perceive it just as fun and karting when, in fact, it's a professional mini-industry.'

So, Anthony and stepmum Linda both took the huge gamble of taking redundancy in an effort to do all they could to advance their son's progress.

But, while the family concentrated on fostering Lewis's karting talent, the bigger goal was always on the horizon. At the age of six or seven, after his parents divorced, while Lewis was with his father at weekends, they both took to watching the televised Grand Prix racing. Gradually, Lewis became interested in the personalities and atmosphere of Formula One and started to understand the nuances and structure of the sport. However, he has few memories of races involving the British hero of that era, not really taking to Nigel Mansell (whose demeanour did not provide the natural role model for a six-year-old). The young Lewis enjoyed watching Ayrton Senna drive for McLaren and the Brazilian's battles with Alain Prost. He has studied his books and videos and has called Senna his 'icon'. He has also told how he was proud to be racing for McLaren because it was the team Senna had raced for and he tried to emulate the way Senna 'diced around the track and overtook the other drivers ... It feels I am continuing his legacy in a way.'

But, although he hoped that he learned something from the great man, Lewis was never a Formula One fanatic. Unlike many young men who take an interest in sport, he didn't develop an all-embracing devotion to Formula One. But, ever since he first became aware of Grand Prix racing, Lewis has been enchanted by the prospect of steering the awesomely powerful yet rapier-light racing machines of Formula One on the great tracks of the world and he wanted to drive for McLaren. When he hit his teenage years, his attraction evolved into a passion and his knowledge and interest in Formula One deepened.

Lewis's karting CV seemed to foretell his future: at 15, he had won every round of the Formula A European Championship, the World Cup in Japan and the junior section of the Elf Masters in Bercy, Paris; he was also crowned the sport's youngest ever number one – a record he still retains. But, of course, it was his talent, not his youth, that really singled him out. However, he has another quality that enhanced his notoriety. Ron Dennis has said that McLaren have been very aware that Lewis's colour could be used as a headline or could certainly be the first sentence of most publicity or media stories about him. Anthony has been pragmatic about the potential for this, seeing it as something that's there and that, in the future, could be used in a positive way, but he has stipulated only if it's good for Lewis and the people that are interested in him, commenting that he wouldn't want his son's colour taken advantage of 'in an unscrupulous way ... it's got to be done properly'. Anthony recognises that motorsport boasts very few black faces, and as such he feels Lewis can set an example and become a role model for other up-and-coming motor racers. But he is under no illusions, knowing that his son 'first and foremost has got to be a winner'.

But Dennis insists that the colour of Lewis's skin is 'immaterial':

'He's been in the McLaren-Mercedes family for nine years. We don't hide from the fact that he's from a mixed-race background, but this doesn't matter.'

Lewis's position on the subject doesn't seem too far from that of his McLaren mentor, saying, 'I'm proud of where I come from and who I am. But, for me, I feel like every other driver. I'm here to do a job.'

With his good looks, Lewis has been dubbed the 'Black Beckham', partly because of the tens of millions he is expected to earn from sponsorship deals and it was the *Sun* that christened him 'Formula One's Tiger Woods' in terms of his potential impact on the sport. Others have likened him to Arsenal's young gun Theo Walcott (which has a lyrical irony as Lewis is a committed Gooner). Such comparisons have some validity and not just because these young men have made a relatively huge impression at such an early age. All three men have also had their childhood talent lovingly nurtured by their fathers. However, for Ron Dennis, although he understands that the comparison with Woods could be seen as a compliment, the similarities between the two sportsmen are, for him, largely extraneous: 'The sort of Tiger Woods label makes you smile … But it's just not relevant to our objective. He's in our team because he's earned the opportunity.'

But Lewis's arrival in the public consciousness is at least as profound as that of Woods a decade ago, because car racing, and Formula One in particular, is even more socio-economically exclusive than golf. Former multiple motorcycle and Formula One World Champion John Surtees has told how he has been appalled to see good drivers being left on the sidelines because they haven't come up with the huge amounts of money needed to put themselves in a competitive car. And it is even more the case now than it was in his heyday that motor racing is excruciatingly demanding financially. If you think it is difficult to pay your way into any top-class golf or tennis club (never mind be accepted) and to try finding the money for equipment and lessons, car racing, which eats engines and chassis that are massively more costly than golf clubs, looks like a sport reserved for those with bottomless pits of cash. Bank rolling a route into Formula One is a project that is reckoned to be in the several millions of pounds; breaking into the American NASCAR or IndyCars isn't as expensive but those precincts are not exactly havens of diversity either.

For all this, if his success in motorsport continues, Lewis will probably be associated more and more with the likes of Tiger Woods. Like Woods, Lewis has felt himself 'very fortunate' to have a father who has watched over his career not just in a parental way, but as a wise and careful guide in business and career direction. He sees Anthony as being 'very strong' mentally and having a major influence on his own mental preparation for racing. Certainly, the support of those closest to him has been the foundation of his career: 'Possibly I come from a different background to some [involved in motor racing] but the main thing is I have a fantastic family ... outside of motorsport my family is obviously number one.'

As an 18-year-old, Lewis was definite that, without his family's support and input, he would not have got very far. At the time, he declared, 'I want to make my family proud of me. That's what drives me.'

This probably has much to do with Lewis's consciousness of how hard his father worked on his behalf and he has matched his dad's sacrifice; Lewis doesn't drink or smoke, he is unerringly polite and during the racing season he is in bed by 10pm.

According to Ron Dennis, it is not hard to tell that Lewis is a very competitive, single-minded and focused individual, but also 'He's got a complete feet-on-the-ground approach to life. From the time I first met him, there's no arrogance ... We could not wish for a more balanced, focused individual.'

Lewis's father's background contrasts with those of many of his Formula One peers, the likes of Lewis's long-term racing friend Nico Rosberg for example, and Lewis is well aware of his father's hard work and sacrifice. 'My dad has had to work; at one point he had three jobs … I don't think he ever went into debt but he had quite a few jobs on the go. His main job was with the railways but I also remember him putting up "For Sale" signs – he'd get £15 a sign.'

Anthony confirmed this, but has no regrets about the hours he put in for his son's success: 'I had to work very hard, taking a second and even a third job to fund Lewis's racing in the early days. But it was worth it.'

Carmen, Lewis's mother, recalled her son's own efforts to finance his passion: 'He's done all sorts to fund his racing, from working in a clothes shop to bar work. But he couldn't hold down a job because he was always off racing.'

Of course, Carmen wanted to be there when her son made his debut in Formula One, but at the start of 2007 it was uncertain if she would be able to make the first race of the season in Australia, not having the cash to finance her trip and being too proud to ask Lewis for the money. It was revealed in the press that she entered a TV competition hoping to win tickets to get her to Melbourne for the March Grand Prix. In the end she was not lucky and had to watch her son's entry into Formula One from her armchair 10,500 miles away.

Shortly after taking his bow in Formula One, Lewis told how his father is invariably nervous when his son is racing. Of course, he likes to have some assurance that Lewis is safe and when he can't see his lad on the track his anxiety grows. Lewis understands that his dad is very passionate about racing and especially in terms of his son's success, which, according to the Herts racer, has made Anthony 'probably one of the proudest father's there is'. While being conscious of his own achievements and his father's part in those, Lewis seems as glad to see his dad achieve his ambitions as Anthony is for his son attaining his goal of making Formula One: 'It's quite funny to see that and it's good to see him relaxed after all the time he's had to be very stressed and working hard to keep us going. We've already achieved so much and it's sort of an end of a chapter in our lives.'

Although he has a lot of respect for the likes of Tiger Woods, Lewis's earliest role model came from a different cultural background:

the culture of speed. Lewis was just nine when his childhood hero Brazilian Ayrton Senna died. On 1 May 1994, Lewis was involved in weekend racing at Hoddesdon; he was sitting with Anthony in the family's small Vauxhall Cavalier, which pulled the trailer that carried his kart from track to track. The VC was also used as their 'pits' where the family would wait for Lewis's turn to race. It was during one of these waiting periods that Linda came over and told Anthony and Lewis that Senna had just died. The news hit the boy hard. But, as he later said, he never liked to show emotion in front of his dad, 'so I went behind the trailer and cried'.

That was to be a turning point in Lewis's life 'because, when you're so young, you believe people like Senna are invincible. And then you realise that they're also mortal. It made me understand I need to make the most of my talent.'

The passing of Senna was not the only painful experience that built Lewis's will to win. At the age of five, he was bullied at school. It was a horrible time for him, but even then he understood that he needed to look to himself in the face of adversity. He told his dad he wanted to take up karate so he could learn to protect himself. The bullying stopped and, more importantly, he developed real self-confidence.

By the time he was 12, as a marshal artist Lewis earned an intermediate black belt, but he learned more than just physical skills. Karate gave him a sense of humility that comes with confidence. In sport (as in most other spheres), pompous pronouncements and bombastic poses (of the likes made by Chelsea manager Jose Mourinho for example) betray a lack of self-assurance and a sense of inferiority that comes of being surrounded by those one might secretly regard as one's superiors.

There is nothing of this 'compensation response' in Lewis. However, at the same time he has understood that he needs a life separate from his competitive efforts. As such, as a child he learned to keep quiet about his track success. Kids at school would ask him, 'What are you doing this weekend?' and he'd reply, 'Oh, I'm going karting.' The response would nearly always be something like, 'I might see you up the road then' – taking it that he'd be bound for the local kart track. Lewis would just nod because he wanted to keep the real extent of his racing quiet. He reasoned that if no one knew what he was achieving it helped make school feel like an escape. School was Lewis's time to mess about and have a childhood – to be normal. But at weekends he rarely took the opportunities to go to any of the clubs or parties where 'ordinary' teenagers might be found. He confessed that this affected him, as the ties of friendship were prevented from developing beyond much more than a relatively superficial level: 'When you say, "I can't go out because I'm racing this weekend," your friends think you're just blowing them off. Even when, near the end, I'd tell people at school I was going to Japan for a week to race, they'd look at me blankly. It just didn't click.'

So, Lewis shunned the usual teenage male pursuits of drinking, getting high, chasing girls and partying all night in order to pursue his dream. He has trained every day during racing seasons and has stayed home at weekends so that he would not lose valuable sleep that on a race day might mean the difference between life and death.

Silverstone Dawn

On 11 June 2006 at Silverstone, with the sporting eyes of England focused on the World Cup, the attendance at the British Grand Prix was expected to be down on previous years. There seemed to be less than a remote chance for any driver hailing from the British Isles achieving something resembling a measure of success in the big event.

At 9am, the GP2 race began with Lewis Hamilton starting in a relatively lowly eighth place. As the stands began to fill with spectators, the young British racer started to battle a path up the field. His belligerent style was expected by those who knew of the young man and caught the eye of those who didn't as he entered the fight for second place. At close to 140mph, the Monegasque driver Clivio Piccione and Nelson Piquet Jr went through Copse as an item, they accelerated out of the corner to be joined by Lewis.

Piquet held the inside as the trio smashed through the five sweeping bends that make up the intimidating Becketts complex. Hitching on to massive momentum of the outside route on the first left-hander, Hamilton snatched second spot and the racing line as the road snaked right then left again. The Brazilian crashed straight through a temporary advertising hoarding with the cheers from the crowd, which had reached a volume that wouldn't be bettered that weekend, ringing round the circuit, signalling Hamilton's victory and vindicating his philosophy: 'Never give up under any circumstances. It doesn't have to be in racing. It can be in anything … When I'm in a race, if I'm at the back or something has gone wrong, I never give up; I keep pushing and it turns good, even if you spin off. I think once I spun off and I got back and focused and ended up coming second. So you just can't lose focus.'

That day at Silverstone, Lewis had not registered the adoration of the crowd: 'It all went silent at that point because we were so close, and I don't know if my body was preparing for something. You know when, if you're going to crash, your body gets ready to protect itself? I felt my body and the adrenaline all building up ready for something, and when I came out it all relaxed, kind of saying, "Phew, thank God for that."'

At that point, Lewis's mind was set on gaining a seat for McLaren's next Formula One campaign and said, 'It's an opportunity not many people get. If I can get that seat then I think – and I feel very confident – that I can make best use of it.'

Now 'Lewis Hamilton + Silverstone' is one of the most popular searches on YouTube. His lifestyle is adapting as he develops as a racer. He used to drive a little Smart ForFour, excusably a sporty version, as he was swift to point out it was 'a 177bhp, specially tuned Brabus and it's seriously quick. It has a big turbo with all the performance you need. Before that I owned a Smart Roadster for two years.'

But adapting to the heady financial waters that has accompanied his growing status, in 2007 he looked to find a car that fitted his changing profile. In the past his connections with McLaren-Mercedes

(DaimlerChrysler, Mercedes' parent company, holds a 40 per cent stake in McLaren) provided him with a Mercedes C-class, followed by a C-class Sports Coupé. But his graduation to Formula One required something extra special; a Mercedes SLR McLaren supercar.

For all this, Lewis remains an empathetic person who works hard not to let his growing standing detract from his awareness of his humble beginnings: 'When I was just 10 and I'd won my first British championship [in karting] I remember going up to drivers for their autograph, but they never looked at me when they signed, they just brushed past me. So I said that, if I ever got to Formula One, I'd always look at the kid, or whoever it might be, I'd be signing the autograph for ... I just feel privileged to be in this position and I see this as an opportunity to see young kids and help them come through.'

Like many involved in motorsport, Lewis is an admirer of Michael Schumacher. He shared a track with him once during testing in Spain shortly before the world's greatest driver hung up his helmet. Lewis could feel the German's focus and will to win and this had a lasting impact on the developing racer. But the 'Stevenage Spitfire' has something that even the great 'Schu' never had. Anthony has spotted a natural joy his son emits in his racing, something of a personal ethos that one sees only in the greatest racers, the last British example being Sterling Moss. According to Hamilton senior, 'He just enjoys what he does, and when you enjoy what you're doing everything flows normally.'

Watching Lewis over the years, I can certainly endorse that conviction.

The Charioteer is the hero of battle.

RON DENNIS CBE AND McLAREN

But the hero of the charioteer is his teacher.
Though while the earth celebrates he who drove to victory,
That warrior commissions his thanks to he who has saved
  his life
Remote from the war
Ten thousand times

Ancient Egyptian

When I saw Lewis Hamilton racing in Formula Renault some years back, he looked good. But I had seen him perform in karts since he was a child and, having been around that world for many years in my youth-worker incarnation, I'd not seen better, so I might be accused of being biased.

This said, Lewis, in his first season in cars, didn't dominate the field in the same way he had in Formula A for instance. Certainly, when he was considered alongside Danny Watts and Jamie Green, it would not have been immediately obvious to anyone who had not witnessed Hamilton's prodigious performances as a kid racer why McLaren boss Ron Dennis CBE had taken his apparently all-pervading, decade-long interest in the lad.

Dennis understands how much Hamilton is a product of his solid relationship with his family: 'Lewis gets his basic character from his family values, and we have just supplemented them ... There is no arrogance to Lewis ... He is a well-rounded individual who appreciates not just what McLaren-Mercedes have done for him, but also what his family have done for him ... That is down to his upbringing, the values of his family. I've had nothing to do with that.'

Around the time that Lewis was making his first deep marks in karting, following prompting from his father Anthony (who had suggested that Lewis had nothing to lose by introducing himself to Ron Dennis), the young racer took the opportunity of approaching Dennis, the guest of honour at the British AutoSport awards. As usual on these occasions, there was a dress code, and the Hamilton family were forced to improvise. They couldn't afford the stipulated formalwear so Lewis borrowed a dark-green silky suit from a fellow driver who, like Hamilton, had been invited to the awards the previous year for his karting accomplishments; he recalled, 'I even got his shoes.'

Lewis had been invited to the awards because he had won the British Championship and he went around the tables at the award dinner with an autograph book (each page of which was inscribed with an inspiring poem). He managed to get the signatures of Damon Hill, Colin McRae, Richard Burns and John Surtees. However, he was disappointed that he 'was a year too late for Ayrton Senna. He had been there the year before.'

The diminutive Hamilton walked up to Ron Dennis – chairman, CEO and part owner of the McLaren Group, whose drivers have become World Champion a record 11 times – and offered an outstretched hand. A couple of years later, Lewis remembered that moment: 'When I met Ron Dennis, I asked for his autograph in my autograph book. I asked for him to put his address down and his phone number ... I was 10 years old ... I'd just won the British Championship in Cadets, which is the first category starting karting. I had no hesitation ... I just went up to him and said, "Hi. I'm Lewis

Hamilton, I won the British Championship and one day I wanna be racing your cars." ... He wrote in the autograph book, "Phone me in nine years, we'll sort something out then."'

According to Hamilton, Dennis was very laidback and, although he put on a brave front, Lewis was surprised that Ron had time for him because 'some people at that level don't have any time for anyone. He gave me a good 10 or 15 minutes so that was quite special.'

Lewis was already a junior karting champion, but it would have taken courage for the young boy to approach Dennis. He was on the hunt that evening for big names, but, even at that young age, Lewis had never been overawed by so-called 'stars' of motorsport: 'I don't know why it is. If I met Eddie Murphy or a movie star, it would be like "Wow!" but when it comes to motor racing I don't think like that.'

Dennis, who on 1 June 2007 reached 60 years of age, and has been something of a fairy godfather to Lewis, remembered that first meeting and still has a slight sense of incredulity and admiration for the demonstrative but courteous young man, with ambition beyond his years: 'It was 12 years ago at the AutoSport awards. He just walked up to me – not that I'd noticed at the time because he was only three or four feet tall, so he was well out of my sight line – said my name. I looked down and there was this young chap with his hand out.'

As the youngster asked for Dennis's signature, the McLaren boss noticed how the boy looked at him and, without breaking eye contact, told him how he was going to manage his career; how he wanted to drive for McLaren and become World Champion. Looking back in 2007, Dennis said, 'It was then I realised that his focus and his commitment, that it sort of sparkled through his eyes, was really far more ingrained in him than I initially realised.'

It was a lot less than nine years before Dennis was back in contact with the Hamilton family. A week after this initial meeting, Ron had checked out the young man's background and determined to keep an eye on his progress.

Lewis told how events unfolded after his first encounter with the

McLaren chief: 'It was, I think, three years after that, because I'd gone there every year [the AutoSport Awards]. Ron called us, and I remember I got home from school, I was 13 years old, and my dad said to me, "Ron Dennis called today and he's offered you a sponsorship deal."'

This offer of support for Lewis's racing career was a precious moment for the Hamilton family. Anthony recalled the conversation: 'He basically just said that, very short and sweet, "Look", you know, "interested to try and help Lewis, I think he's got a bright future and let me know how much you need, and work out a schedule for the next few years and we'll talk."'

Not long after this, Lewis told television viewers, 'Hopefully, I'd like to get loads of sponsors by Ron Dennis and hope he'd let me drive one of his cars.'

From then on, as Dennis put it, smiling, 'He climbed, we paid … But it was worth it of course.'

Dennis had been prompted to pick up the phone himself to contact his potential protégé after Lewis had won the UK karting title on three straight occasions. He recalled Lewis's response: 'He said, "Yes, that would be great!" Obviously with a smile on. There are some traits there that you see in the greats. By and large, all the great Grand Prix drivers are from karting, it's the right place to start.'

For Anthony, that phone call was the breakthrough he'd been working for: 'That, to a degree, changed, if you want, our whole lives, because all of a sudden Lewis had got an opportunity that we never expected; to make a career in motorsport. And even at that time we never thought he'd become a Formula One driver. We just knew that there was this nice guy who said, "Look, I will look after Lewis and help him through school and everything else … We just wanted to take advantage of that and make sure he stayed on the straight and narrow … It's all too easy to become big-headed … when you've been given an opportunity like that and for your feet to leave the ground and before you know it you've lost the opportunity; you've wasted a potential career.'

In 2007, Hamilton had no illusions about the value of the support he got from McLaren: 'Without that support I wouldn't be in Formula One today; it's such an expensive sport and to go out and find 20 grand at the beginning to throw away on karting it's a lot of money.

'Ron has taken a very keen interest and has guided us, so, when we've stepped up from one class to another, he would have a lot of input to that.'

This interest did not stop when Lewis stepped off the track. As he pointed out, '[Ron] was also very hard on me about the schooling … He said, "If you don't keep pushing hard at school, if you don't finish school, then we'll pull out." So that was another pressure on my shoulders but still, it was worth it … me and my dad made a pact, if I worked hard at school, he would work hard and keep me racing. I think he stuck more to the deal than I did maybe, but that's what you're like when you're a kid.'

Anthony remembered this 'contract': 'If I worked 100 per cent to help raise the money, then he would at least work 100 per cent on his school studies. Well, 80 per cent, anyway.

'I suppose it was inevitable that Lewis's education suffered a bit, but I took the view that, with education, you can always go back. It's never too late to learn. But, if you have a chance, an opportunity, in a sport like this, you have to grasp it when it comes.'

Dennis had his reasons for this focus on education: 'For years I've realised that so many drivers in their determination to get into motorsport do so to the detriment of their education which then gives them a weakness if and when they get into Formula One.'

But, once more, Anthony was always there to support his boy with understanding and a sensible attitude: 'Kids will be kids … today's a bad day, tomorrow's a good day, and the thing is, when you're out motor racing or when you've got somebody like McLaren sponsoring you, every day has got to be a good day.'

Between 1995 and 1999, Lewis had progressed through the Cadet, Junior Yamaha and into Junior Intercontinental A ranks. By the tender age of 13, he was a dominant force in European karting, with a long list of national and international titles to his credit that few could even approach in the history of the sport. But it was his determination and passion that so impressed the McLaren chief: 'I was amazed by his self-confidence, and thought to myself that this boy can really go places.'

The young racer's tenacity and passion had enthused Dennis, and Lewis was to become involved in the McLaren and the Mercedes-Benz Young Driver Support Programme (YDSP) from its inception in 1998. This scheme, established by two of the most powerful names in the history of motorsport, was designed to provide a structured environment for nurturing and developing future Grand Prix talent.

Ron Dennis said of the YDSP, 'The Young Driver Support Programme has been designed to create genuine support for drivers who, without the commercial horsepower that we can bring, may not have made it on their own.'

And, according to Norbert Haug, Vice-President Mercedes-Benz Motorsport, 'Above all else, to be part of the initiative, each driver has to be exceptionally talented and show the potential of winning races and progressing towards Formula One.'

As well as financial and technical backing, the programme provides professional advice to up-and-coming racing drivers and has seen a number of its participants reach the top of their motorsport career – Formula One. These include Nick Heidfeld and Toyota test driver Ricardo Zonta.

Dennis's belief in Lewis's talents was such that the contract he offered the Hamiltons even included an option on the 13-year-old should he ever make it into Formula One racing, in effect making the Stevenage youth the youngest driver ever to have a Formula One contract.

With Dennis's backing, Lewis finished runner-up in the McLaren-Mercedes Champions of the Future Kart series in 1998, the year he joined the YDSP.

Two other drivers who were benefiting from the support of the programme at the same time as Hamilton were Giedo van der Garde (at the time of writing, still with the Super Aguri Formula One team as a test and reserve driver, although Spyker Formula One may also have a claim to his services in a similar capacity) and Chinese driver Cheng Congfu (A1 Grand Prix, Team China). But, from the start, Dennis, a shrewd judge of personality, had seen something exceptional in Hamilton: 'He has a uniqueness and a determination that is rarely seen in drivers and he is prepared to make personal and emotional sacrifices – you have to be mentally able to accept that to become the best, and ultimately we came to the point where he was a real candidate for a Formula One drive.'

Hamilton had taken a huge step in fulfilling his ambitions.

Big Ron

Since the start of the 1980s, Ron Dennis has been the principal of the McLaren Formula One team, ever present on the Grand Prix circuit, running the operation of the team and overseeing tactics. Worth in the region of £90 million in 2006, Dennis was 648th in the *Sunday Times* Rich List. By 2007, he had fallen to 834th with a fortune estimated at around £80 million, but, although lagging behind Bernie Ecclestone, at number 20 with £2,250 million, and Eddie Irvine, in 467th place with £150 million, Dennis remains a financial power in motorsport.

Dennis is renowned for his excessively businesslike and cautious answers to tough questions from Formula One journalists, and this style, which started around 1980, when sponsorship started to play a more prominent role in the sport, became so well known in the motor-racing community that it was named 'Ronspeak' after him. The term is regularly used by the popular magazine *F1 Racing*, and it has become a well-used phrase in the Formula One paddock to describe sentences which consist of unneeded complexity and often unfathomable words.

Dennis hasn't moved far from his Woking roots where he was born and raised. After leaving school at 16, Dennis started work as an apprentice mechanic with the Thomson & Taylor garage at Weybridge, not too far from the famous now defunct motor-racing mecca of the Brooklands circuit. Thomson & Taylor eventually became part of the Chipstead Motor Group, and not long after Dennis moved to the Cooper Car Company (part of Chipstead), which built racing cars.

At the age of 19, Dennis was a mechanic with the Cooper Formula One team. Jochen Rindt was the lead driver for Cooper at that point. Two years later in 1968, Rindt moved to Brabham taking Ron with him. After a year, Rindt was on the move again, to Lotus, but this time Dennis chose to stay with Brabham and he took on the role of chief mechanic for Jack Brabham.

In 1971, following the retirement of Jack Brabham, Dennis and Neil Trundle, another mechanic, started their own team, and just a year later, Rondel Racing was set up in Woking. The team enjoyed some modest successes in the feeder categories of Formula One during the mid-1970s, but the firm's ambition did not extend much further than being a customer team. Dennis persuaded Motul to bankroll the Rondel Formula 2 car, and a Ray Jessop-designed Formula One car was planned for 1974, but the fuel crisis at the time hit racing badly, and the car was taken over and raced as the Token and later the Safir.

Dennis formed the Project Three team in 1975 and his cars once more proved to be race winners. Ron founded Project Four in the late 1970s and this team achieved success in F2 and F3, winning the title in 1979 and 1980 with the backing of Philip Morris (Marlboro).

Following disappointing performances by McLaren in 1980, chairman Teddy Mayer was obliged by John Hogan, an executive with Philip Morris, to agree to a merger with Dennis's Project Four. This was in reality a reverse takeover; the Formula One constructor became McLaren International, which eventually led to Dennis taking control of the subsequent teams. He hired designer John Barnard who started work on the team's revolutionary carbon-fibre composite chassis, the MP4/1, which proved to be a crucial aspect of McLaren's ultimate success.

Building McLaren

In 1980, the team failed to win a single Grand Prix, finishing a disappointing seventh in the Constructors' title with John Watson and Alain Prost. Dennis saw the young Frenchman's latent potential but in 1981 was unable to stop him going to Renault. But, during that same season, McLaren regained the knack of winning races with Watson's victory at the British Grand Prix, and Dennis, together with his business partners, bought out Mayer and Tyler Alexander (the other McLaren shareholders).

Ron persuaded Niki Lauda to come out of retirement in 1982 for the South African Grand Prix, and the two-time World Champion lined up with Watson at the beginning of the season. By the end of the year, both Lauda and Watson had claimed a brace of wins and the New Year started with more triumph when Watson won the United States Grand Prix.

During 1983, Ron convinced Mansour Ojjeh, at that time a sponsor of the Williams team, to take a stake in McLaren International. Ojjeh helped fund the Porsche-built turbo-charged engines that bore his company's name, Techniques d'Avant Garde (TAG). The engines were ready for the Italian Grand Prix in September and McLaren-Ford was replaced by McLaren-TAG. Ojjeh upped his commitment by becoming a 70 per cent shareholder in McLaren, and Alain Prost, at that time a successful driver with Renault, came in to take over from Watson. Alongside the hugely knowledgeable Lauda, they produced a dozen victories in 16 races taking the Constructors' and Drivers' titles. Lauda became World Champion a half-point ahead of Prost – both racers gathered double the points achieved by Elio de Angelis, the third-placed driver in his Lotus-Renault.

In the space of four years, Dennis had transformed his team from at best a middle-of-the-road outfit to a dominant force in Formula One.

In 1985, McLaren concluded the season eight points ahead of Ferrari to claim back-to-back Constructors' titles. Prost made the Championship his own with Lauda taking second place. However, 1986 saw McLaren having to give up the title to Williams, but Prost became a two-time World Champion.

By 1987, it became obvious that the TAG engine was past its sell-by date and this prompted Dennis to talk to Honda, who at that time were working with Williams. Anxious about Frank Williams (the team principal of their then partner), who had recently been involved in a serious car accident, and his reluctance to take on a Japanese racer, Honda dropped Williams and agreed to supply McLaren. This, together with the signing of Brazilian Ayrton Senna as Prost's racing partner, looked to make McLaren favourites for the coming season, and, in 1988, McLaren surpassed their achievements of 1984. Victory in 15 of the 16 Grands Prix secured both titles with consummate ease; however, Dennis's skilled diplomacy out of the limelight had much to do with the team's success. Prost and Senna were a powerful pairing, but the mix of volatility and brilliance was always a potentially explosive combination, and it was only Dennis's excellent man-management that kept both racers on track. However, this was never going to be anything but a temporary arrangement, as Alain and Ayrton constituted a marriage made in hell.

During 1989, it became painfully apparent that even Dennis's best efforts could not prevent his two warriors from taking their differences out on to the track. At the Japanese Grand Prix, the irresistible force collided with the immovable object, allowing Prost to take the title, and causing the Frenchman to join Ferrari. Gerhard Berger, the 'Wörgl Wag', stepped into the breach.

The 1990s

McLaren roared into the 1990s as the masters of Formula One. Senna claimed back-to-back Championships in 1990 and 1991, and at the end of 1992 Mika Häkkinen, a promising newcomer, came into the McLaren fold as test driver. But that year Williams made a powerful comeback, and it would be seven years before McLaren would hold another title. Honda shipped out in 1993, leaving Dennis to negotiate with works partner Benetton and Ford for a supply of competitive engines, and in 1994 a calamitous partnership with Peugeot left Dennis fighting to identify a fourth engine partner in as many years. However, in 1995, he established a relationship with Mercedes, an alliance which continues to this day. The initial seasons of this association were demanding on both sides. The predictable problems that are part of developing a new engine and a mediocre chassis, together with the strange choice of driver for 1995, didn't help the situation. Nigel Mansell didn't even fit in the car at the start of the season, and Mark Blundell stepped in, but, even with a modified chassis, Mansell failed to perform. Häkkinen steadily moved into the number-one spot, but his career suffered a major setback after an end-of-season crash in which he sustained serious head injuries.

Dennis rebuilt his team in the mid-1990s. In 1996, he approached Adrian Newey, then a top designer with Williams, and asked him to take on the role of technical director with McLaren. Newey came on board and in 1998 McLaren renewed their supremacy of the tracks, claiming both the Drivers' and Constructors' titles with Mika Häkkinen looking a giant of the circuits winning eight of the 16 Grands Prix and claiming three more podiums. McLaren held on to the Drivers' title in 1999, but Ferrari triumphed in the Constructors' league; this turned out to be a portent for the next half-decade.

The 2000s

Although made a Commander of the British Empire in 2000, Dennis found he had a bit of trouble commanding McLaren's troops when Jaguar's Bobby Rahal tried to tempt Newey to join his outfit. Dennis managed to hang on to his designer – it was rumoured by agreeing that he could devote some time to working on racing yachts. To add to Dennis's problems, Mika Häkkinen decided he wanted to retire from Formula One. Ron replaced his double World Champion with

Kimi Räikkönen, snatching the 'Finnish Flash' from the clutches of Jean Todt and Ferrari.

Following a disappointing 2004, by 2005, Dennis was once more scaling the heights of Formula One. McLaren produced their strongest showing for several years, but were denied both Championships by Renault. With Adrian Newey joining Red Bull from the start of 2006, it would have been easy to lose morale. But, in December 2005, McLaren teamed up with Vodafone in what was reputed to be an £800 million sponsorship deal starting in 2007. With double World Champion Fernando Alonso joining McLaren for the 2007 season, it seemed that Dennis was gunning for glory. However, 2006 was devoid of victory for McLaren and this constituted a decade low for the team. But, at the start of the 2007 season, McLaren, alongside Ferrari, seemed to be the strongest challengers for the World Championships by a long way, and the excitement was heightened with the debut of their rising star Lewis Hamilton.

TO THE DESERT

Trust your dreams.
They are sweet and beautiful.
Trust your visions.
They are soulful and powerful.
Trust your aspiration.
It is your earth-friend
And
Heaven-brother.
Trust your realisation.
It is your Eternity's real Self.

'Your Dreams', Sri Chinmoy

Bahrain

The sun seemed violent enough to blister even the dry roasted sand of desert as the cars lined up on the grid. The two Ferraris were sheltered in the shade in first and third on the unsoiled side of the grid; the McLarens were in second and fourth on the side of the grid that was grimy in comparison; for the third time in succession, the Woking team had qualified in these positions. The temperature was hovering around the 30°C mark, although on the track it was above 40°C. The air temperature was higher still and the humidity unforgiving. The largest variable was the wind speed that was 3.2mph at the start of the race but this would vary wildly during the race and over the circuit; on the pit-straight, it was running nose-on and at points reaching 4.3 metres per second. This should have favoured the extremely smooth Ferraris that, down the straight, already had a 7kph speed advantage over their McLaren adversaries.

Lewis had trailed the Ferraris in testing on the same track in February but, after completely out-qualifying Alonso (this was the first time he had beaten his team-mate in qualifying) the day before the Grand Prix, it was Lewis who led the charge on McLaren's closest rivals. He claimed a place on the front row of the grid, another first in his three-race career. On the Friday, Räikkönen and Felipe Massa set the best times in the morning practice, and the Finn was quickest in the afternoon, this time with Lewis second. On the 3.363-mile Bahrain International circuit, Räikkönen finished in 1:33.162 in the morning and 1:33.527 in the afternoon. Swirling winds blew sand everywhere to make driving tricky and caused the Ferrari driver to complain, 'It was difficult to find the right balance, partly because at this track the wind makes the car difficult to drive.'

But throughout the practice sessions Lewis had been sharp and it appeared that Ferrari and McLaren were closer than they were in Malaysia.

Lewis said that qualifying had been tough and intense, and that he had needed to pull out 'absolutely everything' in that final flying lap. The wind was constantly changing; sometimes there had been a tailwind, sometimes a crosswind. He thought that he could probably have gone quicker in qualifying but that to go into his third race in Formula One and get a front row was 'amazing … but the lap was not that great. Earlier in the session I had better laps … I feel pretty relaxed about what has happened so far. It feels natural. I am happy to be where I am.'

However, he understood that the race was going to be tough. He knew the first corner of the Sakhir circuit was always tricky, being an extremely tight turn. But he was steeled by the fact that he had been there before and felt a bit more comfortable with the circuit.

Lewis had raced in Bahrain in 2004 when he took part in the F3 Superprix. That produced one of the most impressive races of his young career. He started 11th on the grid and ended the opening lap in fourth and then drove through to win, beating Nico Rosberg to the flag. It was also the first track on which he had tested the MP4-22 in February 2007 (he'd had five days testing in Manama).

The Sakhir circuit, which was staging its fourth Formula One Grand Prix, has an oasis feel that makes it one of the most electrifying new locations in the sport. Being situated out in the desert makes it a unique event and very different from other Grands Prix, providing a challenging 14 turns, while the big straights offer plenty of overtaking opportunities. Overall, the drivers enjoy the test the layout represents.

The track is 3.3 miles (5.412km) long and the Grand Prix is fought over 57 laps. Michael Schumacher holds the lap record (1:30.252) that he set in 2004. In 2006, Fernando Alonso had won the race for Renault.

The initial turn at Sakhir can be hectic, with the whole field trying to squeeze round in first gear. The potential for disaster is obvious as the pack of roaring machines, their drivers dizzied with adrenaline, fight for position. There's been lots of overtaking action over the years. If a driver comes through the apex doing around 50mph and makes just the slightest mistake, a car can go straight across the in-field unimpeded and smash into the sides of cars that have made the turn.

There's a long straight leading into a tight corner at turn four, which, although pretty straightforward, is followed by two very high-speed turns. A racer's line and technique through this sequence is crucial. The power has to be varied according to conditions, chiefly the sand and constantly changing wind direction. Each time a driver starts out on these turns, they have to deal with new circumstances and, of course, this is a big ask of the engines.

Coming out of turn eight and up into turn nine, the corner gets tighter and tighter, forcing drivers to brake as they turn. That corner is among the hardest the race has to offer; the speed and grip level are low and tyres can lock up.

Many thought that, following Sepang, it would be the battle at the Sakhir first turn principally between Massa and Hamilton that would be critical as far as the race result was concerned, but, as the lights were extinguished, the Ferrari racer got away faster on the clean tarmac, leaving Hamilton almost dawdling in comparison, struggling for grip on the grubby surface his car started from. But Lewis did well enough to hold the inside line and maintain second, weaving around a bit naughtily, elbowing himself some space.

As the drivers gathered for turn one, Hamilton and Massa almost touched, but there was no opportunity for Lewis to make a progressive manoeuvre. Räikkönen tried to go round the outside as they turned to make the apex. This was pretty dangerous but the Finn could find no way round Hamilton and the McLaren man blocked the assault. Alonso attacked Räikkönen on the inside at turn four and tucked himself into third place.

The British driver had made his mind up to stay behind Massa, knowing that the Brazilian was going a lap more than him. But Lewis saw himself as 'fairly well matched' with Massa and thought that, if he had got to the front, he would have got away from the Ferrari, the Italian cars having one of their biggest advantages pulling away, but the McLarens generally could find similar pace if not quicker on the run.

But, as the war for supremacy at the front was raging, at the rear of the field an incident provoked the Safety Car to be called into action for the first time in the 2007 season. Jenson Button had been spun round as the swift-starting David Coulthard slammed the door on the steely Somerset speedster, after he'd been shunted on to the dirty tarmac by Takuma Sato.

At the beginning of the fourth lap, the race was on again. The laps immediately following the restart were intriguing, the space between cars varying massively as a clear road was marked out, but, if any driver made a single wrong move on to soiled sand-strewn tarmac, their rear ends could slide unpredictably.

After seven laps, an order had become apparent; Massa and Hamilton were loose at the front of the field, Alonso had fallen back but appeared to be keeping Räikkönen at bay. Massa posted the fastest lap of the race (1:35.209) 0.9 of a second ahead of Hamilton who had 2.2 seconds on Alonso. The Spaniard led Räikkönen by 0.6 of a second, but just four seconds separated these first four. However, Alonso was the slowest of the leaders, and would remain confined for the rest of the race. Lewis demonstrated that this relative sluggishness was not a McLaren syndrome when he set the fastest lap on his eighth circuit with a 1:35.137 and then repeated the feat two laps later.

A blue haze had been coming off Hamilton's engine since the early laps and was a cause for worry as there was still a long way to go.

Massa responded to Hamilton on lap 13 with a 1:34.776 round, and a lap later he clocked 1:34.693. Alonso was having a torrid time, sliding his rear tyres. His car was handling so poorly that Räikkönen almost struck the reigning World Champion under-braking on lap 15.

During that same lap, with plenty of space around him, Hamilton produced another FL (1:34.607); he was now seven seconds better than his team-mate; a couple of rounds later there was nearly 10 seconds between first and fourth and Lewis turned the screws with a fastest lap of 1:34.490. Lap 18 saw him lower this to 1:34.270 (five times in the opening stint, on laps eight, nine, 15, 17 and 18, Hamilton set the fastest lap) and at the conclusion of lap 19 he was the first of the front-runners to pit.

Hamilton seemed to be fuelling for a long time. At the end of lap 21, Massa followed him in. Alonso pitted after the 23rd lap and Räikkönen and Heidfeld waited until they had finished lap 24. Although the Brit had been stationary longest, he had made a big enough gap to retain his second place, but Alonso lost out to Räikkönen and came out of the pits to find himself in fourth and soon had to deal with the threat of BMW's Nick Heidfeld closing on him as both McLarens appeared slow in the middle stint.

Hamilton began to haemorrhage half a second a lap to Massa and 0.3 to Räikkönen who little by little started to pull the rookie in. By the 26th lap, Massa and Hamilton were still leading the pack, followed by Räikkönen, Alonso and Heidfeld. Four circuits on, Massa had generated an eight-second lead over Lewis while Räikkönen continued to shut down the space between himself and the Briton.

In lap 32, Heidfeld made an intelligent move on Alonso; down the straight the BMW driver closed in on the McLaren. The 'Oviedo Overlord' was forced to go on the defensive into turn one. He paid the price for this by making a slow exit from turn three. Heading to turn four, Alonso yet again adopted a defensive line on the inside but the German, in a gloriously simple move, went round the outside of the Spaniard.

Lap 34 saw Massa with a 10.2-second advantage over Hamilton who was 2.1 seconds in front of Räikkönen. Heidfeld followed 4.4 seconds later in front of Alonso by a margin of 1.5 seconds. Once more, the World Champion was the slowest driver of the first five.

The gaps stayed constant towards the finish of the second stint. But by the 36th lap Räikkönen was just 1.4 seconds behind Hamilton and it seemed that the 27-year-old from Espoo would pose a serious threat to the Brit.

Massa and Räikkönen sped in for their last pit stops on the 41st and 42nd laps. When Massa set the FL on lap 42 (1:34.067, 0.203 seconds better than Hamilton), few would have bet against a Ferrari one-two. Alonso pitted on the 43rd lap but failed to get back out in front of Heidfeld. One lap on, Hamilton pitted and unexpectedly came out a second in front of Räikkönen.

Although the McLarens had looked comparatively slow during the middle stint, they were now moving faster than the Ferraris and, rather than Räikkönen tugging in Hamilton, Lewis started to get closer to Massa, edging the gap down. But the McLaren racer wasn't helped by the fact that the engine of Anthony Davidson's Honda blew right in front of him, splattering his visor with a coating of oil. For all this, Massa seemed to have the speed to resist any onslaught that Hamilton might have had in mind.

On the 47th lap, Hamilton had crept up to within 6.7 seconds of

Massa. Lewis kept Räikkönen 2.7 seconds behind him. The Finn was 5.7 seconds in front of Heidfeld who was 1.6 seconds ahead of Alonso and, although the Spanish Champ did close in on the German, he was nowhere near getting past him.

Massa, having led from pole, took full advantage and had eked out enough of a margin during the race's middle phase to resist Hamilton's charge on the harder tyre over the closing laps and claimed his first win of 2007. It was a relatively comfortable victory that saw him bounce back from his terrible display in Malaysia. The Brazilian claimed the welcome 10 points for his treble (he posted the best lap time of the race to add to his pole position and race win) and revitalised his faltering campaign. But it was Hamilton, just a couple of seconds behind the Ferrari man, who showed that he was able to overcome handling difficulties that seemed beyond his McLaren colleague. Just after he crossed the line, Lewis's radio told him that he was 'the current leader of the World Championship, not too bad for a rookie'.

Hamilton laughed and said, 'Not too bad, guys, not too bad.'

After the race Lewis told how he had managed where Alonso had floundered: 'I was able to keep up with Felipe in the first stint but I really struggled with the balance of the car in the second. I had a lot of under-steer and wasn't able to brake as late as I would have liked. However, after the second pit stop, when I changed to hard tyres, I was able to push again. I really enjoyed the race today and with a few more laps I might have been able to challenge Felipe for the lead.'

His team-mate had a more straightforward tale to tell: 'I couldn't keep up with the Ferraris and Lewis.'

When confronted with the rhetorical remark by a reporter 'another great race for our man Lewis', the reigning World Champion replied 'Yes' in a tone something just short of curt, and seemed to be trying to find a polite smile from somewhere.

The Spaniard, although notionally leading McLaren's 2007 challenge, fought to master his car's under-braking and struggled with the balance of the vehicle throughout the race; he could not get anywhere near his junior partner despite a clear advantage in the pits – Lewis pitted on laps

19 (9.9 seconds) and 44 (7.1 seconds); Fernando pitted on laps 22 (8.4 seconds) and 43 (6.6 seconds).

At the start of the season, McLaren could not have thought they might be protecting Alonso from Hamilton, but, brake problems notwithstanding, the man thought to be the understudy in the McLaren team had crushed his erstwhile superior. But Alonso remained a redoubtable enemy, a proud athletic bull-fighter of a competitor. Both he and Massa, like Hamilton, had risen through the ranks of motorsport. For all this, he would not have anticipated being on the end of Hamilton's talent so early in both men's Formula One career with McLaren. Previously he had not been bettered by a team-mate in Formula One. His reaction when challenged by Giancarlo Fisichella and Jarno Trulli in the past was cold and efficient. But there would be no better place than Barcelona and his home country to hit back.

However, in Bahrain, Hamilton had been quickest in the final phase of the race. Had tyres utilised in the second stint not mysteriously drained performance from his car, McLaren believed Hamilton would have been celebrating his first victory in the desert; Ferrari had the edge on the softer compounds, but on the harder wheels, which were used in the last stint of the race, Hamilton seized the advantage.

Reflecting on events after the race, he smiled and commented, 'I worked extremely hard and I've just been told I've made history! I couldn't feel better. We potentially had the fastest car ... the second stint I struggled on my second set of tyres, perhaps we should have gone out on the hard tyre. I don't know what the reason was for the lack of pace there, but the first and the last stint were clearly quicker and it was close ... we really wouldn't have expected this six or seven years ago. When I was doing karting, you just couldn't imagine standing on the podium where Michael Schumacher and all the greats have been. I just beat Kimi Räikkönen! It just doesn't seem real ... Felipe did a great job of the first corner and he took the lead but next time we'll be working even harder to be at the front.' He smiled and winked.

As it was, Lewis became the first driver in Formula One history to finish on the podium in his first three races and claim a share of the lead of the Drivers' World Championship.

Räikkönen finished a secure third and Heidfeld got another creditable fourth place. Alonso, having struggled throughout, was just fifth.

The race had not been as explosive as many had anticipated, but it did throw the World Championship wide open. At that point Hamilton was a clear challenger to Alonso and Massa and had the edge on Räikkönen in terms of overall performance.

McLaren's chief executive Martin Whitmarsh, not a man prone to gushing, was swift to praise Lewis's achievement: 'Three races in to be a contender for the World Championship is phenomenal ... We all have to conclude now that Lewis is a serious title challenger. He'll want to go better now and win a race. I don't think anybody doubts that he will do that this season.'

Strictly speaking, Alonso was the leader of the Championship given his results (a victory and a runner-up spot). Räikkönen's win in Australia kept him second on a count back, but the concern for both was the fact that Lewis had hardly been pushed over his three Grands Prix outings and no one knew the measure of his capacity. Unlike Malaysia, where he had at least been physically and mentally tested, fighting off the Ferraris, Hamilton looked strikingly fresh and untroubled in the heat and dust of Sakhir.

As Lewis jetted out of Bahrain to fulfil a sponsorship engagement in Shanghai, he was expected to return to Britain a few days later; he had been away from home for nine weeks. McLaren declined to say when exactly he'd be back in the UK, in the hope of maintaining some control of the Hamilton story. It was probably too late for that, but Ron Dennis summed up the team's weekend well enough saying that, even though it was not a perfect day, they would leave Bahrain leading both the Manufacturers' and Drivers' Championships and he saw this as 'a great achievement for the team'. He admitted that Alonso had struggled with the balance of his car and that McLaren hadn't managed to perfect his set-up. However, he confirmed that Hamilton had been more comfortable with his car and had a great race. He concluded by saying that McLaren's intensive R&D programme would 'change up a gear and hopefully deliver a performance step that will make us even more competitive at the Spanish Grand Prix, and, of course, we are already looking forward to the start of the European season in Barcelona'.

In Melbourne, Lewis had been the surprise turn; in Malaysia, he had defended like a tiger and was a revelation; in Bahrain he was 'Hamilton the Hunter', chasing down Felipe Massa in the closing laps of the race and leaving double World Champion Alonso in the dust.

As the stands at Sakhir emptied, three drivers were equal on 22 points and Massa was close behind on 17 but Lewis was not deluding himself. He was still not a winner. However, he seemed in no doubt that he was in a position to challenge his team-mate for supremacy both in the Championship and in the context of the McLaren set-up: 'I don't see why not ... I seem to be as quick as him. I know I feel a lot more comfortable now. We just have to make no mistakes and keep pushing.'

After Hamilton's triumph among the dunes, Sir Frank Williams, the man behind Britain's last World Championship success in Formula One when Damon Hill won the title in 1996, compared Lewis to the seven-time World Champion Michael Schumacher: 'I thought after we got rid of Michael, "Now we've got a chance again." But then another superhuman turns up ... Michael was many things, but he was also a very simple human. Hamilton is a different character, but, purely in terms of calibre or quality of skill, what I'm seeing so early in this man's career is remarkable ... Hamilton is still a baby, so to speak, but he is dishing out loads of trouble already ... I mean that in the nicest possible way. I cry he's not in a Williams, but I rejoice for Formula One.'

Hill himself thought that Hamilton was bound to win at some point: 'Somewhere between now and the end of the season, that's going to happen and then he'll grow in stature and start to see himself differently, and we'll all start to see him as a Championship contender. I think it's real.'

Three-time World Champion Niki Lauda, who was also in Bahrain, said he believed that the young driver's 'education' in motor racing by Ron Dennis was the key to his success: 'He had a perfect build-up, which nobody has ever done before ... Ron, or somebody, took care of him since he was 12 and then they realised the talent in him and made him race in one category after another in such a perfect way that he won most of them.'

Sir Jackie Stewart, who didn't make the podium until his eighth race (Monza, 1965), after witnessing Hamilton's performance in Bahrain, declared, 'He is, of course, driving for one of the best teams in the world at the present time, with a competitive car, but nevertheless he's been able to accomplish more in a shorter time than any driver I've ever seen.'

Stewart went on to say that Lewis could become Formula One World Champion in his debut season and, although he saw it as 'not unusual for a driver to do very well in his first year and have a bit of a dip in the second year', he was confident the Stevenage lad would certainly win the title within three seasons.

However, according to another former British Champion, Nigel Ernest James Mansell OBE, Ayrton Senna and Michael Schumacher did more to impress at the start of their motor-racing careers. Mansell believed that Lewis had struck lucky by driving the top-of-the-range car that McLaren had developed: 'Lewis has lucked into a fabulous car ... What he's done has been very impressive but it's what he should have been doing anyway.'

For Lewis's dad, Anthony, 'It was crazy getting his first podium, crazier getting second in Malaysia and then leading the Championship with Fernando Alonso and Kimi Räikkönen at the same time – you couldn't write it ... I thought, "If we end up sixth or seventh this year, I'll be happy," but this is absolutely out of this world ... I am frightened what's going to happen next! ... There is a lot said in Formula One about young drivers not being able to cut the mustard. Well, hopefully we have done some good for some other young drivers who are good enough to sit in the seat.'

Lewis's stepmother and his brother Nicholas were also in Bahrain. Nicholas summed up what the rest of Britain was feeling when he said he had enjoyed the race 'so much, it was the best race I've ever seen. Just to see him closing the gap on Massa was amazing and to come away with second is great!'

Garage, Pit, Sim

Since Ayrton Senna's death, the rules of Formula One racing have changed. In modern racing, cars don't get dragged along in the slipstream as much as they used to and now have bigger tyres. Lewis complains about the latter: 'They are higher off the ground, so have less down-force on them and are slower.'

Lewis believes today's racing does not compare with the 1990s, for him the glory days of Formula One: 'They used to overtake a lot more. Now there is a bigger problem with down-force and it is harder to overtake.'

There is a lot in Hamilton's view that the long-term fan finds it hard to argue with, but Formula One in the 21st century is a sport that is no longer totally about the individual as it once was. The joust of yesteryear is now a war of attrition between opposing armies, who, although they field champions at the head of their battle wagons, rely on a whole apparatus of technology and know-how in their fight for supremacy.

A Grand Prix team can be around 100-strong excluding the test team, and Lewis is quick to acknowledge those around him who have contributed to his success. He has confessed that there are times when he hasn't even noticed changes his engineer has made, but understands his 'engineer is so smart and he understands what I say and the way I communicate', and for Hamilton that is 'a great feeling' because, 'when someone understands what you're talking about and is able to translate that into your car, it runs better'.

Phil Prew is Lewis's race engineer. At times, he has looked more nervous than Lewis in the garage just before the driver takes to the track. Hamilton shakes his team's hands and seems to bring a feeling of calm to the garage. McLaren are a warm, friendly team, and Lewis fits in well with this ethos.

During practice, testing or racing, Hamilton is constantly tracked from the pit wall by Prew, who monitors all aspects of the car's performance and his driver's condition and responses. The relationship between driver and engineer is powerfully symbiotic: working as a tight pairing within the wider team, intent on exploiting the full potential of driver/car combination. For Lewis, as with any rookie, the engineer also plays a big part in style development and racing technique.

While on track, Prew advises Hamilton via the radio link between the car and the pits. This is how the driver finds out about how the race is developing tactically and gets feedback on his own performance.

According to Prew, there is a dual focus to the preparation of a driver, the actual racing and the nature of the circuit to be raced on. As soon as Hamilton was officially named as a McLaren driver in November 2006, he and Prew began to work on an extensive and exhaustive development programme to guarantee Lewis's proficiency in particular areas that apply to any race, for instance competition tactics and strategy for pit stops. Among many other things, Hamilton also needed to be able to provide tremendously precise feedback on the feel of the car and how it reacted to minuscule changes.

Preparation for particular circuits offers different sets of challenges. Although Lewis has raced at some of the tracks in other Formula, it doesn't help much as racing at Formula One is a different experience, so Hamilton had to start from the beginning and even *unlearn* some stuff. Familiarity can help, but sections that seemed straight in a GP2 car can feel like a corner when driving a Formula One vehicle.

For Lewis, 'Formula One is so tough and the cars are so much faster.' This means a driver's reactions need to be sharper.

Preparation is intense. Prior to a race, a massive amount of telemetry data from the past couple of years has to be analysed and compared with the video footage. Prew and Lewis look at details like where drivers have gained or lost lap time, where they start their braking and their approach to the corners. In-car videos of other teams' drivers are also looked at, but, without the relevant data, it is difficult to identify their mistakes or determine how well they are doing.

According to Prew, Lewis's driving style is developing all the time, which makes it imperative to attempt 'to keep his mind open' about how to deal with certain turns and make sure he understands that some corners have more than a single line, each of which has its particular outcomes. Making a choice of line is difficult to prepare for, as conditions of track, car and race vary so much. That's where experience and skill take over and it has to be said that, although he is building these all the time, Lewis is at a disadvantage relative to more practised drivers and, as such, at least for now, has to rely on instinct and innate physical and mental capacities to make up the difference.

Lewis has gained a lot from time spent on the state-of-the-art simulator secretly developed by McLaren at their Surrey technology centre. Prew and Hamilton have used it to meet many of the new challenges of Formula One racing. For Lewis, although there is no substitute for 'real-time' experience on a track, it is a 'great tool'. The simulator enables a driver to familiarise himself with circuits and work on the set-up of the car. The machine provides all the details one would find in a car and replicates the particular conditions of any given track and car performance. This is particularly helpful when looking to identify reference points (features of a circuit) to aid a driver to maintain consistency in terms of lap time.

Prior to arriving at a track to walk with his engineer (a vital part of race preparation), Lewis receives a detailed file from his engineering team that provides him with an exhaustive summary of anticipated features and expectations of a circuit.

The dossier also has details of gear ratios, maps, historical information and a weather forecast. Following a race, the driver gets another pack that goes over his performance and that of the car. It details every aspect including mistakes and mishaps.

Prew has said of Lewis that one of his strengths is his 'openness and willingness to listen' to both positive and negative observations: 'If there is something he needs to improve, we say so. It's as simple as that. There are no airs and graces about him and he's not set in his ways either. He's just eager to learn from everybody around him, including Fernando Alonso. Having a team-mate of his calibre to learn from has already been of huge benefit to Lewis.'

Hamilton's Team

Personal trainer – Adam Costanzo
Australian – joined McLaren's human performance laboratory programme in 2006.

No2 mechanic – Karl Lamenranta
Joined McLaren five years ago. Formerly a Formula 3000 mechanic. Looks after the front end of the car during races.

Race engineer – Phil Prew
Been with McLaren a long time – used to work with Kimi Räikkönen. Cool under pressure.

No1 mechanic – Chris Thompson
Very experienced, long time with McLaren – responsible for preparing Lewis's car at Grands Prix and at testing.

Study

During a party hosted by Swiss watchmaker and McLaren sponsor Tag Heuer in July 2007, Lewis told how his time had been devoted to books over the previous nine months, only taking breaks to watch DVDs and talk about the car to the McLaren team.

He talked about how the cars have huge amounts of software, so there were considerations apart from mechanics. It is not just a case of getting into a Formula One car and roaring round the circuit. Among other things, a good knowledge of aerodynamics is needed and Lewis had been studying this from September to March. Each circuit on the Formula One schedule also needed close and detailed scrutiny.

Willy Ribbs

Hamilton's sensational entry into Formula One has the potential to revolutionise the sport. His youth and his background have a lot to do with this, but, despite all efforts to skirt round the issue, the fact that he is black is at least a significant part of his impact. But he was not the first man of African descent to break into Formula One or to make a powerful contribution to motorsport as a successful participant.

William 'Willy' Theodore Ribbs Jr was born on 3 January 1956 in San Jose, California, to Geraldine and William T Ribbs Sr.

Ribbs's love of cars and racing began at the age of four. As a nine-year-old, Willy worked as a ranch hand on his grandfather's ranch. But, following his graduation from high school in 1975, having been taught how to drive fast by his father, rather than managing the successful family plumbing business founded by his grandfather, Henry Ribbs, in San Jose in 1927, Ribbs went to Europe to race in the Formula Ford Series. In his first year of competition, he won the highly regarded Dunlop Championship. He returned to the United States where NASCAR owner Will Kronkite took Willy on to drive his Winston Cup car and he became one of the only African-American NASCAR racers.

However, Ribbs was guilty of two unexplained absences from practice sessions, and was replaced with Dale Earnhardt. But Willy went on to race Formula Atlantic cars, winning the pole in the 1982 Long Beach FA race. He led the race, outpacing veteran drivers, before engine failure dashed his chances of winning.

In 1983, Ribbs won five races in the SCCA Trans-Am Series as a rookie and was honoured as Pro Rookie of the Year. He had 17 more victories over the next two years driving for Jack Roush.

Willy attempted NASCAR again in 1986, running three races in the DiGard Motorsports' #30 Red Roof Inns car. His best result was his debut race where he finished 22nd at North Wilkesboro Speedway. Lack of sponsorship ended his season.

In January 1986, Willy became the first black person to test a Formula One car, with the Brabham team in Estoril, Portugal. He was a guest of the future Formula One potentate Bernie Ecclestone, then the Brabham team owner and someone who has always had a feel for the needs of Formula One and knew how to create headlines.

Ribbs became the first black driver to experience the power of a modern Formula One car, but he never got the chance to show what he could do in a Grand Prix. Brabham were sponsored by the Italian Olivetti company and, unsurprisingly, started the 1986 season with two Italian drivers. Competing for another drive against the likes of future Formula One Champion Nigel Mansell, Willy was never in with a shout.

After three successful years with Dan Gurney in IMSA, Ribbs moved to Indy cars. In 1989, Bill and Camille Cosby stepped in and funded the Raynor-Cosby Motorsports team with Ribbs as the top driver. With one of the world's top black entertainers sponsoring him, Ribbs won two top-10 events in his 1990 Championship Auto Racing Team (CART) Indianapolis debut. Sadly, during his first CART season in 1990, he was involved in a collision at the Vancouver street circuit in which a marshal was killed.

In 1991, Ribbs became the first African-American to qualify for the Indianapolis 500. For Willy, 'The Indianapolis 500 is the biggest race in the world. When you walk into the Indianapolis Motor Speedway, it's the Taj Mahal. You cannot not feel something.'

Ribbs achieved the same feat a second time in 1993, starting 30th but finishing a creditable 21st.

However, by 1994, it was clear that corporate sponsors were not yet willing to back an African-American driver, despite Cosby's offer of free television commercials in return for sponsorship. Ribbs was released from his Indianapolis 500 contract and spent the year competing in the CART series, finishing in the top 10 at Michigan and Denver Grand Prix races.

Ribbs got back into racing in 1998 when he ran the NASCAR Street Race in Los Angeles, where he competed against Mark Martin for the lead.

During 1999, Ribbs raced in the Indy Racing League (IRL) event at

Las Vegas Motor Speedway. He crossed the line in 26th place following a crash. In 2000, he signed with Victoria Motorsports SCCA Trans-Am team. He had three top-10s and finished second at Long Beach, third at Detroit and fourth at Las Vegas. He was awarded the Johnson Triple Crown.

Willy signed to drive the #8 Dodge Ram for Bobby Hamilton (no relation to Lewis) racing in the NASCAR Craftsman Truck Series in 2001. Driving 23 out of 24 races, Ribbs had a best placing of 13th, and finished 16th in points. He was the first African-American in the modern era to compete full-time in a major NASCAR division.

In May 2006, Willy provoked controversy by referring to NASCAR as Al-Qaeda or 'Neckcar' or the WWE (World Wrestling Entertainment). He has consistently questioned the governing body and its commitment to minority drivers and criticised NASCARs diversity programme: 'When I raced, there was no such thing as a diversity programme. I think that's just a public relations programme. I think NASCAR, they have to take a look at themselves in the mirror and ask what do they want … You're not a big player until all people can compete in the sport.'

In contrast to his NASCAR experience, Ribbs remembers fondly driving in the CART series and calls racing legend and 1978 Formula One World Champion Mario Andretti an 'awesome man' who Willy grew to admire 'because he is as tough as a tiger now as he was 20 years ago'.

Another fond recollection for Willy is how comedian Bill Cosby called him out of the blue to sponsor him.

Willy's Indy Car earnings amounted to $1,241,952.

Originally taught to shoot by his grandfather, Willy is now competing full-time in the San Antonio-based National Sporting Clays Association. His highlight, he says, is winning a preliminary division for the Kruger Cup. One of the things Ribbs loves about the sporting clays is the sense of control: 'It's just like having a golf club in your hand or a baseball bat. It's just you. You have 99 per cent control of your success, whereas, in auto racing, with the way the sport has become, as a driver you have 15 to 20 per cent control of what you're going to accomplish.'

Willy is divorced and has teenage children, a daughter Sasha and a son William Theodore Ribbs III (Theo) who also is an aspiring shooter.

Willy still boxes with heavyweights such as Ray Mercer to keep in shape. Columbia Pictures and actor Michael Douglas purchased the rights to Ribbs's life story for a future movie and he has received a Sports Image Award. He says that if he hadn't been in racing he would have become a jazz musician. In the past he has occasionally 'moonlighted' as an extra on the set of *The Cosby Mysteries*.

Willy loved the thrill, the speed, the high he got from defying the odds and winning and living to tell about it, his description of what it takes to race fast in cars is not too far from how Lewis Hamilton might see things: 'When you roll out of the pit lane and out on to the track, you are absolutely switched on like a computer. You are thinking. You are not driving out of control. You are very, very precise with everything you do. And at high speeds you have to be very precise. It's like a surgeon. When a surgeon is in the operating room, he's got on those glasses and that mask, and he's focused on what he s doing. He knows, if he makes an error, it could result in someone dying. Well, it's the same thing with driving a race car. You absolutely must be in a zone, in your own world. You don't become emotional about it, or you will end up in the wall. Or crash.'

While Willy might never have climbed the heights Hamilton has the potential to reach, he exemplifies the difficulties, social and financial, involved in a black driver getting to the top of motorsport. Perhaps it is too easy to say that he lived in another time and that things are different for the likes of Lewis. But it is clear that what Ribbs had to say about NASCAR is equally true of Formula One – you're not a big player until *all* people can compete in the sport. It is probable that Lewis is bringing this home to many people and making it an inescapable fact that the time is over when Formula One can wait until some rich kid emerges from the fields of wealth. But with the news that four-year-old Ben Kasperczak, being hailed as 'the next Lewis Hamilton', became the youngest ever driver to be signed to a manufacturer (*Motorsport World*) in April 2007, although not yet able to ride a bike without stabilisers, one cannot help but wonder if the sport is not about to jump from one extreme to another.

Willy T Ribbs's Racing Career

1977 – Paid his own way to England. Rented Formula Ford ride, finished third in the race. Won his second race. Finished second in fourth race ahead of fellow driver Nigel Mansell. Produced six wins in eleven starts and series Champion.

1978 – Had sole ride in Long Beach Formula Atlantic race. Promoter HA 'Humpy' Wheeler invited Ribbs to Charlotte Motor Speedway to attempt to qualify for World 600, but competitive ride failed to materialise.

1982 – Ran Red Roof Inns-sponsored Ralt in Formula Atlantic. Won pole at Long Beach against competitors Michael Andretti, Al Unser Jr and Geoff Brabham.

1983 – Stepped up to Trans-Am Camaros. Won five of twelve races and SCCA Rookie of the Year.

1984 – Ribbs won more races (17) than any other Trans-Am driver during 1984.

1985 – Went to Indy with deal constructed by boxing promoter Don King. Last-minute preparation, handling problems and lack of speed led to cancellation of plans to qualify.

1987 – Won four races and IMSA Driver of the Year honours.

1988 – Three more victories, again winning IMSA Driver of the Year title.

1989 – Drove developmental IMSA GTP Eagle HF Prototype. Announced in November ride with newly created Raynor-Cosby Motorsports team with financial support from entertainer Bill Cosby.

1990 – Made PPG Cup debut at Long Beach. Did not attempt to qualify at Indy.

1991 – An improved PPG Cup season, finishing 17th in points in nine starts with Walker Motorsports team. With McDonald's sponsorship starting at Indy, became the first black American driver at the Speedway. Finished in the points in five races including an IndyCar career-high sixth at Denver after qualifying 13th. Also drove Toyota HF 90 IMSA GTP car in 24 hours at Daytona and 12 hours of Sebring endurance races.

1992 – Started one event at Laguna Seca for Walker Motorsports.

1993 – Started 13 races with Walker Racing in competitive season with full-time sponsorship from Service Merchandise and Pepsi. Scored five points-paying finishes.

1994 – Started 15 races with Derrick Walker Racing. Scored a season-best finish of seventh at Michigan. Scored three other points-paying finishes. Will not return to Walker this year.

Best career finishes:
6th – 1991: Denver.

Points standing:
1990: 3 (26th)
1991: 17 (17th)
1992: 0 (57th)
1993: 9 (20th)
1994: 12 (22nd)

THE CONSUMING THRILL

The gemmy bridle glitter'd free,
Like to some branch of stars we see
Hung in the golden Galaxy.
The bridle bells rang merrily
As he rode down to Camelot:
And from his blazon'd baldric slung
A mighty silver bugle hung,
And as he rode his armour rung
Beside remote Shalott.

'The Lady of Shalott', Alfred Tennyson

Espana Por Favor

On Sunday, 13 May, the Gran Premio de España Telefónica 2007 started on the Circuit de Catalunya, north of Barcelona, in front of an expectant and partisan crowd of 140,000. It was the best-attended race of the year and the spectators had been queuing for five hours (all the way back to Barcelona) hoping for great things from Spain's top sportsman Fernando Alonso. The presence of his team-mate in row two could not have been a comfort to the homeboy. But the local lad lost the race from the start after a struggle between himself, Hamilton and Massa. He took the risk of holding the Brazilian, covering the inside on the first turn, but it was just good fortune that he didn't turn over into the gravel. Räikkönen and Hamilton took advantage and Lewis slotted into second place.

Alonso took over in third after Räikkönen was forced to retire on lap 10 following problems with his car, but the Spaniard found no way to pull Hamilton in. However, Lewis was faring no better in cutting space down between himself and Massa, who gradually improved his lead to almost 10 seconds by his first pit stop on lap 19. Alonso also came in at this point, but Hamilton carried on for a further three laps. He could get no closer to the Ferrari after rejoining the race following his own stop.

With the initial pit stops completed, Alonso's already faint hopes of claiming victory in front of his compatriots for the second year in succession were fading.

McLaren used the harder tyre for his middle stint, but the rest of the field held on to the soft option, looking to the harder tyres for the final assault. The idea seemed to be for Alonso to consolidate mid-race and leave his charge for the concluding laps. However, all seemed lost when Hamilton was clocked better than 10 seconds ahead of him during the laps immediately after the stops, the Spaniard's tyres taking time to warm up.

The winning criterion for the irascible Iberian leaked away as he lost more ground to his team-mate over the entire second stint. The man who was looking less and less like McLaren's number one was adrift of Hamilton by more than 16 seconds by lap 47 as Lewis made his second stop.

A lap later, Alonso followed him in and began to close on his partner after rejoining the chase, but in the final 10 laps the gap became a constant. At the front, Massa had put himself in an unassailable position to win his third race in four outings, but Lewis became the first British driver to lead the World Championship since David Coulthard in 2003 and was the youngest driver to do so since Bruce McLaren (the founder of the McLaren team) but he was the first driver in the history of Formula One to get four podiums in his first four races.

The Race and the Racer

Talking of motor racing, Lewis has said that, if he didn't love the sport, he is certain that he would not be the performer he is today. He feels he would not have invested the extremes of effort he has exerted into the pursuit of his evident excellence. Looking back on his initial years in karting, he told how he thought there were drivers who relied almost totally on their God-given abilities and 'don't do the hard yards'. But, for Hamilton, the youthful mind does not fully understand that success is reliant on a 'work hard and see the result' ethic and that it is too easy to fall into a frame of mind that leads to a 'I can't be bothered to work hard now' cul-de-sac that leaves you struggling and complaining: 'But if you really put the effort in you see the result. Even if you don't do well you know you've done the work, so next time you can improve on it.'

The consuming thrill of motorsport, despite what the purists might tell you, is premised on the inherent potential of disaster built into the pursuit. How can one take pleasure in such an atrocious prospect? Perhaps the answer to the question is too complicated to express in words. But I don't know if those addicted to the spectacle of Formula One racing actually enjoy it in the customary sense; motor racing isn't wholly based on blood lust; and it is not a game or an activity in the usual way that that most sports are thought about. Many a sporting psychologist would not agree with me when I say that motor racing can't be understood by writing about it as a metaphor; we can argue that it can tell us things about the world, but that will not explain why the likes of Lewis Hamilton as a boy mourned the death of his track hero Senna but continued to want to emulate the fallen warrior, take the same chances he took and risk the same ending.

For all this, motorsport for the fan is always going to have a symbolic meaning; for the watcher it will express something beyond itself, as if its distinctiveness was just an ellipsis, or representation. One can of course argue that life is a metaphor for Formula One; human existence as a race with its shunts, crashes, drop-outs, overtaking, mechanical faults, pit stops, flags, safety cars, winners and losers, all unresolved, again the finishing line and, once more, me and my rival, perfectly matched. It is easy to perceive that your adversary is you: and the battle, set over a circuit, enclosed by barriers as in a corral laid out to the elements of heat and cold, wind and rain, under the gaze of an expectant and demanding audience, sometimes tens of thousands strong. Life is like the contests of the track in countless disconcerting ways. But, at the same time, motor racing is just like motor racing ... and nothing else. If you have watched a thousand races you have borne witness to a thousand contests, they share particular facets but this is not what intrigues the crowds in the stands or the millions of television viewers or those who write and read about the race, hours, days or years later. But it has to mean more; it has to have a relationship with something 'real' in life to make it worthwhile. Any sport that is *just* an end in itself will quickly become a very sectional thing and finally disappear altogether; we need to *identify* with what we are watching in order to become or at least feel *involved*.

According to perhaps the greatest racer of the golden age of the Grand Prix, Juan Manuel Fangio, 'The driver of a racing car is a component.'

But for the Brazilian World Champion and twice winner of the Indianapolis 500 Emerson Fittipaldi, 'The racing driver's mind has to have the ability to have amazing anticipation, co-ordination, and reflex. Because of the speed the car goes.'

As such, the driver *is* the race; the winning driver is the individual who most becomes part of the car and, at the same time, bends it to his will to tackle the circuit by intellectual and physical means. Fangio recalled, 'When I first began, I used to grip the steering wheel firmly, and I changed gear so hard that I damaged my hand.'

This person is totally identified with the race in a very physical way. It is this 'tenet of the track' that Lewis Hamilton is completely tuned into: there is no separation between himself and the competition he is involved in; winning is his confirmation that he is living, and that his life has meaning. This intimacy means that those who spectate, in identifying with the race, at the same time identify with the racer who is thoroughly merged into the race.

The Making of a Champion

When Lewis began racing, he achieved a string of magnificent results. Journalist and former racer Adam Jones was introduced to Hamilton in 1994 by Martin Howell, the then owner of Playscape, an indoor kart track in Clapham that has over many years now played a huge part in inducting young people into karting. Jones runs 100ccPR, a public relations agency that specialises in working with kart racers. Howell opened the formality by saying, 'This is Lewis – he's going to be a Formula One World Champion.'

Jones shook the lad's hand, saying, 'You're going to be a Grand Prix Champion, eh?'

Lewis replied, 'Yes, I am,' and Jones has admitted his thoughts were something like, 'Yeah, right!'

The PR man was not really too impressed by Lewis's seemingly precocious confidence, but there was something in the tone of Howell's introduction that struck him. The Playscape owner was well used to dealing with young racers (the Clapham track was a Mecca for youth workers bringing their adolescent hopefuls to 'fulfil their potential'), and Jones was not able to detect any condescension in Howell's prologue. Jones saw that Howell was serious and he was soon to understand the gravity of that introduction, which was much more the judgement of an educated eye than the opinion of an interested party.

Almost every potted biography that you will come across will mention Hamilton's karting experience, but they hardly ever communicate the level of excellence he achieved. Lewis has not come from out of the blue (as many people seem to think); he and his talent have been around for something more than a good while.

In 1997, the then *Observer* reporter Michael Eboda interviewed Anthony and Lewis at Buckmore Park kart track. He arrived at the track and asked where he might find Lewis Hamilton, to be told,

'He's the only black kid here and he'll be about three laps ahead of everyone else.'

Eboda recalled meeting a confident and polite 12-year-old in the rear seat of an old Peugeot hire car. Lewis had not wanted his dad to be part of the interview. Eboda, the current editor of *New Nation* (a newspaper for the black community in the UK), was astonished by the almost existential reply he got after questioning how the young man drove so fast: 'I don't know why I'm so quick ... When I come to a corner, the answer just comes. I take what the answer says and it makes me take it as quickly as possible.'

Going fast is a lifelong trait of Lewis's. Kieran Crawley is chief of M-Sport, a leading kart team in the UK, who worked with Lewis as he advanced in the karting world. He recollected Lewis proving how fast he might go while taking part in the Junior Intercontinental A Class race in Belgium. Crawley told how Hamilton had a habit of stalling the kart, but the regulations allowed for team organisers to wait by the side of the track with an engine starter. As they rolled on to the grid, the M-Sport boss noticed that Lewis was looking for him. Crawley was convinced this meant Hamilton had stalled and got the starter into the side pod just as the lights flashed to green. Lewis took off from the rear of the grid and was immediately trailing by half a lap. But the young 'Stevenage Speedster' pulled himself back to the pack and eventually claimed fourth place. He had competed against some of the best drivers in Europe, Robert Kubica (now with BMW's Formula One team) included.

In 1998, Lewis graduated up the karting ladder to the Junior Intercontinental A level. He finished second in the McLaren-Mercedes Champions of the Future and raced in the Italian Open Championship, finishing fourth.

Hamilton continued his Junior Intercontinental A success in 1999. He was Vice European Champion, Trophy de Pomposa winner and once more finished fourth in the Italian Open Championship. That year Lewis also raced in Intercontinental A and won the Italian 'Industrials' Championship.

Lewis had progressed through the Cadet (1995–96), Junior Yamaha (1997), Junior Intercontinental A (1998–99) and Intercontinental A (1999) to move into Formula A ranks in 2000. In all, it had taken him just six seasons to reach the top of the karting tree.

In 2000, Lewis became Formula A European Champion (winning all four rounds); he won the World Cup in Japan, was World Number One, won the Elf Masters at Bercy in France and the second round of the Italian Open. Recognising his success, the British Racing Drivers' Club made him a 'Rising Star' Member.

Formula A (FA) is the Formula One of karting and requires heavy financial commitment. At the start of the 21st century, to have any chance of competing, backing of around £60,000 a year was needed.

Usually drivers compete in national karting competitions then graduate to international racing in the ICA or JICA (Junior ICA) classes where they are required to finish in the top 34 to qualify to compete in FA. Once involved in FA, drivers either compete for a few years, improving their skills before moving on to car racing or they enter the world of professional kart racing and race in FA until they retire. Many open-wheel racing drivers started their careers in karts.

Although from 2007 Formula A used the cheaper 125cc Touch-and-Go (TaG) engines to increase participation, getting to the top in the class continued to require substantial financial underpinning. Starting in January 2007, Formula A was renamed KF1.

As Hamilton's reputation grew, he began to receive floods of offers to race in other series. He had been well prepared for the conversion from kart to car. As soon as he signed with McLaren, they had sent him a steering wheel so he could learn all the controls and the sequences for the start. Looking back, he recalled, 'I just kept it in my lap. When I got to the first race, I wasn't nervous about the start because I knew everything.'

Opting for the conventional next step from karting for any aspiring champion, Hamilton got involved with Formula Renault and took part in the highly competitive British Formula Renault series. Fears he wouldn't cope with such an upswing in horsepower proved short-lived. Attacking single-seat racing with the same resolute determination that had borne fruit throughout his karting days, from 2000 to 2001 Lewis made the transition into car racing, and competed in the British Formula Renault Winter Series, finishing fifth overall. From this point on, Lewis knew he was entering a different dimension of racing. He found that, even compared to the relatively fast karts he had raced in, the cars were 'so quick, and you have the gears also … it's just fantastic, the adrenaline when it gets going is just unbelievable.'

Hamilton's first full Formula Renault UK season was the 2002 campaign, competing under the Manor Motorsport banner (based close to Sheffield).

Team boss John Booth recollected Lewis's early impact: 'Even though he crashed on the third lap of practice, it was obvious he was a natural driver.'

It is pretty clear what Booth was getting at here, but as 19 podium and dozen-time Formula One Grand Prix winner Mario Andretti had it: 'Desire is the key to motivation, but it's determination and commitment to an unrelenting pursuit of your goal – a commitment to excellence – that will enable you to attain the success you seek.'

It was Lewis's possession of these qualities that marked him out and 'incubated' his innate gifts such as touch, reflex and a relatively high body strength/weight/height ratio. Aki Hintsa, McLaren's physician, helped make Lewis physically and mentally prepared for Formula One competition. Having worked with Olympic athletes, including the Ethiopian long-distance runner Haile Gebrselassie, Hintsa declared that Hamilton had the potential to be a great athlete, regardless of whatever sport he had chosen to compete in.

But a telling marker of greatness in any sportsperson or artist is the individual's capacity to enhance what is already there with what they put in. The likes of Ali in boxing or Best in football are exemplars of the blooming of inherent ability. From the same sporting environments, Bobby Moore and Marvin Hagler had to do more to *make* themselves. At very rare points in time, there are instances where a perfect balance emerges; Sugar Ray Leonard, Sterling Moss and Carl Lewis achieved such equilibrium of intrinsic talent and an instinct to win set within a cradle of effort. Those (like myself) who have watched Lewis Hamilton materialise out of the realms of speed see in him the same sort of symmetry of aptitude and concentrated endeavour evident in the latter group. I have met both Ali and Moore. I have reams of notes from interviews and conversations with the latter and from the stands at Upton Park and Old Trafford I have watched him foil even the great Best on many occasions. I was ringside when Ali dissected Henry Cooper (a great natural talent himself) and I have followed 'the Greatest's' career since the 1960 Olympics in Rome. Hamilton is like a coming together of these two in terms of his capacities. His personality is much closer to Moore's but I suspect his spirit is akin to Ali's.

In the summer of 2002, at just 17 years of age, Lewis claimed his first victory in the hotly contested category he had chosen to take him from kart to car. It was only his ninth car race. He finished his season third overall, winning three races plus one Formula Renault Eurocup race. He scored 274 points, not too far behind Champion Danny Watts (who made 333) and was just five points adrift of second-placed Jamie Green.

Formula Renault UK, which is widely regarded as one of the world's principal junior single-seater categories, has started the careers of many top racers, the likes of Kimi Räikkönen, who in this ferociously competitive feeder category was propelled from the status of unknown rookie to a McLaren Formula One star in little more than 18 months. Other famous names who have graduated via Renault UK include former Williams Formula One driver Antonio Pizzonia and Le Mans 24 Hours winner Guy Smith. It attracts the biggest race-day crowds in Britain and is part of the support package to the British Touring Car Championship; the Renault Championship also links up with the British round of the World Series by Renault at Donington Park. In 2006, this event drew a crowd of more than 100,000 fans over the weekend. The average season budget for any entry is up to £130,000, inclusive of all races and testing.

By the time he graduated from karting, Lewis had a treasure trove of trophies acquired from his earliest years. Only nine years after he had started kart racing, he was being mooted as a Formula One star of the future and in 2002 he was putting as much faith in McLaren as the Woking-based outfit were putting in him. He saw that McLaren had helped him shape his future and provided him with a structure within which to work. Following his success in Formula Renault, he said, 'Where I go beyond Formula Renault is more down to their guidance because they have the organisation and know-how.'

At that point, Lewis saw two years in Formula Renault as his best way forward. He felt that his first full season had been an opportunity to learn about the tracks and that the next campaign would be geared to building himself up to the level of the other drivers in the Championship. He commented, 'I'm just looking to do the best job possible and get as much experience as I can.'

It cost McLaren around £150,000 to finance Hamilton's Formula Renault programme. At the same time he received off-track coaching in promotional and PR techniques and he showed himself to be a gifted exponent of these arts. What this demonstrates first and foremost is that, if the financial playing field is levelled, you get not just diversity in participation, but diversity in those who succeed and potential sporting celebrity. However, given McLaren's commitment, Lewis's growing experience, innate aptitude, personal resolve, confidence and maturity was producing a driving talent well beyond his tender years. He elucidated on the technicalities of his development from karts to single-seater racing cars with an impressive eloquence: 'It's quite a challenge adapting to car racing. I've learned a lot about how the car works during pre-season testing and the few races we have done so far this season.'

Lewis tended to try to set his car up to reproduce the feel of a kart, so he was able to throw it into a corner in the same way he might when racing a kart, powersliding it, controlling the back end on the throttle.

Lewis had ambitions to move into F3 by 2004, being anxious that F3000, which supplied the major supporting events at the majority of European Grands Prix, might have been a fruitless dead-end for him. He told how he was worried that many Formula One teams failed to pay enough attention to F3000 and felt that he would be better served using F3 as the springboard to a Grand Prix career.

In retrospect, this was an insightful and wise analysis. Although F3 helped produce the likes of Juan Pablo Montoya, the 2004 season was the last F3000 campaign, partly due to falling field sizes. In 2005, it was replaced with the GP2 series, with Renault backing.

Lewis went on to win 10 of the 15 races in the Formula Renault Championship in 2003, but it took him until the fifth round, at Silverstone, to take his first win. But from there on, he dominated, winning all but one of the next 10 races. Hamilton stormed to the title with 10 wins, nine fastest laps and 11 pole positions.

The title was Hamilton's with two races remaining. He amassed nine fastest laps and 11 pole positions, picking up the Championship title in only his third season in the category. At the age of 18, he was the youngest ever Formula Renault Champion, driving at speeds of up to 160mph. Anthony said at the time, 'Put him in a car and he does what comes naturally. He's an 18-year-old kid but when he gets on the racetrack he's not any age; he's just a consummate professional.'

The year after his Championship-winning season, Lewis passed his driving test at the first attempt, having had just six lessons. He paid for his own tuition as he didn't think his dad was the best person to teach him: 'He thinks he is the best driver and even now when I'm at the wheel I still get instructions on how to do it!'

Hamilton's Renault Championship triumph, beating Alex Lloyd with 419 points to 377, was something stronger than convincing. His progress was being monitored unobtrusively by the McLaren management. Martin Whitmarsh had recently journeyed to a Silverstone club meeting where Hamilton had to start 28th on the grid, following engine problems in practice, for a 20-lap race on the national circuit. Whitmarsh was impressed; Lewis had climbed through to ninth at the finish and was very decisive when it came to overtaking his rivals. Whitmarsh saw the performance as 'a good index of his talent. In four or five years he might well be in a Grand Prix car, although nothing is certain in this business and certainly not at this level.'

Whitmarsh stuck his neck out and said of Hamilton, 'If you're asking me whether he can win before [Jenson] Button, I'd have to say yes. I think he has the capability to win.'

Up to his achievements in Formula Renault, Hamilton's success was premised on the composed and intelligent approach of his father Anthony. He reflected on his son's development saying that, when Lewis started racing, he was just part of a 'middle-of-the-road family' looking to give their son a chance of racing karts. For Anthony there had never been any pretensions or thought about where Lewis's talent was leading him. But, when he won his first cadet race at the age of eight, Anthony was conscious that 'everything developed its own momentum'. Lewis was blossoming and it was as natural as daybreak and the gentle Mediterranean breezes that blew over the streets of Monte Carlo as they awaited the 'Herts Hurricane' in the spring of 2007.

5

TRYING TO BE THE PERFECT DRIVER

Once more unto the breach, dear friends, once more;
Or close the wall up with our English dead.
In peace there's nothing so becomes a man
As modest stillness and humility:
But when the blast of war blows in our ears,
Then imitate the action of the tiger;
Stiffen the sinews, summon up the blood...
Henry V, Act III, Scene i, Shakespeare

Monte Carlo or Bust

After his impressive performance in Spain, Hamilton moved with McLaren and the other 10 teams that contest the World Championship to the Paul Ricard circuit (at Le Castellet, near Marseille, South of France). The former home of the French Grand Prix is now the most sophisticated test track on the face of the earth, primarily because it is owned by the billionaire Caesar of Formula One, Bernie Ecclestone.

A dozen hours after starting testing, Lewis had completed 98 laps, recorded the fastest time by better than a second and alongside his mechanics undertaken a two-and-a-half-hour analysis of the car's performance.

I was among the few dozen people that were present, a far cry from the several tens of thousands that can attend race days. Strange echoes fill the air and at times you can hear the most intimate conversations from a long way off. But the proceedings are worth watching and there is an atmosphere of concentrated effort that permeates the great empty spaces and gives a feeling of controlled expectation. In many ways, as an observer, this is as close as it gets in terms of experiencing how Formula One racing works and its deeper labours that constitute intricate rehearsals that address every imaginable aspect of driver, car and support performance. There is time for jokes and passing chats, but the job at hand is never lost; racing is all.

Between his exertions on the track, Lewis spent time in the back of the McLaren bus entranced by a cosmos of facts and figures rolling down a computer screen; even Grand Prix racing has its moments of comparative stillness.

Around 60,000 spectators lined the tight streets of Monte Carlo for the 65th running of the Monaco Grand Prix. Monaco is the race that most drivers want to win. Its street circuit, continental setting, history, prestige and romance make it the epitome of what Grand Prix racing should be.

Lewis was second on the grid, facing the 78 laps and something like 4,000 gear changes he would encounter before the race was finished. He had suffered his first crash of the season on the previous Thursday. Steering problems during his second practice session caused him to smack into the barriers at the first turn. He was unhurt but the car was damaged on the left-hand side.

Earlier Lewis had posted the second-best time of the morning session (1:17.601); Alonso, the winner of the race in 2006, clocked the fastest time.

From the start, it looked as if Lewis had made his mind up to run a defensive race, tucking almost immediately behind Alonso in pole. Making no attempt to pass the Spaniard in the opening laps, the scenario had many of the hallmarks of a choreographed affair, except that Lewis looked unusually tentative initially.

For all this, the tight turns and cityscape, together with both McLarens showing commitment to take risks in terms of speed and race hard as a team, made it an entertaining event up to the first pit stops, although Lewis effectively blocked out any chance of assault, hogging the narrow roads and protecting his team's position.

However, no other car in the Grand Prix had been able to match the sheer pace of the McLaren-Mercedes. Although Massa had been competitive during the first stint, holding third place, he fell a minute behind Hamilton but was the only driver not lapped by Alonso and Lewis.

Hamilton patted his car as he walked away from it after the race as if to say 'it wasn't you that let me down'. He had never lost a race at Monaco and now he had led every Grand Prix he had driven in. It was McLaren's 150th Grand Prix victory and their 14th in Monte Carlo. They were then well clear of their Italian rivals at the head of the Manufacturers' league.

Emerson Fittipaldi had won his first Grand Prix at his fourth attempt and Hamilton had hoped that Monte Carlo would be the place he would stand on the podium for the first time as a winner.

Lewis had five laps' worth of fuel more than Alonso from the start of the race, but the team had told him to come in earlier than he had expected, as he was readying himself for a rush of speedy laps to ram home the advantage he had over his team-mate, who had already stopped (Hamilton was pulled up two laps after Alonso pitted). This altered his tactics and effectively opened the gate for Alonso to claim back-to-back wins in Monaco and his 17th Grand Prix victory.

Hamilton showed signs of frustration that reading between the lines came from his belief that he had given up a chance of victory, as he slipped to second place in the chase for the title, although both drivers were on 38 points. A win in Monaco is considered among drivers as 'half a World Championship' in terms of status. He declared, 'I made sure I brought the car home ... I was actually quite surprised because I was fuelled to do five laps, maybe six laps, longer than Fernando and they stopped me with three laps to go ... There wasn't much time to pull out a gap or improve my time; I wasn't really given much time for it. I came in two or three laps after him [Alonso]. That was unfortunate, but that's the way it goes.'

At the press conference after the Grand Prix, Lewis seemed to brush a tear of frustration from his left eye at one point. In the last part of the race there had certainly been a moment when he looked ready to sacrifice all to chase Alonso. Kieran Crawley, who knows Lewis from his karting days, said before Lewis raced in Asia, 'In Formula One we haven't seen him come from the back, but that's when he's at his most dangerous. When he makes mistakes, just watch him go. I want to see him make some mistakes – then you'll see just how good he is.'

In a way, Lewis might have thought he had been conscripted into a mistake, certainly in terms of his own position in the race. There is probably little doubt that left to his own devices he would have attacked Alonso no matter how far ahead the Spaniard had been and put the Manufacturers' prize on the back boiler to be thought about at another time.

Hamilton has more than once shown this propensity in his career; most recently prior to Monte Carlo, he had charged through in Istanbul in GP2 during 2006, when he spun and worked his way up from 18th to second at the chequered flag, less than three seconds adrift of the race-winner and with a fastest lap, almost a full second quicker than anyone else in the field. He has claimed to 'rarely make mistakes in races' and that the Istanbul incident had been one of the few mistakes he'd ever made. This said, he seemed to look back on his achievement in Turkey with not a little relish. Smiling broadly, he stated, 'It was great! But I was struggling in the car. The rear end was not right. Straight after that [the spin], I somehow extracted a little bit more from the tyres and I had this boost and everything's right, the car was great and things need to be ... I love those experiences. I love coming from the back.'

As such, it is not too much to speculate that a veto had been put on his instincts in Monte Carlo. Not long after the Monaco result, Dennis, who had claimed McLaren had been cruising from lap 10 onwards, was obliged to deny accusations that McLaren had given Hamilton orders to hold back and manipulated the race, which would fly in the face of Formula One regulations that had come into force after the Austrian Grand Prix of 2002, when Ferrari told Rubens Barrichello to let Michael Schumacher overtake him to win the race. Ron made his denial forcibly: 'We are scrupulously fair at all times in how we run this Grand Prix team ... We will never favour one driver, no matter who it is. We don't have team orders; we had a strategy to win this race. There will be places where they will be absolutely free to race, but this isn't one of them.'

That ultimate line was seized on by the FIA and an investigation of 'incidents' concerning the McLaren team during the race was inaugurated. For a short time things looked ominous for Dennis and his team. Bernie Ecclestone declared that McLaren 'could be excluded from the Championship or they could have points deducted'.

Alonso had finished 4.095 seconds ahead of Hamilton. Lewis reflected on the situation after the race: 'He was obviously close to me, and I was told to take it easy ... At the end of the day, I am a rookie. I am in my first season in Formula One and I have finished second in only my first Monaco Grand Prix, so I really can't complain. I've got number two on my car, I am the number-two driver; it is something I have to live with.'

But the Surrey men were cleared of any wrongdoing by the FIA.

NASCAR racer and cultural icon Dale Earnhardt has insisted, 'To win more Championships and stay alive in this sport, it's very, very, hard and it's hard to understand how it works.'

Ayrton Senna claimed that a driver touches his limits in racing: 'Something happens and you suddenly can go a little bit further. With your mind power, your determination, your instinct, and the experience as well, you can fly very high.

Double World Champion Formula One racer (1962 and 1968) Graham Hill, as a driver, saw himself as 'an artist. The track is my canvas, and the car is my brush.'

His son Damon, who was World Champion in 1996, declared,

'You should never feel comfortable. There is something wrong if you are. You should always feel under threat, on the edge of your seat and pushing yourself. Win one and you want to win more. It's never-ending.'

Jacky Ickx, six times the Le Mans 24-hour race winner, who from 1967 to 1979 took the podium 25 times in Formula One races (including eight times as a winner), when talking of his experience as a driver said, 'The existence is a tremendous curiosity, within the course of the years, the discovery of yourself in your inmost evolutions. With the age you feel better than you are, what you represent. Which means a little at the planet's scale.'

For Emerson Fittipaldi, 'The first thing a driver must have is excellent anticipation. He must know what is going to happen before it is going to happen … When I began to drive Formula One in the 1970s, the odds of surviving were 7 to 1. Incredible high risks. The odds of surviving now are like 800 to one … You are going in one second the length of a football field … You had to decompress the pressure before the race. I taught my heart to relax. I lay down before the race. It gave me more energy just before the race … You have to visualise a second or two ahead of your car what line you are taking, what you are going to do, before you get there because it comes too fast.'

As such, it can be seen that, in motorsport, drivers' minds must be attuned to their bodies in exceptional ways. The difference that exists among drivers in terms of these qualities parallels the unfairness of life. In theory, the finely regulated nature of Formula One contests has been engineered to prevent one manufacturer being advantaged over another. However, in practice, this merely puts a premium on the mental and physical gifts of the driver. In the modern era, this makes it possible for an ambitious racer with a high degree of talent to aspire not only to be a champion but to be a great champion. This translates to emulating the likes of Michael Schumacher, Alberto Ascari, Fangio, Jack Brabham, Graham Hill, Mika Häkkinen, Jackie Stewart, Niki Lauda, Alain Prost, Nelson Piquet, Ayrton Senna and

Fernando Alonso to become a double or triple champion, to make himself an immortal.

Talent is not the only requirement or variable. In order to maintain his competitiveness, the driver must watch his diet, sleep well, undertake an appropriate exercise regime and becomes a master of timing, as race preparation, doing the right and not doing the wrong things prior to an event, is crucial. Lewis Hamilton has thus far shown himself to have both the physical and attitudinal make-up of a champion; he has the body of a true racer: he is not tall, but carries not an ounce of fat, being built of lithe, solid muscle. His mind reflects his physique. His temperament and mental demeanour have been honed by the requirements of the track and, while his intellectual and emotional discipline was detectable during his time in karts, it was when he graduated to F3 that this became an obvious feature in his armoury.

In 2003, Lewis made the move to F3, taking part in the end-of-year Asian races. He finished fifth in Macau, and at the conclusion of the season took pole position on his first visit to Korea for the Superprix event. But Hamilton's debut appearance in British F3 with Manor Motorsport was less than successful. At Brands Hatch in the final round and the finale of the 2003 season, at a speed of around 100mph, he went off the track in the first race. In the second event, he collided with team-mate Tor Graves and was knocked unconscious. On coming round, he found he was unable to move his legs and was rushed to Sidcup Hospital, but fortunately it was only an overnight stay.

Hamilton and Manor advanced to the 2004 F3 Euroseries, which forms part of the support programme to the DTM (Deutsche Tourenwagen Masters) series, in a car powered by Mercedes-Benz engines. It was Manor's rookie season in Europe and Lewis won just one race in this highly competitive environment, at the Norising. But he made four further podiums which gave him fifth place overall behind Champion Jamie Green, Alexandre Prémat, Nicolas Lapierre and Nico Rosberg. In December, he had his first test in a McLaren Formula One car.

Lewis defected to the powerful 2004 Champions ASM for the following season, which was a prelude to another destruction of the opposition just as he had in Formula Renault two years earlier. He dominated the Championship in a Silver Arrow Dallara Mercedes.

However, at the end of the 2004 season, Lewis and Anthony wanted to move into GP2 racing but McLaren wanted their protégé to stay in F3 another year and win the Championship. There was some friction about this divergence and it was this that led to Hamilton competing in the Macau F3 Grand Prix without McLaren's backing and seeking another sponsor to race in GP2.

In November 2004, in the Macau F3 Grand Prix Qualification Race, Lewis stamped his authority on the field after grabbing the lead on the opening lap and remaining unchallenged throughout the 10-lap encounter. He looked untouchable and ended the day more than a second clear of his nearest rival.

Having soared to the top of the timesheets from the start, Lewis had consistently improved his advantage despite a rash of incidents that twice provoked the red flag. At one point, he ran wide on the dust and was lucky not to hit the wall. After the race he reflected, 'That was close. Considering that was my only scare in 45 minutes of running is not too bad, and I think I even impressed myself. I know what I came here to do and whether I am two seconds clear of the rest or one-tenth doesn't really matter. Every lap I was doing out there was quicker and, considering we did not use any new tyres, there should be more time to come.'

In the next qualifier, Lewis eventually finished 2.2 seconds ahead of Nico Rosberg, with Alexandre Prémat taking third place. This ensured him a front-row start position for the 15-lap race on the Sunday. But, despite this, Lewis could only manage 14th place.

It was a creditable performance but Hamilton failed to attract alternative backing and eventually decided to go back to McLaren and heal the rift. Ron Dennis would be proved absolutely right.

The leading F3 drivers and teams came from Europe, Asia, Australia and America to fight out the first Bahrain F3 SuperPrix. But the opening day at the desert racetrack was hit by rain, making the challenge faced by some of the world's best up-and-coming racers all the more demanding.

The drivers first took to the circuit on Wednesday, 10 December 2004 for three practice sessions. In the opening half-hour encounter, Nico Rosberg set the pace driving the Opel-powered Dallara. His 2:05.068 lap headed the 31-car field. Richard Antinucci of the USA was the next fastest, putting Lewis and Fabio Carbone behind him.

Ripping nearly a second off his opening session time, Antinucci headed the timesheets in the next practice session, as the rain continued to ask questions of the racers. Lucas Di Grassi of Brazil was just 0.032 seconds behind Antinucci. Ronnie Quintarelli, Franck Perera, Fabio Carbone and Lewis rounded out the top six.

The going was difficult because the rain was on a start/stop programme; although the track offered a lot of grip, in the wet the drivers had to lift off the throttle on corners that were going to be easy flat out in dry conditions.

As the conditions got worse, most of the field opted out of the third practice session. On Friday, 12 December, the intended 10-lap qualification race started the day, but the contest was red-flagged with two laps to go after Antinucci, the pace-setter from the previous Wednesday, went into a spin and stalled his Toms Dallara.

Englishman Jamie Green won the shortened eight-lap event, three seconds ahead of Fabio Carbone of Brazil who finished two seconds clear of Nico Rosberg. Hamilton, from 22nd on the grid, charged up the field to qualify in 11th place. Despite this powerful assault, it was a poor qualifying result for Lewis. However, in the Grand Prix, with a mixture of work and finesse, he created himself a path to fourth position during the opening lap. From nowhere, he had put himself into a space where he might mount a challenge on the leaders. But with the arrival of the safety car he was forced to reassess.

In the crush following the exit of the safety car, Hamilton was able to push through the tightly clustered cars to win by less than a second in front of Rosberg. The Englishman, who headed a one-two-three of

F3 Euroseries drivers, told the world that he was overwhelmed: 'I was just trying to preserve what I had in third. I couldn't even stay with Nico.'

As such, the Hertfordshire lad was happy to see the safety car bunching the field: 'I anticipated it just right. Nico and I have been friends and team-mates for a long time and it is fantastic to come away first and second.'

It was now clear that in 2005 Hamilton would be a major player and in fact no one would touch him in the Euroseries.

The 2005 calendar included events at the historic circuits of Pau (France), Spa-Fracorchamps (Belgium), Zandvoort (Holland) and Monaco.

Drivers from 13 countries made up the entry list. For the first time racers from Argentina, the Czech Republic and the USA were competing. The team competition was between France, Germany, Britain, Austria, Italy, Holland, Luxembourg and the Czech Republic.

After a promising debut season at F3 level, Lewis was regarded as the Championship favourite. But no one would have dared to predict the way he would control and command the competition.

Early in May 2005, Hamilton was victorious in the Pau F3 Grand Prix in France from pole position. At this point, Martin Whitmarsh had good reason to feel confirmed in his initial impression of Hamilton. He had seen the young man as an extraordinary talent who, with technical approach, was developing year by year, getting stronger mentally. He had named Lewis as a McLaren driver in the future: 'We have paid his entire budget for the last eight or nine years and put a lot of time and effort in with Lewis. We wouldn't have been doing that unless we thought he will one day win a World Championship in a McLaren.'

To be like Ayrton

Lewis, ever on the lookout to learn, has drawn inspiration from the genius of Ayrton Senna. Prior to competing in Monte Carlo, alongside his engineers he watched a video of Senna racing at

Monaco. He concluded that it was much more difficult to be a Formula One driver in Senna's time. Hamilton had noted that the Brazilian had driven one lap practically one-handed and had to correct the car four or five times. But he was still a second quicker than anyone. For Hamilton, 'That's how he drove – on the very limit or just over it. That's what makes me want to be like Senna. Like him, I'm trying to be the perfect driver.'

There are drivers who have tremendous instinct and/or a mysterious insight. Watching them, you might believe they are recollecting every race they have been a part of. There are drivers who compete dexterously, but almost automatically, unable to invent or create when a competitor changes their tactics. Some drivers, including a few of the greatest, at the zenith of their powers, comprehend, perhaps halfway through a race, that they do not, never have and never will have enough. Their careers finish unexpectedly and irreversibly as we watch.

But, occasionally, a driver emerges possessed of an exceptional and disturbing consciousness. Not only do they seem to foresee every manoeuvre (anticipated or carried out) an opponent might make, but also the minute changes in the humour of spectators, for which they appear to feel personally accountable. Lewis Hamilton is such a racer.

The exceptional dramas that Grands Prix are come to life not needing words, are crushed into the space it takes to devour the laps. Although nothing astounding might occur, the performance remains an exercise in mental and emotional tension; there is always the expectation, even the likelihood, that something will happen. The race rejoices in but at the same time warns of the humanity of those who drive. This is the essence of the drama of the potential and limitation that is the Grand Prix; it is always tragic and moving. This stage seems made for Hamilton, or he for it. In him you can see each act played out and that he would be the emptier without it.

The Grand Prix, although it is an event without words, speaks. Its linguistics can be found in its vicious, primeval incoherence, which is articulated in the motion and speed of technology that makes the race possible. The idiom, a discourse among drivers, is carried out at a neurological level, on a mental plain: a dialectic of reflexes in a collective reaction to the inexplicable demand of the crowd which is always that the race will be a battle for survival and all that makes the setting – the pits, lights, flags, stands, safety cars, even the crowd itself – be expunged from and lost to memory. Just like in a place of worship or theatre, the actual environment evaporates as the 'spectacle' fills the vacuum. Race commentators might link the action with words, but the Grand Prix is closer to music or dance than a mere word-filled report.

For a routine event to be transformed into the 'greatest race in history', that race that we want to witness more than any other, at Silverstone or Monaco or wherever, is to move from merely watching to a sort of participation, and that too is part of what brings us to the track in the hope of seeing the great encounters of sport. In the Grand Prix, so much comes about so quickly and with such shocking grace, it cannot be completely grasped in real time. We are often restricted to a still powerful consciousness that something intensely extreme is happening in a venue not translatable into words.

In his glory year in F3, this was exemplified by Lewis's performance at Monaco. In May 2005, he was in pole position for the 40th Monaco F3 Grand Prix run as a support event to the annual Formula One race in the principality – the first in eight years. In the initial race of two, the Brit made a powerful start and controlled the contest on a course that lived up to Monte Carlo's reputation as a venue that offers scant opportunities to pass.

In the seventh lap, Hamilton's progress was curtailed after the safety car was called upon while Thomas Holzer's car, which had skidded into the barriers on the exit of the Swimming Pool chicane, was removed from the circuit. Following a couple of ambling laps, at the restart Lewis leaped back in front, and dominated the race to claim his fifth victory of 2005. He created the drama by way of the acts and scenes supplied by the circuit and the other players.

For Hamilton, to win in Monaco, a place with a history and

atmosphere that makes all drivers want victory there, was, 'just fantastic ... something very special. Adrian [Sutil] was extremely fast and it was really difficult to keep him behind. I had to work really hard to be the first to take the chequered flag.'

Hamilton had held the lead for the entire 18-lap race. As a consequence, most of the field remained in procession from beginning to end. Lewis came home 1.777 seconds in front of McLaren-Mercedes stablemate Sutil. The following day, race two, despite his seven-second winning margin, was no cakewalk for Hamilton, but he continued his domination of the F3 Euroseries by taking his fifth win of the year. But Ron Dennis's protégé was unable to command the Saturday race in the same domineering way as he had the day before. Indeed, he was probably fortunate after contact with the wall at the exit of the Swimming Pool chicane. In the lead, his right rear wheel struck the barriers hard, but amazingly the suspension stood the test and Lewis stayed out in front.

But the mistake allowed his team-mate to close the gap between them. However, as the German tried to get by Hamilton at Ste Devote, he banged into the tyrewall and was obliged to retire.

Reflecting on his sixth win of the season, and his second in what turned out to be a weekend of supremacy for him, Lewis said, 'To win both Monaco races is far more than I had dared to dream of. I made a big mistake in the second race and, for a moment, my heart stopped beating when I made contact with the crash barriers. I thought that was that, but fortunately my car survived and I had the chance of finishing the race in a focused style to grab the win.'

Winning both of the races at the prestigious Monaco event from pole position had lengthened his already strong lead in the series after only eight races.

Fay Taylour, perhaps one of the most famous pre-war female racing drivers, was once asked why she took part in the sport. She answered, 'I think about racing all the time. I talk about it all the time. I do not write poetry, but every race is a separate tale and gives rise to its own legends.'

Drivers are on the track to create a supreme and extreme event, a communal exposure of how far personal limits might extend; the racer will understand facets of themselves that for most of us will remain uncharted zones; they will explore the furthest reaches of their corporeal and spiritual abilities and be obliged to acknowledge the depths and shallows their own capacities.

Racing at speed is a deeply personal pursuit that involves drawing its participants out of reason's reach into a realm that exists in the abstract, an atmosphere of potential wherein agony (*agon* is Greek for 'contest') in one form or another is the probable outcome. Out on the track, the main players are ruled by the same instincts as the chariot racers of old. All competitors have to muster their total consciousness because by their motion they fight the power of time; the winner will 'go the fastest'. To do this competitors must call on all that they are; both their strengths and their weaknesses will be laid bare and even the most covert and hidden elements of their make-up will be open to the mass gaze. The material self, together with that which defines their identity is exposed to reveal the very basic fibres of the personality and soul. Every race is a test of the spirit and, for Lewis, the 15th F3 Marlboro Masters in Zandvoort, Holland, in June 2005 was no exception.

Lining up with 37 drivers from 16 countries, in front of a crowd of 40,000 and with live TV coverage being piped into over 5,000,000 Dutch homes, Lewis had betrayed not a single chink in his armour as he took pole in Europe's most prestigious F3 race, looking to emulate previous Masters winners that included Formula One drivers David Coulthard, Takuma Sato and Christian Klien.

Hamilton was in a class of his own on the dunes of the Dutch coastline; having commanded the qualifying sessions, he scored a lights-to-flag win over team-mate Sutil, taking the victory with a comfortable margin of some 6.5 seconds. In the process, he broke the F3 lap record at Zandvoort by half a second, with a time of 1:32.866. At the press conference following the race he told of his tactics: 'I conserved my tyres for the first 10 laps and once I'd opened up a big enough gap it was a matter of staying consistent and not making any mistakes.'

At the conclusion of the season the British magazine *Autosport* featured Lewis in their 'Top 50 Drivers of 2005' issue, ranking him 24th.

Lewis had beaten Sutil to the Championship by 172 points to 94 (Hamilton had almost doubled the German's total), winning 15 races from 20 starts. He had achieved 13 pole positions and recorded 10 fastest race laps. He had won the series with four races remaining and been the most powerful element in ASM's retention of the F3 Team Championship title that it had secured in 2004.

The Fracture of Possibility

At this stage in his career, Lewis felt it was important to keep racing because he saw that as being what he did best. Both he and his father believed there was a need to keep the momentum going rather than risk stagnating and jeopardising his push towards Formula One. Anthony was driven by the understandable perception that racers were seen as being only as good as their last race and, as such, 'You have to make it all count.' At the end of that season, Lewis became a free agent and, although his loyalty and commitment was to McLaren, Anthony said, if they suggested that Lewis went in a certain direction, he and his son would consider it seriously, but would choose to go their own route if it just didn't fit with what the Hamiltons expected.

After all the help and support McLaren had given to Lewis, Anthony's reaction might have sounded a little ungrateful. But Grand Prix races as tales are contrary narratives. They become understood as events wherein anything can occur, sometimes in a fraction of a second. There is no other sport where so much can happen in such a short time span, with such permanent and atrocious consequences. This being the case, a driver, and anyone involved with them, must, almost by instinct, be open to any possibilities.

The great Scottish parliamentarian Henry Campbell-Bannerman

believed: 'Scare answers to scare, and force begets force, until at length it comes to be seen that we are racing one against another after a phantom security which continually vanishes as we approach.'

This is a realisation that, while competition might not be an end in itself, in the last analysis its meaning and purpose are unclear. But we almost *have* to do it in some way or another. However, the reason *why* we do it, despite the trophies, the glory and the prize money, is often intangible. To climb into a machine that is more than able to kill you, and many others, in the process is to place your own existence in jeopardy and, in doing so, turns a sporting crowd into possible witnesses of death.

For Lewis, 'When I am driving at 200mph, if I lost focus then I could die, so it kind of puts it into perspective.'

According to Ayrton Senna, 'I don't know driving in another way which isn't risky. Each one has to improve himself. Each driver has his limit. My limit is a little bit further than others' … The danger sensation is exciting. The challenge is to find new dangers.'

So, the audience might identify with the drivers but racers do not act or live in the same way as 'ordinary' people. In racing, on the track, nothing is totally 'natural' – everything is mediated but, if there is a moment when the mediation shatters, nothing is left but raw skin and bone; the 'normal' person does not habituate such a condition. Unless you are acclimatised, it will kill you very, very quickly.

For the car racer, technology plays a decisive role. Even the best drivers cannot find victory in a relatively poorly performing vehicle. But this does not negate the role of the individual with the wheel in his hands. The better the car, the better the driver required to drive it. The best car is going to be a complex machine, generating a performance of almost unbelievable potential. The 'jockey' is as such obliged, over every inch and every second of every lap, to manage, control and tame this inanimate yet wild thing that will take him to his triumph or demise. To come first over the bumpy, tight streets of Monaco, negotiating the 13 corners of the circuit at an average speed of 93mph (150kmh), the driver has to have a level of skill and awareness that puts him on the very edge of human capacity.

Friedrich Nietzsche, that dark and crazed philosopher of nothingness, claimed that, 'if you gaze for long into an abyss, the abyss gazes also into you'. Perhaps this is the 'contest' (the agony). Take away the rage of rivalry and humanity would deteriorate; nothing to live or die for, nothing to strive to achieve, nothing to overcome, nothing but the abyss. There is the threat of physical oblivion, but overcoming that is the prize, and the likes of Hamilton, having understood this, would find life hard without the meaning it gives to living.

Jacky Ickx once lamented, 'In the past, two colleagues died each season. It was generally accepted this could happen.'

In the Grand Prix, even in the modern era of super-safety, dying at the wheel is a constant threat. This is the reason why most of us prefer to *watch* motorsport than actually take part. The first man I saw die in a Grand Prix was Piers Courage in the summer of 1970. I saw Senna die in 1994 at San Marino. Both these men perished, at least in part, because of their innate courage. Damon Hill made the point that Formula One would not survive today if drivers were being killed at the rate they were 30 or 40 years ago. He feels. 'It would have been taken off the air. It is beamed into people's living rooms on Sunday afternoons, with children watching.'

In the 40 years between 1954 and 1994, 28 drivers lost their lives in Grand Prix racing (including eight Britons); there have been no fatalities for the past 13 years. This demonstrates that death on the track is not a likely outcome; however, the potential for death is always there. But spectators have also died at motor races. In 1955, dozens were killed at Le Mans when Pierre Levegh launched his 300SLR into the crowd, and horrific injuries were inflicted from the exploding car. A couple of years previously, the first South American round in the World Championship, the Grand Prix of Argentina, held on the Buenos Aires circuit, attracted more spectators than the venue could hold. Many sat right at the edge of the track; the inevitable occurred and at least 15 spectators were killed and many others injured as a result of a crash.

Immediately after a death in Grand Prix, it is not uncommon for the fatality to be portrayed as an almost arbitrary event that could not have been foreseen – literally an accident. But later, after the conditions and the car have been studied and analysed, it is invariably shown that the racer's death was probably avoidable. But death haunts the track; among all the glitter, the sheen of life, it is the most omnipresent aspect of the sport. This being the case, the drivers can only make the decisions that they and those interested in their progress consider best for them. In the last analysis, Formula One, although entered by teams and having a team championship, is not a team sport. It can never really be that as it is not the life of the team, but the individual that is being literally laid on the line at the start of the race.

At the end of 2005, the Hamiltons had no illusions about any of this, and their decision was always going to be more about Lewis and the future than about McLaren and the past – the past is by definition departed, a time complicit with death. Life is played out only in the present and the future.

...wis collects his thoughts during a test session at the Montmelo track,
...rcelona, Spain.

Celebrating another race,
another sweet victory.

p: HRH the Prince of Wales meeting a 14-year-old Lewis at McLaren's Formula One ·tory in Woking.

low left: The support and drive behind Lewis is his father Anthony Hamilton.

low right: Young Lewis was a UK karting star before exploding on to the Formula ·e scene.

Proud race winner Lewis
Hamilton smiles on the
podium, Nürburgring,
Germany, 2006.

p: Who do you think you are? Stirling Moss?

low: Lewis with his brother Nicholas and stepmother Linda Hamilton.

The look of a calm and composed young man who has the world at his feet.

Above: Karting star Lewis and Ron Dennis, the McLaren team boss.

Below: Lewis listens to his team manager give instructions during a practice session.

Top: Anthony Hamilton embraces his son in celebration at the Circuit Gilles Villeneuⱽ in Montreal.

Bottom: Lewis holds the winning trophy that realises his dreams after his first Formula One victory at the Canadian Grand Prix, 2007.

6

WOULD YOU BET AGAINST HIM?

Now set the teeth and stretch the nostril wide,
Hold hard the breath and bend up every spirit
To his full height. On, on, you noblest English.
Whose blood is fet from fathers of war-proof!
Fathers that, like so many Alexanders,
Have in these parts from morn till even fought
And sheathed their swords for lack of argument:
Dishonour not your mothers; now attest
That those whom you call'd fathers did beget you.
Be copy now to men of grosser blood,
And teach them how to war.

Henry V, Act III, Scene i, Shakespeare

Montreal

Should Lewis Hamilton have had the chance to look at a Canadian newspaper on the morning of 10 June 2007, he would have seen his own face mirrored in the front pages. He was born seven years after Gilles Villeneuve won the Canadian Grand Prix at the Circuit Ile Notre Dame, what is now the Circuit Gilles Villeneuve, the venue of the 2007 race, renamed in honour of the Québécois racer, father of

World Champion Jacques, who in 14 podium finishes stood victorious on half a dozen occasions.

Lewis took his first Formula One pole position on a beautiful Montreal day. The wind speed was 2.0 m/s, the air temperature was 27°C, on the track it was 53°C and humidity was 54 per cent as Alonso, who won the race for Renault in 2006, joined his team-mate in the front row (it was the fifth time in six races that the Spaniard had claimed a place in the leading rank).

Hamilton had never seen the Circuit Gilles Villeneuve 'in the flesh' before he arrived in Montreal but he had prepared for the race by using the McLaren-Mercedes driving simulator at team headquarters in Woking.

It is an unusual track. It asks 70 laps of its 4.361km (2.7-mile) circuit, the lap record for which has been held by Rubens Barrichello since 2004 (1:13.622). The corners are fairly nondescript and the track is made up of high-speed straights that command heavy braking, which, in turn, demands stability as drivers plough through the circuit's many chicanes – traction out of these is critical. On the Circuit Gilles Villeneuve, drivers spend about 20 per cent of each lap (around 18 seconds) pushing the brake pedal. It is crucial that cars are stable in the braking zone.

At Montreal, it's easy to go into the wall. The final chicane is entered at around 200mph but the anchors have to be slammed on to come down to 75mph at its kernel. There's a big area of tarmac on the outside that almost invites drivers to cover it, but, if you come in a bit too smartly and still try to make the chicane, there's a dangerous mound of concrete at its edge. A Formula One car hitting that, there being very little travel in the suspension, will be launched into the air and bounce into the wall on the inside of the track. In 1999, Michael Schumacher did just that coming into this (the 13th) turn – he was immediately followed by Jacques Villeneuve, who did almost exactly the same thing. The wall, which bore the slogan Bienvenue au Québec (Welcome to Quebec), has become known as the 'Wall of Champions' as Damon Hill, Fernando Alonso, GP2

Champion Nico Rosberg, CART Champion Juan Pablo Montoya, and Ricardo Zonta (at the time, reigning sports car champion) have all had too close associations with the structure. This is part of the reason why when racing at Montreal the presence of safety car has to be factored into team planning.

Hamilton would have expected Alonso to push him hard, and his racing partner got away well, but Lewis fended off his fellow McLaren driver. BMW's Nick Heidfeld, who looked menacing and had made the best start of the front four, considered attacking the Brit on the outside, but thought better of it before he had committed. While Lewis was occupied with the BMW man at the first turn, Alonso went wide on the outside, firstly on to the tarmac and then over the grass (which was just as well as, if he had continued to the tarmac road beyond the greenery, he would have been penalised). His route took him across Hamilton's path, who if he had not had his wits about him would have ploughed straight into the side of the World Champion. Indeed, Alonso was doubly fortunate; if Heidfeld had got round Hamilton at the start, he would almost certainly have connected with Alonso as he crossed the circuit. As it was, the Spaniard found himself on the far side of the track, watching Heidfeld fill the second place he had just given up. Seemingly having damaged the underside of his car on the kerb as he returned to the track (and maybe getting some grass in his radiator), Alonso was once more fortunate to slot in behind the German. Although some saw Alonso's opening gambit as typical of his 'do-or-die' attitude, the fact was that the whole of this episode made him look clumsy; it was at least an extremely costly mess-up on his part. He'd gone way too deep into the corner with cold front tyres and ice-cool brakes; he was never going to be able to kill his speed fast enough. But at this point he had a BMW in front of him and Massa's Ferrari too close behind him; the World Champion seemed to have lost the race almost before he'd started it.

While all this was going on, Hamilton had capitalised and held a decent lead for so early in the proceedings. Alonso would have known that at best he would need to stay close to Lewis and attempt to beat him in the pit-stop phase, but that now looked very much like a plan that was dead in the water.

At the conclusion of the first lap, Heidfeld was 1.5 seconds behind Hamilton who was pushing even harder, looking to build a decisive gap. He was easily the faster driver on the circuit in the first two sectors. By lap two, Lewis had a lead of 2.1 seconds; the following lap, the divide between him and Heidfeld had not changed, while Alonso looked to be losing touch. There was a long way to go, but Hamilton was lapping a second faster than his team-mate and by the fifth lap he had a lead of 5.5 seconds, 7.4 seconds ahead of Alonso. In lap 14, the latter ran wide again on turn one, back on to the grass. It cost him at least two seconds and put him 12.4 seconds adrift of Lewis. It may have been that the possible damage to the underside of his car sustained at the first bend was the root of his problems, and it might well have meant a loss of down-force, but Alonso looked unfocused and careless by this point. This was emphasised when, again on turn one, Massa dived across the grass in front of Alonso to take the McLaren driver out of the first three.

Meanwhile, by lap 20, Hamilton looked supremely cool at the front. Coming into the pits, he was 19 seconds ahead of Heidfeld and 21 seconds better than Alonso – a full pit stop ahead. He returned to the race in fourth place, with Massa, Alonso and Rosberg in front of him.

The first shunt of the race happened when Scott Speed clipped the rear wing of Alexander Wurz's Williams-Toyota. The American entered the hairpin with broken suspension. But the safety car needed to be deployed when Adrian Sutil's Spyker crashed at turn four on lap 22. Lewis had pitted just prior to the coming of the safety car. At that point, the pit lane was closed but Alonso and Rosberg pitted anyway. The McLaren man had been low on fuel and had no option but to make his first stop, but in doing so he broke the rule that dictates that drivers may not pit until the field has formed up behind the safety car.

Both drivers were given 10-second stop/go penalties and Alonso lost all hope of a win. But the coming of the safety car was also bad news for Lewis. As the drivers lined up for the restart, all his good work had been wiped out.

After the pit lane was reopened and the rest of the field pitted, stacking and some confusion took a toll – Massa and Fisichella exited the pit lane while the red light was still on, and both were later black-flagged from the race.

Following his punishment, Alonso was in 13th place. But, in an attempt to get back towards the front, he started to lap at record pace. He was also helped by more safety-car periods. The race had restarted on lap 26. On the approach to the hairpin on the following lap, Robert Kubica struck the rear of Jarno Trulli's Toyota; the Pole was travelling at about 160mph. The collision shunted Kubica on to the grass at the edge of the track, and a bump launched his car into the concrete wall just before the hairpin; the impact would have been about 50G. Most of the nosecone and front suspension was wiped out by the first impact. The BMW violently rolled down and across the circuit and came to rest against the armco in the run-off area on the other side of the track. Medics needed some long minutes to extract Kubica from the car, and he was rushed to Montreal hospital. Initially, messages came through that the Pole had broken his leg, but, in fact, he sustained only a sprained ankle and concussion. His manager, Danieli Morelli, put many hearts and minds at rest when he announced the driver was 'fine'. Unfortunately, Trulli was not privy to this information as he viewed the crash in his rear-view mirrors. Losing focus in his concern for the other driver's welfare, the 'Pescara Panther' crashed on the exit of the pit lane after his second stop.

Hamilton continued to look the most composed man on the circuit. On his second pit stop, at the conclusion of lap 48, he was half a minute in front of the field. He took on the soft tyres, which had proved to be three-quarters of a second a lap faster than their harder cousins when new, although they tended to wear more quickly.

The last restart came with 10 laps to go. The cars that had survived the race to that point were on the same lap and this created claustrophobic racing conditions. But Hamilton had sustained his pace despite all the incidents and got himself well ahead of Heidfeld in the last part of the race, claiming his first Grand Prix win with comparative ease.

Alonso had got close to Räikkönen and seemed as if he might better Ferrari's flying Finn. But struggling for grip he dropped back, all fight seemingly drained from man and car. Lewis's Championship position was made more secure after Takuma Sato, in a Super Aguri, got by the Spaniard for sixth place, racing around the reigning Champion outside of the final chicane. Alonso had not made a battle of it, wanting to avoid the chance of colliding with the Japanese racer.

The race had been a battlefield with two disqualifications and a total of 10 drivers failing to finish, six of them because of accidents. A number of cars were damaged: Alex Wurz's rear wing was crunched in the incident that took out Scott Speed and Anthony Davidson, in third place at the time, had struck a groundhog.

The resulting safety-car interventions (four in all) could have been disconcerting for some drivers, but Lewis showed the calm maturity that had thus far characterised his season to maintain his leading role.

Hamilton had performed perfectly in a race that had been one of the most challenging seen on a dry surface, packed with incident, cut and thrust, to claim his first Formula One win at only the sixth attempt. Hamilton, leading what had been a dramatic race from start to finish, drove with a coolness that belied his years as the field fragmented in the interventions by the safety car behind him. BMW's Nick Heidfeld, who had trailed Hamilton for the most of the race, followed him in for his sixth podium, with Alexander Wurz and his Williams Toyota making third (the Austrian achieved his third career podium in the race that marked a decade since his entry into Formula One). It was the first time in the 2007 season that a driver other than the four Ferrari and McLaren men had made the podium. Alonso could do no better than seventh.

As his winning driver came across the line, Ron Dennis's radio message was sanguine but typically understated, although there might have been some cryptic message harking back to Monaco: 'Well done, Lewis. You won fair and square.'

The victorious racer's reply was a high-pitched cheer somewhere between a 'hooray' and a 'whoopee'.

Hamilton's victory gave him the Championship lead and the prospect of his winning the title in his first season looked much more than a dream. He declared, 'I've been ready for this for quite some time, ready for the win – it was just a matter of where and when ... it's difficult to grasp ... It was a fairly simple race ... the challenge was to keep heat in the tyres. The safety car is so slow, it's so easy to go off line and crash and hit the wall.'

Lewis was also swift to thank all the watching British supporters, particularly those who had come to Montreal.

Felipe Massa was full of praise for the Championship leader, saying, 'Lewis is a fantastic driver.'

Alonso, looking somewhere between angry and dejected, perhaps because he was now eight points adrift of Hamilton in the Championship, gave a weary, curt and none-too-generous assessment of the winning driver's performance: 'Very good. Very lucky. The safety car worked for someone at least.'

McLaren stood at the top of the Manufacturers' table with 88 points. Ferrari, their nearest challengers by a long way, had 60 points.

As Lewis was dedicating the result to his father in the post-race press conference, Anthony told television reporters that he felt 'drained', but that he had seen 14 years of hard work come to fruition in Montreal. He saw the event as being the product of 'lots of karting experience' and 'severe determination', and said it demonstrated that if a father and son 'both give 100 per cent you'll be surprised what you can achieve'.

Reacting to Lewis's Canadian performance, Martin Hines, his

childhood karting sponsor, told London radio station LBC News 1152 listeners that it was no more than he had expected of Lewis: 'It's the only Lewis I've ever known, one that goes out and wins ... He's cool, calm, knows what he's there to do and goes out and does it ... Would you bet against him? If you can get a decent bet on, I would, for sure; I think he's going to win it.'

Hamilton's victory made him the first ever driver of African descent to win a major (of global status) car race. You have to go a long way back to find anything approaching Lewis's historic victory in Montreal. In 1963, Wendell Scott won a NASCAR Grand National race on a dirt oval in Jacksonville, Florida, although NASCAR was not then what it is now and at first officials had declared Buck Baker to have been the winner.

Over the following 44 years, not a single black driver won a major race. However, notable drivers like Willy T Ribbs and more recently drag racer JR Todd did make their mark. In 2006, Todd became the first black driver to win in the premier Top Fuel class of the National Hot Rod Association series, scoring three wins. In major oval or road racing series, George Mack (17th in the 2002 Indy 500) and Bill Lester, who is a regular on NASCAR's Craftsman Truck support series, have made attempts on the Nextel Cup tour. Stock car racing has reigning Supercross Champion James Stewart as its top candidate to be the sport's first black winner since Scott. But these men sit in the history of motorsport as rule breakers in terms of the 'colour code' rather than exemplars of change.

After the Australian Grand Prix, Sir Frank Williams had described Hamilton as a unique talent. The Williams team boss, winner of nine Constructors' titles, who has been associated with seven World Champions, including Nigel Mansell, Alain Prost, Damon Hill and Jacques Villeneuve, claimed Lewis's instant impact on the sport was unmatched: 'I've never seen anyone arrive and be so successful so quickly ... from his first race. It is quite remarkable ... I am looking hard to find fault with him and he is very nice, which is quite unusual, too.'

Williams, who has been in motorsport for close to four decades, was asked if Hamilton reminded him of any other racers. His reply was concise: 'Nobody!'

Really Outstanding Stuff

Dale Earnhardt once told of how when his son, Dale Jr, was a boy (Dale Jr would become a two-time Busch Series Champion – one of six people to win back-to-back Championships – and was the winner of the 2004 Daytona 500) that 'hunting and racing are a lot alike. Holding that steering wheel and holding that rifle both mean you better be responsible.'

Almost every decision a driver makes in motorsport has serious consequences; in the driving seat or off the track, what you make your mind up to do is important. But the 1995 Le Mans Class winner Mario Andretti insists, 'Do it no matter what! If you believe in it, it is something very honourable. If somebody around you or your family does not understand it, then that's their problem. But if you do have a passion, an honest passion, just do it.'

In 2006, Lewis Hamilton made a crucial choice in his racing future, joining the ART Grand Prix team to contest the GP2 series (the 'second league' of Formula One) alongside Alexandre Prémat, who had won races in 2005. Like ASM in F3 when Hamilton joined them, ART were reigning Champions, having taken the 2005 GP2 crown with Nico Rosberg.

It was expected that Lewis would have a learning year and that he was not going to overcome the likes of Prémat, Nelson Angelo Piquet (son of the former Formula One World Champion) or Ulsterman Adam Carroll in his first season. This seemed a fair assessment given the experience and ability of the competition, but right from the start Hamilton was impressive and by the end of the season he had outshone Prémat. But the pair's first challenge was to secure the team's second consecutive GP2 title.

Lewis replaced the previous year's Champion Nico Rosberg in the ART team, the former having moved on to race for the Williams Formula One team.

Nico was Hamilton's closest friend when both drivers were racing prodigies and karting team-mates in Italy for two seasons. They were also competing for the prize of becoming the youngest ever driver in Formula One. According to Lewis, Nico got there first because he had a season in GP2 while Hamilton was in F3. For Lewis, 'GP2 is vital because the set-up of the car is very similar to Formula One and on some tracks we hit the same speed at the end of a straight.'

Prior to his first GP2 campaign, in mid-January 2006, Hamilton told how, although he had only managed around 10 days' experience with the car, he was looking forward to the coming campaign 'after the fantastic season we had last year and I'm sure the team will do a fantastic job this year'.

Lewis made it his goal to win races and looked to take the Championship as well. But his focus was more pragmatic than idealistic: 'I have to work hard and make sure we maximise the time we have to develop the car.'

In March 2006, Nicolas Todt, the son of Ferrai's CEO Jean Todt, the principal of the ART team, made it clear that ART GP's first season was exceptional in terms of results, and that they were at that point able to continue their charge in the series with the same dynamics by ensuring they had a pair of exceptional drivers, such as the combination of Prémat and Hamilton. Todt stated that Lewis had proven in all the lower formulas in which he had competed that he had a natural talent for driving and had displayed great professionalism. He made it know that ART were 'thrilled to be able to count on his pure speed and maturity when it comes to defending both our Drivers' and Constructors' crowns'.

Frenchman Frédéric Vasseur, General Manager of ART Grand Prix, said it was a great pleasure to sign Lewis and that his joining ART was a logical continuation for the organisation following his title in the F3 Euroseries the previous year. Entrusted by McLaren, Vasseur went on to say that Hamilton had integrated very well into the team and that he was happy and proud to be able to count him as one of ART's drivers.

During the winter, before his new challenge, Lewis had spent time catching up with his family, girlfriend and friends. He had also done a bit of travelling, starting off by visiting New York with Jodia. They went to the top of the Empire State Building, visited the Statue of Liberty and of course they couldn't go to New York without doing some shopping! Then Lewis moved on to Bermuda with some friends for a week. Although it was the island's winter, it was still warm and Hamilton found it to be a beautiful, very relaxing place, which was just what he needed before the start of the season.

Apart from spending off time in Bermuda, to relax Lewis plays guitar, dabbles in basketball and, in recent years, has been looking to turn his hand to golf.

In March 2006, Lewis was looking forward to getting back to testing, saying it had been too long since he'd been in a racing car: 'The last time I tested was back in early December of last year at Paul Ricard, although it wasn't a full test day as there was heavy rain, so it was cut short. I've been itching to get back to it since and was really looking forward to getting back to it this week.'

And, before his first official test with ART at Paul Ricard, Lewis told how it was great to be back at the circuit where 'the facilities are world class. It is very good for testing because of the different configurations available and it is very safe.'

The test went well and it was a productive session for Hamilton. He covered over 180km on the first day and set the fastest time. On day two he set the second fastest time. He reflected, 'There are three more tests, at Ricard, Barcelona and Valencia before the start of the season, which is 8–9 April in Valencia, so I will be spending some time with the team in France and training when I am at home in preparation.'

This was Hamilton's first test with Alex Prémat as an ART driver, as he hadn't been at the tests late the previous year; however, they did race together in 2004 in the F3 Euroseries when Alex was with ASM. Lewis recalled, 'I was in my first F3 year with Manor Motorsport. Alex is a nice guy and we get on fine.'

The previous season, Prémat had performed well in GP2 and had been competing in A1 GP, appearing to be the driver to beat; as such, Hamilton was 'looking forward to having a strong and competitive team-mate again this year, as with last year in Adrian Sutil. It is always great to have this situation as you can really push and challenge each other and work together as professionals.'

When asked about the differences between F3 and GP2, Hamilton said that, other than the obvious differences in the size of the car and the power output from the engine, he didn't think the two cars were that dissimilar to drive, although he understood there are characteristics that are slightly different, for example the inability of a GP2 car to carry the same speed into a corner as a F3 car. But he pointed out that the GP2 car is able to power out of corners. For all this, he saw the ART GP2 car as being 'really fun to drive, it is very tricky, and it has so much power behind it. Because there is so much more power, you have to make sure you are always on point, particularly through the high-speed corners. It is definitely more demanding, both physically and mentally.'

This said, he told how he was relishing the coming challenge and stepping up the racing ladder.

Just before a race Lewis gave an insight into his preparation, having just returned from a week of fitness training with the Mercedes-Benz DTM squad in the Algarve in Portugal, alongside Mika Häkkinen, Formula One World Champion in 1998 and 1999, Jamie Green and Bernd Schneider (the former Formula One Zakspeed and Arrows driver) among others: 'To see guys such as Bernd and Mika who have achieved so much already and they still have a massive desire to push and do more was quite inspiring really.'

Some of these men were nearly twice Lewis's age and he expressed the hope that he would be as fit and inspired as them when he got to their age: 'It was a good week of training and bonding, and we did all the exercising together so it was a great motivation, it is like a big family with everyone pushing everyone else.'

Hamilton was starting his day at 7.30am on the beach. A break at

9am for breakfast until 10am was followed by another session up to a 1pm lunch. At 3pm it was back to training until 7.30pm. For Lewis, 'It was a tough week but great fun.'

But, according to Nigel Mansell, 'I've tried everything other than jumping out of a plane, but nothing gives you an adrenaline rush like racing a car.'

And this is what Hamilton wanted to be doing.

Hamilton's main rival for the Championship would be Nelson Piquet Jr, who was in his second year of GP2. The very first round set the tone for the season with Piquet winning from Hamilton.

From the outset Lewis's performance in competitive GP2 racing was impressive. It was plain that his considered approach put him a cut above the majority, showing himself to be a strategist with the courage to take risks.

During the third weekend of the season at the Nürburgring, he won both races (in spite of a penalty for speeding in the pits during the first race) to become only the second driver in the history of the series (after Champion Rosberg) to 'do the double' during a single event. The first of his two victories was more than just a win, it was a devastating performance that demonstrated his superiority to all around him. He lapped over a second quicker than his rivals.

Following Lewis's performance at the Nürburgring, McLaren's Martin Whitmarsh was upbeat about the young man's potential and, despite earlier having voiced the intention of wanting 'to keep pressure and the sense of anticipation off Lewis', on Monday, 8 May 2006, he stated that Hamilton's effort the previous Saturday was the most phenomenal performance he had ever seen in a GP2 race. He went on, 'If he continues like that, he could decimate the entire field through the remainder of the year and this is doubly impressive when you consider that most of his strongest rivals are in their second year racing in the category. It was really outstanding stuff.'

Coming from a taciturn Formula One set-up in a hard-hitting industry which relies on logic, science and facts more than hysterical hype, these comments were unexpected. Looking forward to the following season, Whitmarsh added that McLaren had made no secret of the fact that they would prefer Kimi Räikkönen to remain in the Formula One team with Fernando Alonso in 2007 and that, together with Hamilton, McLaren obviously had a good stable of drivers signed up, which also included Juan Pablo Montoya and test drivers Pedro de la Rosa and Gary Paffett.

From the start of his GP2 career, Hamilton was most eagerly looking forward to the race in Monaco, having been victorious there the previous year in the F3 Euroseries. Lewis told how he enjoyed the whole track and there was not one section that stood out for him 'because it is all great'. However, he saw the tunnel as being unique to motorsport, the experience of driving through it, the roar of the car engines bouncing off the walls being 'great'! For Hamilton, racing in Monte Carlo is 'just the most immense feeling as it is such a legendary track. To be going faster on the Monaco circuit will be amazing; I just can't wait.'

Starting from pole, Lewis was once again victorious in Monaco. Ron Dennis, usually a dispassionate spectator, was almost moved to tears.

Lewis, the GP2 new boy, was driving for the most successful team, but, although his dramatic winning style was remarkable, even more striking was the way he humbled his team-mate's efforts. Prémat, a man who had a year of GP2 experience and was pretty evenly matched with Nico Rosberg in 2005 was being put in the shade by Hamilton. Lewis looked to be in a different league and, on the evidence of the exceptionally positive reports about Rosberg's performance with Williams, the 'Tewin Typhoon' seemed likely to make even more of an impact on Formula One if he got the opportunity in a quality car.

Hamilton saved two of his best GP2 performances for his home crowd at Silverstone. The 'Hertfordshire Hurricane' made a dramatic start in an aggressive contest, but his cool style gave him a distinct advantage in the heat of the fight and he won in commanding fashion. For Lewis, the race was 'a superb victory ... Again it was emotional, like Monaco, but I think this tops Monaco. England won the football today [England had beaten Paraguay in the World Cup in Germany] and for a British driver to win as well, for me to win as well, here at Silverstone, it's a really special feeling for me, and I'm really happy with it.'

The second heat at Silverstone the next day was one of the drives of the 2006 season. His win in the first race gave Hamilton eighth place on the grid.

At the start Alex Prémat, in third position, stalled, calling for a second formation lap. As the lights went out, Felix Porteiro flew off, he was followed by Clivio Piccione, Giorgio Pantano and Nelson Piquet Jr, who moved swiftly past the Italian into third place. Meanwhile, Hamilton was starting his attack. Passing Timo Glock at the start, he quickly found a way round Adam Carroll, making good use of the slipstream on Hangar Straight, sliding past into Stowe. He now had Pantano well in his sights; however, the Italian wasn't going to give way without a fight, and Piccione was responding in a similar fashion to a series of charges by Piquet not many metres up the track. Further down the field, Michael Ammermüller took out team-mate Neel Jani, necessitating the entry of the safety car.

By lap eight, the cars were once more clear to go and Porteiro managed the pace brilliantly. Hamilton saw his chance to go beyond Pantano and the duo ran side-by-side down the straight, but the British driver gained the position into Copse. Now he would deal with Piquet who was still attempting to pass Piccione. Into Maggotts, Piquet dodged to Piccione's left and, with Lewis to his right, they ran three abreast into the corner. Hamilton came out best after an impudent move, dashing past his adversaries as Piquet slid off the track, letting Piccione and Carroll through.

Lewis rapidly caught Porteiro, but the Spaniard was driving an excellent race and held the Championship leader off for several laps. But, eventually, with 11 laps to go Hamilton made his move. He glanced up the inside of Bridge but Porteiro held his line, obliging

Hamilton to alter his strategy into Brooklands. Once more, Porteiro held position before Lewis made an elegant charge up the inside of Luffield. The Englishman had taken the lead and he pulled out a second a lap until the flag fell. The ART driver had produced an amazing race.

1st Lewis Hamilton – ART Grand Prix. 37:27.225
2nd Felix Porteiro – Campos Racing. +9.060
3rd Adam Carroll – Racing Engineering. +10.040

Lewis gained the point for the fastest lap, and as such he finished his home weekend just missing the pole-position points which would have given him the perfect total. After his fine victory, he expressed his hope that the result was just a continuation of his success and his drive to get to Formula One: 'I'm working my arse off not only to do the best job possible, but also to get that seat at McLaren; I really want that, and it's an opportunity that not many people get.'

Lewis was to see coming from eighth and winning at Silverstone as a 'special' memory of his year and his career thus far. But, for him, 'Each year something new happens. It's not necessarily better. To win my first race at Monaco in F3 was quite special for me.'

These comments are typical of Lewis. Like Alain Prost, who once told how he 'would look at Michael Schumacher on the podium next to me and he'd be very happy and I understood how he felt. But very often my mind would already be on the next race.'

Hamilton tends to look to the future rather than over his shoulder. However, he had demonstrated that he was not only lightning fast, but also a brave driver of the old-fashioned style. His passing move driving around the outside of two other drivers during that second race was a breathtaking manoeuvre that no one who saw it will forget.

Lewis has an aggressive attitude to racing and is a natural competitor. He overtakes in Formula One like a GP2 driver but often when Anthony talks of his son's racing style, particularly when analysing his first-corner manoeuvres, he tells how he often applies skills he learned on kart tracks. I recall watching Lewis as an 11-year-old win a race in cadets at Buckmore Park. Much smaller than most of his rivals, he smacked out a superlative final lap, producing an overtaking manoeuvre from fourth place to grab an improbable victory. His timing was perfection, his confidence shocking and his positioning just short enough of reckless to be massively skilful. Caroline Hoy, a former kart racer and now an organiser of the BRDC, had recognised Lewis's potential early on. She claims that she has seen his karting background coming to the fore in his later career and believes that 'karting taught him how to race'. She recalled how as a boy he had a knack for overtaking in a style similar to taking a corner; it was a very smooth and natural action that just kept going. This seemed to indicate he knew the move would come a relatively long time before he actually made it. So, on the point of overtaking, he wasn't really thinking about it in the way that others might. He had thrown his vehicle round at Silverstone with much the same panache. It is hard to recall a driver who has carried so much from karts to cars. And it works to such an extent that watching him sometimes I think it shouldn't; those unused to carefully scrutinising his technique might mistake his feel for the physics of a car for careless distain. However, any opponent might do well to understand that, as long as Lewis is left with the authority to meld his inherent sensitivity into a growing depth of knowledge, his driving is going to be a melange of unique endowments and a well-practised and informed mosaic of skills.

Hamilton's double win supporting the British Grand Prix at Silverstone delivered a critical blow to Nelson Piquet. Flying past the Brazilian and Clivio Piccione in a fine move at Becketts, a series of high-speed (up to 150mph in a GP2 car) bends where overtaking is rare, had nailed his colours to the mast and probably did much to destroy Piquet's confidence. The crowd had roared in approval of Hamilton's skill and daring. Lewis became the first GP2 driver to win both heats at two races.

Following Silverstone, in July 2006, Ron Dennis was saying that it was close to 'inevitable' that Hamilton would find his way on to the Formula One grid the following year. But he tempered his remarks with a lengthy analysis, starting out by saying that 'it would be jumping into the deep end if we put him into one of McLaren's cars' and that he didn't want Lewis's career 'to go wrong when he is so close to achieving his goals'. However, he went on to state that McLaren had 'what they believed to be the most exciting driver line-up in Formula One for many years. Alongside Fernando, we have the excitement of the debut year for Lewis. We have of course worked with Lewis for a decade, so he is very well known to the team. His level of preparation and commitment is unprecedented. He has not only excelled, but exceeded our expectations with all the challenges that we have set him to reach this point.'

It was clear that Dennis had great faith in Lewis and at that point rated only Alonso and Kimi Räikkönen above the young man from Stevenage.

Lewis was impressing in the highest circles. In August Formula One mogul Bernie Ecclestone said, 'He's won every single racing series that he's entered. I want to see this young guy on the starting grid next year … he'll win a Grand Prix some time – sooner rather than later.'

Turkey Twizzler

Talking about his preparations for Turkey, the penultimate race of the season, Lewis gave a clue as to how he would approach this new track and his diligent approach to racing in general by telling of how he planned to go to the ART workshops in France and analyse Prémat's and Nico Rosberg's data from 2005. He'd seen the Istanbul circuit on TV so he had an idea how it ran. He commented, 'There looks to be some really exciting corners there so I am looking forward to it.'

Late in August, in the first race, Lewis once more demonstrated his overtaking prowess and, although he failed to win, his nerve, survival instincts and will to strive for victory were firmly demonstrated. Lewis was in seventh place when it all went wrong. He spun and had to wait for everyone to go past him before he cut across the rest of the traffic. This cost valuable ground; he went down to 21st or 22nd place.

According to Niki Lauda, 'Giving up is something a Lauda doesn't do ... I always go extreme ways.'

There is something of this in Hamilton's attitude and he showed it in Istanbul. From 21 laps out, he set about practically starting again, turning a reverse into an attack and a rush for the front.

With two corners to go, Lewis was in second place: 'Even though I finished second, it felt like a win.'

Hamilton had put on a spellbinding performance; he had shown the kind of racing spirit that makes people attend car racing. After his magnificent accomplishment, he told of how he had turned his day and the event around: 'I made a mistake ... But I think that throughout the season in GP2 I just showed consistency and determination which is key ... I came from the back ... got myself together, took all the negative, turned it all into positive and drove to the front; I really dug deep and drove with my heart.'

Bonza in Monza

The records of the final races of the season in Monza are a testament to Lewis's racing wisdom. Piquet cut Lewis's Championship lead down to just eight points by making pole position for the first race. The Brazilian was joined on the front row by Giorgio Pantano, who just got past Hamilton to take second place in the closing minutes of qualifying, but the Italian was unable to match Piquet's best time of 1:30.161.

When the lights went out to start the last contest of the season, polesitter Piquet made a sluggish start; however, a flat line through the initial chicane enabled him to snatch back the lead when he glided by Pantano. Hamilton stalked the leading pair, observing and waiting for an opening. But the local driver refused let anyone by; not many corners on, he powered a path beyond Piquet to hit the front of the pack.

As the field completed the first lap, at the head of the race Adam Carroll, who had settled on Hamilton's rear wing for most of the lap, smoothed past his countryman over the long front straight.

But Lewis was not in a frame of mind to shift his focus from Piquet, and overtook his compatriot the next time past the pits and retrieved third place. However, the time spent trailing Carroll had consequences; Pantano and Piquet were locked in conflict well in front of Lewis.

The leading pair upped the level of attrition to a war footing, alternating for the prizes of the fastest laps, while putting more and more time and space between themselves and Hamilton. At that point the Englishman was the only driver able to approach the pace the two leaders were setting. It appeared that the race would go to the duelling duo in first and second place, but on the ninth lap Carroll came in for his stop, as did Alex Prémat and Jose Maria Lopez; this was the start of what seemed like the usual pit stops throughout the field. The Ulsterman came out 10th, but his right rear tyre came loose halfway round the track, forcing him to retire. However, the rogue tyre bounced frighteningly in front of the oncoming cars.

The situation forced the safety car to take to the track, and most of the field were obliged to come to a standstill, including the leading three drivers. The order into the pit lane was Pantano, Piquet and Hamilton, and that was the order out as well, although Fairuz Fauzy and Jason Tahinci (who had yet to pit) were on the track between the title contenders.

On the 14th lap, the race once more went green. Piquet made a forceful charge up the inside at the initial chicane, dramatically locking his tyres, but he cut the corner as he stampeded through. He was forced to allow Pantano back through to dodge a penalty, and the hunt was back on.

But, as the race wore on, Pantano and Piquet were once again leaving Hamilton. It began to look like Piquet would keep the title chase going into the next day, but things took a dramatic turn in the

23rd lap. Hamilton snatched the fastest lap and with a possible points difference of seven the title would be his.

From the restart Piquet's tyres had been shot, but he continued to press hard with everything he had to grab the crucial point for fastest lap: he set fastest first sectors, he set fastest third sectors, but he was unable to turn this work into the FL he lusted for.

However, Pantano did achieve the fastest lap on his last circuit, so rescuing Piquet by keeping the contest open.

Pantano, Piquet and Hamilton made the podium, but the points difference between Hamilton and Piquet was now down to only half a dozen: to win the title Piquet had to take victory in the second race, make the fastest lap, and hope that Hamilton would finish out of the points.

Pantano did just what he said he would do the day before, but the fastest lap on the final circuit had been crucial to the Italian. That Hamilton had gained the fastest lap for much of the closing stages of the race, which would have provided him with a seven-point cushion over Piquet, and given him the title, must have been a hard pill for the young Brit to swallow.

However, although Pantano had won the penultimate race at Monza, and set the fastest lap on the final round, initially taking this bonus point from Hamilton, it transpired that the Italian had set his time under a yellow flag, indicating to the officials that he had not slowed enough to avoid potential danger. This meant he lost the fastest lap, which instead gave Hamilton the single point he needed. Lewis was Champion with a race to spare.

But there were still points to prove and a moral victory to be won. The fight was on to prove Hamilton a worthy champion or otherwise. On Sunday, 10 September, Giorgio Pantano flashed past the seven men in front of him on the grid to head the field at the first chicane, Hamilton stuck on his rear wing, having been assisted by the slow start of polesitter Hiroki Yoshimoto. The Japanese racer blocked the way causing the field behind him to bunch up, which allowed Hamilton and Pantano to fire to the front.

The three fastest men of the day before demonstrated that they had held on to their alacrity. At the front Pantano and Hamilton took turns in grabbing the fastest laps and Piquet spent little time or effort passing the cars in front of him and got right up behind P3 Piccione by the conclusion of the second lap.

While the leading couple sped away from the field, Piquet was anxiously struggling to find a means to pass Piccione in order to hunt down the front runners; however, the Monegasque driver was determined in his resistance and, as the laps went by, in spite of all his efforts, the Brazilian could not find a way round Piccione.

Piquet's task became more pressing when Hamilton ran well wide at the Lesmo corner, causing a veneer of gravel to engulf his tyres and he slid back to within touching distance of Piccione. With his deadly rival in sight, Piquet maximised his effort, but, as he hurtled into the first chicane, down-force deserted the front of his car and he lightly twirled through the corner.

Pantano was six seconds ahead of Lewis, but the belligerent Brit was now producing a series of fastest laps while Piquet, in eighth place, was fighting to find some redemption for his mistake that looked all the more costly as the race progressed.

Piquet, having got by Luca Filippi at the chicane, shifted himself back into the points and on the tail of Yoshimoto. However, the Nippon racer had not forgiven himself for his embarrassing and disastrous start and did all he could to deny the Brazilian.

At the sharp end of the race the space between Pantano and Hamilton was telescoping. Hamilton caught the Italian and got past him at the Ascari complex. However, as Lewis cut the corner, he had no choice but to allow Pantano back into the lead. From then on, the Italian's concentration did not falter and he managed to hold Hamilton off as they went over the line nose to tail. The man from Padua was just 0.4 seconds in front of Lewis and added his name to the short-list of double race winners over a GP2 race weekend. Pantano drove a splendid race under inexorable pressure from Hamilton, running an inch-perfect racing line for 21 laps to claim his third win of the season for FMS International.

Piccione was the next home. Piquet finished in sixth. Lewis gained the added point for fastest lap that put a nice finish to his Championship-winning experience.

Lewis had won the GP2 Championship. That the title victory was achieved at his first attempt, and the fact that he did it with five victories out of 22 rounds, emphasized his talent. He had overcome stiff opposition from more practised rivals who had raced in GP2 in 2005. Although all drivers in GP2 have access to the same machinery, Hamilton proved capable of regularly lapping over a second per lap faster than his rivals.

Hamilton drew deserved satisfaction from his achievement. On the Saturday evening, he was still with the team in the paddock preparing to race again on Sunday, when the news came that Pantano had lost his fastest lap for that day's race, so passing Lewis the Championship. But he knew that the following day he'd have to beat Nelson Piquet to prove that he deserved the title.

Lewis rather modestly considered that he'd 'done pretty well; I am happy with it ... It was hard, by no means an easy thing.'

He reflected that he did not go into a season expecting to do so well, but thought his team had the right approach. He saw himself as fortunate to be with one of the top teams and said that ART had done 'a great job'. Hamilton told how he had confidence in the team and that for him it had been 'just about learning as much as I could from my team-mate. When I got there I was immediately ahead of him. Step by step we improved.'

The five-time World Champion racer Juan Manuel Fangio once declared, 'You need great passion, because everything you do with great pleasure, you do well.'

This was confirmed by Lewis when he was asked if he had any regrets about choosing to devote time to GP2, he replied, 'Absolutely not. It was a fantastic season.'

Lewis confessed that he had found the experience a bit more

demanding than F3, but had learned many lessons in a short space of time and 'there were a lot of good guys out there. It was intense because you had about 10 laps to learn a new track.'

After Lewis had won the title Norbert Haug, Vice President, Mercedes-Benz Motorsport said, 'This is the greatest day in Lewis's career so far and, after Formula Renault and the F3 Euroseries, the third important Championship he has won in the last four years at the age of 21. We have known Lewis since he was a little boy and Ron [Dennis] had the idea that both McLaren and Mercedes should support his racing programme starting with karting nine years ago. Since then, Lewis has become a real part of the family.'

Winning is What Matters

In the furore surrounding Michael Schumacher's victory and retirement announcement at the Italian Grand Prix, Hamilton's GP2 success went almost unnoticed. Yet it was probably the key to the door of his ultimate ambition. He certainly saw his achievement as pointing to his next step: '2006 was a fantastic year, a year in which everything I had learned through karting, Formula Renault and F3 all came together in GP2. I learned a great deal in GP2 and thank Frédéric Vasseur and everyone at ART for their support.'

Lewis's secret to success in 2006 was based on a very straightforward attitude to competition that seems to be based on giving oneself feasible goals: 'When you go into a race, you have a certain amount of confidence because you know what you can do from where you are starting ... you don't go into a race in GP2 thinking of winning when you start eighth on the grid. Each time I overtook someone, I thought, "I'm sure I can get a couple more places."'

According to multiple World Champion motorcycle racer Valentino Rossi, 'I race to win. If I am on the bike or in a car, it will always be the same.'

This is an attitudinal trait of winners and Hamilton is no exception; in the last analysis, the sport for Lewis is about one thing: 'Some wins are better than others. Winning is good. Winning is what matters.'

But wins lead to new challenges and probably the search for even greater success. Shortly after his triumph in Monza, Lewis said, 'I saw Ron [Dennis] on Sunday and he was very happy with the work I've done this year. Right now I'm training as usual, and waiting for him to call.'

Not long after, rumours that Räikkönen was going to move to Ferrari if Schumacher retired prompted Hamilton to comment, 'If Kimi's smart he'll stay at McLaren.'

But if the gossip was true Lewis saw that the situation could work in his favour: 'It gives me a much better chance if he does go. But look at Alonso. He started at Minardi, so I expect to do something like that [to be loaned to a team at the back of the grid]. But if I end up alongside Alonso it definitely would not intimidate me. I've never had a team-mate who's beaten me over the course of a season. So I would love that challenge.'

Looking to the future, much was now expected of Hamilton and his potential move up to Formula One was already causing excitement. But GP2 is notionally a single-make formula; everyone involved takes their place on the grid in cars that are equal in terms of performance. However, in actuality, like its predecessor F3000, in GP2 there are teams that prepare and set up cars better than others. For a time in F3000, it appeared that driving for Arden guaranteed the title; the ART seats in GP2 have had the same type of kudos. For confirmation about the difference between the teams, one only needs to note how quickly Timo Glock's performance improved when he switched from the BCN Competicion team to Isport.

But Hamilton's superiority in GP2 suggested he could have outperformed the opposition in any car. His race pace and skilful consistency provoked comparisons to a young Fernando Alonso and at his very best he had stunned onlookers with some spectacular performances, outshining his more experienced team-mate Alexandre Prémat and a resurgent Nelson Piquet Jr with his bold driving style. Lewis had won the title and, perhaps more importantly, the paddock's admiration. However, the glory was much more of a stepping stone for Hamilton than an end in itself. He conceded he had a fantastic season defeating some very experienced drivers, but at the same time felt he had nothing left to prove outside of Formula One.

In 2006, Nico Rosberg performed well enough in Formula One but he had never dominated his ART team-mate Alexandre Prémat in the same way that Hamilton did, despite Prémat's advantage of being in his second year in the series. However, total command in the lower levels of racing does not automatically translate to success in Formula One. Erik Comas was almost untouchable in F3000 in 1990 but didn't achieve much in Formula One. In 2003, Bjorn Wirdheim took all before him in F3000 (although the quality of the F3000 field that year was below par) but was a modest performer with Jaguar in Formula One competition. Ricardo Zonta defeated Juan Pablo Montoya to take the title in 1997, but again, like so many of his predecessors, he was unable to follow this up with notable success in the top echelon or racing. Smashing all the records in British F3, Jan Magnussen was christened by the UK motorsport media as the new Ayrton Senna, understandably perhaps since no one had dominated F3 like Jan had since Senna. On the basis of his F3 profile, Magnussen was taken on as a test driver by McLaren, and was later given a full race seat at Stewart; the Dane disappeared off the map.

This said, Hamilton won in a relatively strong GP2 field and the F3000 and F3 grids were not always as impressive as they perhaps might have been. Lewis also had Ron Dennis on his side, a fact that should not be underestimated. But, for all the excitement and hype that surrounds Lewis, the question 'Is he the next Senna, Schumacher or Alonso?' is a little unfair. The evidence up to the conclusion of his GP2 career was impressive. Drivers who get as far as Formula One status are the ones who have impressed in F3, F3000 and GP2, although few had shown Lewis's kind of 'muscle' so young.

The truth is that the hard-fought and enthusiastic world of GP2 is not really comparable to the ultra-professional realm of Formula

One and that before 2007 Hamilton was yet to confront the likes of a Räikkönen, a Schumacher or Alonso in heat of competition. For all this, Anthony was looking towards that goal when he shared the pretty obvious news that Lewis's next aim was to get into a Formula One car. He saw sticking with McLaren-Mercedes as paying them back for their loyalty. But he went on to say that, if Lewis could become a Formula One winner, that would be the time to 'fully exploit his commercial and marketing opportunities'. Hamilton senior had no doubt that could happen at some stage because his son had become a proven winner, but he also understood that his progress had to be managed and planned properly so that it had 'the right effect'.

STYLE AND HUMILITY

And you, good yeoman,
Whose limbs were made in England, show us here
The mettle of your pasture; let us swear
That you are worth your breeding; which I doubt not;
For there is none of you so mean and base,
That hath not noble lustre in your eyes.
I see you stand like greyhounds in the slips,
Straining upon the start. The game's afoot:
Follow your spirit, and upon this charge
Cry 'God for Harry, England, and Saint George!'

Henry V, Act III, Scene i, Shakespeare

An American Dream

On the Thursday before the 2007 United States Grand Prix, Hamilton arrived at the Indianapolis Motor Speedway for what may be the last time (as Bernie Ecclestone seems to have an eye for Las Vegas in 2009). His entrance was practically anonymous, with no admiring fans, no autograph hunters or photographers. 'I've only been recognized a couple of times,' he said. 'Once by a Spanish couple, and by a couple of English fans. I've been able to relax!'

This evidenced the level of interest in Formula One in the United

States, but then four days after his Indy 500 victory no one had recognised Dario Franchitti roaming around downtown Chicago.

On his cool-down laps at the end of practice and qualifying for the United States Grand Prix, Lewis waved to the fans around the 13-turn Indianapolis Motor Speedway Formula One circuit. He commented, 'You exit the garage, and you see everyone stand up and give you a clap ... I appreciate all their support, and I appreciate them coming and supporting everyone here ... It is nothing for me on my in lap to give everyone a wave. I am sure it makes them all happy. I get a lot of energy from all the crowd.'

Just seven days after Lewis had claimed his first Grand Prix win in Canada, the 2007 United States Grand Prix was awaited with huge anticipation given the publicity about favouritism within the McLaren team, allegedly instigated by Alonso talking on a Spanish radio station. Hamilton had denied the theory saying he found it strange that his team-mate should say such a thing, feeling that ever since they had joined the McLaren Formula One team there had been equal efforts to push both drivers towards winning. For Lewis, Ron Dennis and others had worked very hard to make sure each of the racers had similar opportunities. Hamilton told of the 'great relationship with the guys' from his first days with McLaren as a 13-year-old, but claimed that when Alonso had joined the team they had been 'extremely excited'. As such, Lewis felt that, although his team-mate might have considered that he had not been treated fairly, he didn't agree that was in fact the case.

Dennis denied that any driver had received preferential treatment, although Alonso, the youngest Formula One Champion when he first took the title in 2005 at age 24, must have been taken aback at Lewis's meteoric rise. It had certainly surprised the majority of people in Formula One. Many rookies have been given their Formula One debuts with top teams, but they have not been instant winners. Hamilton had done this and at the same time demonstrated his potential to become an all-time great. And the plaudits coming his way from former British Champions would have made almost anyone feel a bit 'out of it'. The honest and plain-speaking Damon Hill claimed, 'Lewis is probably the closest we've got to a guy who can dominate and be at the top for a long time. This guy has been on four wheels since he was five years old. It doesn't matter whether it's a GP2 car, a go-kart or a flippin' Morris 1000, it's as if it's part of his body. A Formula One car is just a bit bigger and a bit faster and he's not intimidated ... He fits the template ... He is in the right place, with the right team at the right time.'

And Sir Jackie Stewart eulogised, 'Lewis is exceptional ... He has the mind for it, the attitude, the God-given skill, but he is already recognising that he needs something else.'

For Stewart, that was why he was in the factory every day, and why he was already more popular than many British drivers who had won World Championships. The great Scot saw that Lewis was 'doing it with style and humility' and forecast that 'he is going to rewrite the book'. The ex-World Champion claimed that Lewis would create the new benchmark for a whole generation of drivers, and, although Niki Lauda and James Hunt had changed the culture of racing drivers, they were not role models because 'they said nothing, didn't give a damn'. However, for Stewart, 'Lewis Hamilton can become the role model. Everybody needs one.'

Considering Alonso's possible reaction to his success, Hamilton told how he very much doubted the Spaniard had expected him to do as well as he had: 'He's a two-time World Champion. He's not really been challenged so much and by someone as close as me, and by a good friend off the track. So it's a very difficult situation.'

Although Anthony Hamilton claimed that there was no problem and his son and 'El Rápido Fernando' were 'best buddies', and could be seen together in the back of the McLaren camper van, playing computer games, the consequent sniping between the two drivers had accompanied McLaren's preparation for the battle at the Indianapolis Motor Speedway. However, even more expectation was generated for the meeting of the two McLaren men, particularly among British fans, when Lewis took pole (on the right of the track) for the second time in succession with his team-mate in the next best position (on the left). Hamilton had earned his place at the front of the grid with a 1:12.331 lap, running round at 129.643mph. He was just 0.169 of a second quicker than his McLaren team-mate.

Analysing his first experience of the Brickyard (the nickname given to the Indianapolis circuit – a yard of the brick paving that the whole circuit was once made of still exists at the end of the grid) Lewis said, 'The really tricky bit is the mid-section as it's very tight and twisty.'

Alonso had led the field in both Friday practices and the Saturday-morning practice preceding qualifying.

Although, for Lewis, 'Pole was unexpected,' he saw his qualifying performance as 'a fantastic feat … Getting my second pole is even better than last week. When I came across the line and the team said I had P1, I was screaming in my helmet. The crowd here has been fantastic. It's great to see a lot of British flags here. Also, a lot of support from the Americans.'

He also told how he was 'trying to eat way at Fernando bit by bit', which gave a good impression on his ambitions. For all this, on the occasion of Lewis's first Grand Prix at Indianapolis, the fact that 'Hamilton fever' had reached 'the home of the brave' was evident by the much improved attendance of the event. A huge crowd had turned up at the Brickyard and the whole of the pit straight was sold out.

If Lewis was ready for America, it was certainly ready for him. For some time, NASCAR's 'Drive for Diversity' programme had been putting young minority drivers in the pipeline, but they were still years away from what might be seen as a notable degree of success. At the same time, most of the drivers from minority groups had been hit by a lack of financial backing and it has to be said that NASCAR hadn't dug too deep into its deep pockets to fund the programme. For all this, NASCAR had raised the issue of race in American motorsport and welcomed Hamilton with open arms on to the front pages.

Before the weekend of the US Grand Prix, Lewis hadn't even been on the McLaren simulator for Indianapolis and had only experienced the circuit on computer games and recorded TV footage from previous races. Although he had looked at data, he confessed to not knowing what to expect. However, he expressed the intention of approaching the race with an open mind and to do the same sort of job he had done in Canada.

Lewis had seen the famous Indianapolis 500 races on television and in 2007 viewed and admired the way Dario Franchitti took victory for Britain. The admiration was mutual. The Scotsman said of Lewis, 'I've known Lewis since he was eight years old and it's great to see Lewis do a good job ... He grew up racing against my cousin [Paul Di Resta], and he's done a wonderful job.'

Indianapolis Motor Speedway is one of the oldest tracks in the world, but the infield section was built for Formula One only eight years ago. The track's banking is a unique characteristic in Formula One but it doesn't have a huge impact on the cars.

Ferrari had won six out of the last seven US Grands Prix, but, with their wind tunnel at the Maranello factory in trouble since April, they had started 2007 struggling to respond to McLaren's pace, although the Surrey-based vehicles were 10kph (6mph) slower down the main pit straight than their Italian rivals, they were faster over a whole lap. At the end of June, the Italian team boss Jean Todt admitted, 'We had a problem with the rolling road and we lost about two weeks' development, but that's not an excuse ... it's up to us to have a wind tunnel that doesn't break.'

In Indiana, the heat and degradation in the tyres was going to be crucial as would be the run down to the first turn. Indianapolis is a relatively wide track but at the initial bend there isn't as much space and it acts as a type of filter – that's when the cars can start to bump.

The seventh race of the Formula One season, on 17 June, was run over the 4.192km (2.605-mile) in-field road course. This 70-lap circuit included the long straight stretch from the final to the first corner that would take the drivers around 23 seconds to cover; most would probably hit the 200mph mark on this. Schumacher had won the event for Ferrari in 2006 but the track record went back to 2004 (1:10.399, held by Ruben Barrichello). The first two turns would be crucial. The US Grand Prix had not been won by a British driver since 1982 when John Watson (driving for McLaren-Ford) had finished in front of Ligier-Matra racer Eddie Cheever of the USA. Hamilton was once more accompanied in the front row by his McLaren partner. Alonso had staked a place himself in the top of the field for six of his last seven races. The Ferraris were just behind them.

With a wind speed of 2.2 m/s, the track temperature was 54°C (air temperature was 35°C) and humidity at 33 per cent, the cars were slow to form up on the grid; those at the front were held up for the best part of a minute before the lights went out. Hamilton had a slight edge in the first couple of seconds, but had to deal with Alonso's attempts to hustle him off the grid; however, the Brit, using his now expected early pace, pulled away to open a lead from the start. But the Spanish 'McLareneero' stayed close behind, followed by the Ferraris. He seemed to give a thought about another big sweep around the outside, but it never happened. Through the first two corners, the Spaniard did his best to distract Hamilton, but the Brit was not fazed and didn't even look in his mirrors, although he was obliged to drive defensively to keep his team-mate behind him.

Early on, only Hamilton was doing better than 1.13 laps; everyone else was on 1.14 plus. Lewis extended his lead over Alonso to 1.5 seconds and by lap 6 he was 1.7 seconds better.

Following their earlier than expected initial pit stops (one lap apart), the reigning World Champion attempted to get by Lewis, who, not for the first time in the season, had got himself entangled with the tail-enders resulting in three slow laps.

In the 39th lap, picking up speed in his team-mate's slipstream, Alonso dragged himself alongside Hamilton as the two McLarens roared down the main straight at 190mph, but, as he had shown in his GP2 days, Hamilton was not one for being intimidated. Lewis positioned himself solidly on the inside and then braked with grace. So the Championship leader shook off the World Champion on turn one.

Falling back behind his team-mate, Alonso swerved violently

sending a message to the pit wall, an obvious expression of anger and evidence that his Latin emotions were getting the better of him. Hamilton had fuelled longer than Alonso who had come in first on the second pit stop. As such, the latter was on a shorter stint and, if this was going to work for him, he needed to get past Lewis who was going longer in that stint. Hamilton had not given way as a number-two driver might have been expected to. It was now becoming more apparent that the rumours about Alonso no longer sharing his race strategies with Lewis might be true.

After that encounter, the McLarens did not cross swords again throughout the race and Lewis held on to the lead to win his second-ever Formula One Grand Prix and log his first back-to-back victory at the top of motorsport. He completed the race in 1.31. 9.965, at an average speed of 125.145mph. It was also his first triumph (it being his first visit) at Indianapolis. The Ferraris (Massa and Räikkönen) took third and fourth place.

Hamilton had produced yet another astonishing performance in a McLaren one-two. Just after he crossed the finishing line, he told his team over his radio, 'Fantastic, guys! I love you all.'

The reply from Ron Dennis was: 'I love you too.'

This was the second time McLaren had been victorious in the US GP at Indianapolis. Mika Häkkinen won for them in 2001. Hamilton led for 66 of the 73 laps, tying with Michael Schumacher's record number of laps led in the race set in 2000.

As he mounted the podium for the seventh time in seven races. Hamilton said, 'What a dream! ... To come to two circuits [Montreal and Indianapolis] that I didn't know and to really come out with such pace and to see the team moving forward is great ... They've done a fantastic job. I'm so thankful to them. It's the perfect team. I'm really happy I could put the icing on the cake.

'The last 15 laps seemed a lifetime, but I was in the lead, I was able to do it and I'm very emotional now. It was very tough, Alonso fought very well but at the end I managed to pull a gap which I was able to maintain and control the race.'

But, for all his analytical prowess, Lewis was still in awe of the position he found himself in: 'I never expected two in a row.'

Alonso looked anything but happy, even though he had never done better in the USA: 'I think the start was the key point of the race, after that who was second would be second in the race ... My start was good but we both braked in more or less the same place. I tried to overtake but I didn't want my race to finish in the first corner ... Eight points are better than nothing. We increased the gap on Ferrari which is one of the main things at this point in the Championship.'

Lewis's triumph at Indianapolis made him just the fourth rookie (the others were Jacques Villeneuve, Nino Farina and Juan Manuel Fangio) to taste victory in at least two races in their debut season. Among British racers, Nigel Mansell and Damon Hill had both won their second Grand Prix immediately after their first; both, of course, are former World Champions. Another good omen for Lewis was the fact that, in 9 out of the last 10 years, the driver who finished race six of the Championship as leader of the drivers' table has won the World Championship.

As he took the podium, Lewis said, 'It's hot out there,' and then kissed the TV camera lens that was transmitting his victory back to his homeland and across the planet.

Alonso had taken the battle to Hamilton but Lewis had defended and made not a single mistake. The same could not be said of his team-mate, although he looked much more focused than he had in Canada.

With 10 races to go, Hamilton was 10 points clear of Alonso in the Championship. He had held off the other McLaren racer until they were 15 laps from home, at which point Dennis had instructed them to turn their engines down. With 106 points to 71, the Manufacturers' league was still a two-horse race, but the prancing one was looking decidedly second best.

With his North American tour of duty concluded, Lewis was getting homesick and Anthony (on Father's Day, the day of his son's victory) told how they were both looking forward to returning to Britain and sharing a Sunday roast.

Before the race, Ron Dennis had stated that he expected drivers to drive for the team first and themselves second and that the team was focused on winning. He had also said that there were no issues in the team. After the Grand Prix, he made an emotional statement that seemed to be something of a response to Alonso's temper tantrum on the track and perhaps his comments on Spanish radio before the race about Lewis being favoured by McLaren: 'Everyone wants us to race. The consequence of racing is that you get more pressure in the team. They were only asked to turn their engines down 15 laps from the end. We're delighted to come first and second. We never care who wins and we give every driver the opportunity to win, but there has to be someone who comes second, inevitably that person is not going to be as happy as the guy that wins.

'It was a great race. You saw the fight, it was clean. At the end of the day it's motor racing – that's what we're here to do.'

Sebastian Vettel, not yet 20 years of age, became the youngest driver ever to score a point in Formula One. Things happen fast in many ways in Formula One and the young German made Hamilton seem like a veteran. The Hertfordshire racer was certainly gaining the respect of his fellow drivers. Red Bull's David Coulthard as always was candid in his view. Reflecting on his seven races and 10-point lead, he considered Lewis to be 'well on his way to a world title' and that he had been 'flawless', not having made any mistakes in the eyes of the Scottish track veteran. He went on to say that it was interesting to watch how Hamilton had adapted to McLaren, a team he's been familiar with for the best part of a dozen years, and how Fernando Alonso didn't appear to be quite as comfortable as the Englishman. For Coulthard, 'Fernando is the one feeling the pressure at the moment.'

Renault test driver Nelson Piquet Jr, who had raced against Hamilton in GP2 in 2006, declared that Hamilton could win the Championship, having found the right moment at McLaren, getting the seat in a car that no one else seemed able to beat: 'He is always going to be first or second in races … He's doing a good job and has a car that's capable of winning the Championship for him.'

Sir Jackie Stewart pointed out that Lewis has been well brought along and developed as a young driver, and that, having been successful in every formula he had participated in, he obviously had an enormous natural ability. However, he was particularly impressed by the maturity of his 'mental management' given his relative youth and expressed his belief that Hamilton would create the 'benchmark for a whole generation of drivers'.

David Richards, Chairman of Prodrive, who will enter a team in Formula One next season, told how he had known Lewis since he was eight when he was kart racing with his son, Jamie. He declared that what Hamilton had achieved since then had probably surpassed all expectations: 'But, nonetheless, we always knew he was phenomenal. My son put a bet on him at the start of the season to be World Champion – and he got very good odds!

The Cherry on the Cake

Hamilton, aged 22 years and 161 days, became the first rookie to win the United States Grand Prix and the second-youngest driver to win a major event at the Indianapolis Motor Speedway. Only Troy Ruttman, who won the 1952 Indianapolis 500 aged 22 years and 80 days, was younger when he took the chequered flag. Hamilton also became the first black driver to win a major race at Indianapolis.

As Lewis looked back towards Europe and his date with the French Grand Prix, he might have seen himself having continued to lay a path of dreams. But the effects probably spread much wider than his own individual ambitions. NASCAR, which dwarfs Formula One in the American consciousness, got a severe smack on the arse in its own backyard. Hamilton had received a relatively tumultuous welcome and his victory shouted out an obvious truth: diversity does not develop on minimal investment.

Humpy Wheeler, one of the leading NASCAR promoters in the US, commented that it was unfortunate that NASCAR do not have as many black drivers as it should have and that Hamilton is 'the exact example' of what had to happen in NASCAR: 'He started out at an early age. And his path is exactly the path we've got to get our kids on – we've got to get black kids at an early age ... start them out when they're 10 or 12 years old, in something like our Bandoleros.'

The Bandolero car might be thought of as being between a kart and a car, a racing car designed for drivers as young as eight years old.

McLaren and Lewis had questioned the whole of American motorsport and, in effect, proved it wrong. But this message carried an underlying political hit, because what is true of car racing has a bearing across the whole horizon of society – achievement needs to be nurtured and talent fostered. Empty gestures, weasel words and penny funding do not make the cradle of success – they just confirm prejudice in that they change nothing.

But as Lewis's mother Carmen puts it, 'I'd like people to see beyond the colour. The fact that he's the first black driver is going to be the cherry on the cake.'

Clearly an Option

Following Lewis's fine performances in GP2, speculation about his possible transition to Formula One became endemic, but, in his own words, 'I think I managed it quite well. I tried not to read too much into the reports. If you get too into it, you can lose your motivation. I needed to win. And it got harder as the other teams were getting better.'

It was clear that Hamilton thought he had acclimatised sufficiently to make the leap to Formula One: 'In GP2, you are racing on the Formula One weekend so you still get a feeling of the high life in the race world.'

He told the press, 'I haven't heard anything official yet. But I'm ready to get into a Formula One car and to start testing. As far as the drive being mine to lose, well, it's not mine in the first place. It's Pedro de la Rosa's.'

However, Martin Whitmarsh saw Hamilton as 'clearly an option' for the Woking-based team, after ruling out looking beyond current McLaren-contracted drivers for 2007. But, after Lewis's performance in

Turkey, Whitmarsh commented, 'Performances like that make it very difficult, don't they?'

He was to name Hamilton as his choice for a place in the team, even at the expense of Colombian Juan Pablo Montoya, but cautioned that it was 'a big jump and a big responsibility to jump into a seat at McLaren, and we have got to make sure we don't put too much pressure on him'.

After his season in GP2, few would have argued that Formula One was not Hamilton's natural habitat and he looked historically set for that destination. Alain Prost was victorious in seven of 12 Euro F3 rounds in 1979. Ayrton Senna won 12 of the 20 British F3 races in 1983 and Mika Häkkinen triumphed nine times in 17 outings in 1990. All three catapulted themselves straight into Formula One. According to Lewis, 'Every driver is going to be biased and say "I am ready", but I think I am, in terms of confidence and experience.'

Hamilton argued that he had three times as much experience as Kimi Räikkönen had when he went into Formula One and more than Jenson Button had when he made the move up. He also made the point that in GP2 he had proved that he could go into a quick car and 'be right on it'. He told how, 'At the end of each year, I sit down with my manager and we review and evaluate the year and come up with a plan for the following year.'

For Hamilton, 2007 would be no different to any other year in this respect. Once he and Anthony have made a plan, they have always followed it to the end. Lewis let it be known that he understood that he had to work harder to be stronger mentally and physically and to prepare himself for whatever may come his way in Formula One, but he made it abundantly clear that he was 'ready and relishing the challenge'.

Nico Rosberg, Hamilton's friend, had made the transition to Formula One the previous year. Lewis found this a hopeful sign, but by no means a guarantee that he would get the same treatment: 'I don't think it gives me extra confidence but it proves it is possible.'

Rosberg and Lewis were team-mates in karting and he was always one of Hamilton's main competitors. For Lewis, the Finn had done a fantastic job in Formula One but it was strange for Hamilton to see his friend and Robert Kubica doing well. Just five years previously, they were all in karting and all struggling in one way or another. Rosberg and Lewis were experiencing difficulties with their equipment, while Kubica was having financial problems. Looking back, Hamilton confessed that he 'never thought that five years down the line we'd all be in Formula One'.

After all his success, Lewis hoped that he would be granted a test drive with McLaren with the view to making a start on his Formula One career: 'I'm hoping I'll get the call to do a test, but we haven't yet sat down. They're very busy preparing for the next race and I've got a lot of time. But I'd obviously love to go ahead and test a Formula One car.

'I feel good about the situation with McLaren. I feel there will be something for me ... that's extremely positive. My goal in the first place was to get a test seat ... If I couldn't get a race seat, a test drive would be the next best thing. But I'd much rather get into a race seat and be able to prove myself in that way.'

At that time, many thought that it was likely that Hamilton would be loaned to another Formula One team to gain some experience in competition, and, if that all went well, he might make a start for McLaren in the 2008 season. Even Lewis admitted it would be a risk for McLaren to give him a Formula One race drive in 2007; he understood that it was a risk because he had yet to test the car, so no one knew if he'd be quick or not. Lewis appreciated that his future depended on whether McLaren were willing to take that risk: 'It's a tough decision for the team and Mercedes ... I understand how tough the challenge is going to be and that you have to make some mistakes to learn ... At the end of the day it's the team's decision, but I feel I've got a good relationship with everyone on the team and feel they'd be happy for me to drive as a test or race driver. The majority of drivers have come through the ranks after getting a test drive; that would be one of the options.

'In the past they've been very loyal to me, so we'll just have to see what happens ... I will be preparing myself the best I can both mentally and physically but obviously the biggest pressure is the one I put myself under.'

Any Formula One racer is one of few. Over a season it is rare that more than 25 compete. The unusual conditions of a driver's existence mean his mind must work atypically. Danger is a constant but so too is the money and notoriety. Other ever present features of this career are the merciless competition, the technical intricacies and the in-depth scrutiny of every facet of a driver's being; what the team is not watching, the media are.

Added to these latent and blatant pressures, in the rarefied environment that surrounds the Grand Prix, natural considerations like impartiality, justice and fairness must be secondary considerations (at best). Formula One is not a simplistic meritocracy. A seat is not handed to an individual just because they abstractly deserve it. At the same time, holding on to a place in a team is not always due to a driver's aptitude. The racer of last month can become the spectator via the workings of political processes or the unpredictable swing of conspiracy. An entire team who have crossed the world to Malaysia or Bahrain and toiled into the small hours to make a vehicle ready for the ultimate test can find themselves watching it dominate for 40 laps only to see all their labours melt due to the failure of a minuscule element, buried deep in the entrails of the great roaring monster they have nurtured so meticulously.

But, whatever the problem, the driver is expected to cope. That might seem unreasonable, illogical or perhaps nonsensical, but the bloke in the seat is expected to drive the car; he is employed to get over the problems and the extent to which he does that is the measure of his tenure. Things can be changed for the next race, for the next season – and that in particular includes the driver.

But Dennis saw the time as right to take advantage of the recommencement of testing at the Circuit de Catalunya, Barcelona, that signalled the start of the 2007 campaign.

Hamilton was given a test drive in the McLaren-Mercedes Formula One car for the first time at the Silverstone circuit on Wednesday, 13 September 2006. Shortly after, he was told that he would begin testing for the 2007 season the following week in Barcelona, Spain. Lewis impressed and he was buoyant with the experience: 'I'm feeling very optimistic. We had some very good testing, the car is looking very good and I'm fitter than ever before so I'm really looking forward to the first race.'

Few expected Dennis to fill his driver vacancy with Hamilton, as McLaren had not started a season with a rookie driver since employing Michael Andretti in 1993 and he had struggled badly. Dennis had also seen the idea fail with Formula One debutant Andrea de Cesaris. However, McLaren had been prepared to act as Formula One midwife to Ayrton Senna but the Brazilian had turned down the offer. Going straight into a McLaren Formula One machine was never going to be an easy task. However, with Renault signing Finland's Heikki Kovalainen, two of Formula One's top-three teams looked to be starting the 2007 season with debutant drivers.

Hamilton's credentials were now hard to ignore: a world and European karting champion, the British Formula Renault Champion, the European F3 Champion and, then, an instant success in GP2. However, in mid-September, he was still waiting for confirmation from Dennis of the date for his first official Formula One test.

A protracted period of heightened speculation started as the European autumn gave way to winter. Conjecture as to whether Lewis, Pedro de la Rosa or Gary Paffett would drive the Vodafone McLaren-Mercedes MP4-22 alongside World Champion Fernando Alonso for the 2007 Formula One season seemed to fill the horizon of the racing media. Britain's authoritative *Autosport* magazine made Hamilton their cover story, describing him as a 'hot prospect' and a 'rising star'. The Stuttgart-based *Auto Motor und Sport* predicted that Hamilton would be named as the man to fill McLaren's vacancy on the grid, claiming that Ron Dennis had 'made the decision' to sign Hamilton. The magazine, however, added that

McLaren had toyed with leaving de la Rosa in place for 2007, after some engineers reportedly expressed concern about Hamilton's feedback about the set-up of the car in his early tests. In London, *The Times* backed up *Auto Motor und Sport* and quoted Hamilton as saying, 'The trust I have in Ron [Dennis] and Martin [Whitmarsh] and in McLaren-Mercedes goes way beyond anything else. They have guided me all the way.'

For all this, there were those who felt that the final decision about the young Brit's inclusion in McLaren's 2007 Formula One plans was taken as soon as Kimi Räikkönen made his move to Ferrari. Dennis had for many years looked to the moment when he might introduce a new name to Formula One, a driver who has dreamed of such a moment all his life. Lewis recalled that, while in Monza, when he won the GP2 Championship, he walked to the front of the Formula One grid. McLaren were on pole. He admired the car, and looked down to the first corner, imagining what it would be like in Räikkönen's position: 'Not many people know this, Ron just came over to me and put his arm around me and pulled me to the side and secretly said, "I'm going to give you a chance. You're gonna have to work hard for it, but I'm going to give you a chance," and it was at that point difficult to know what that was. So I put on a professional face, a professional smile, but inside, obviously, I was ecstatic.'

Lewis confessed to not knowing what to think: 'Was that a race drive? Was that a test or was that going to be a shoot-out to see if I could get the drive or what?'

But soon all would be made clear. Lewis remembered the moment he knew he would be driving for McLaren in 2007. Dennis invited Hamilton to his house and told him, 'You're going to be our second driver for next year.'

'It was just – you can imagine, by the smile on my face just now – it was just an unreal moment. It was a really special moment for me ... I brought out the champagne and celebrated. It was a humongous, a big day for me.

'I began watching Formula One when I think I was six years old ...

I knew at that time I wanted to drive one of those cars. I said, "That'll be fantastic." And now here I am [in McLaren's Woking headquarters], one of those cars is over there that I was watching when I first began watching Formula One. It's just unreal! You dream of having your own car with your name on it, and eventually we got a test and I had my name on the side. But now I've actually got a car that's been built for me and it's mine!'

He smiled and went on, 'Obviously, it belongs to the company, but it's my car and I will drive it and no one else will drive it for me and it's a really crazy feeling. It's fantastic! I'm really excited and can't wait to get out in that car.'

Anyone who knows anything about Ron Dennis understands that *no one* makes up his mind for him. Not even Räikkönen. Hamilton's impressive testing times and mature approach won him a race seat. Although giving Lewis a place in the team might have seemed like an out-of-character move for a traditionally conservative team, it was never a quantum leap. During 2006, Ron had watched as Lewis was crowned GP2 Champion, having won his races with skill, tenacity and a burning desire to dominate his opponents. Although still youthful, Hamilton had been driving for 13 years and, during this time, Dennis had seen him mature. He made his reasoning for bringing Hamilton in for 2007 very clear: 'His domination of the GP2 Championship in 2006 was outstanding. Because we were a team in transit ourselves looking to change one or both drivers, ultimately all of us decided to give him a chance.'

Lewis thought that a defining element of 2006 had been the motivation for Dennis. He said of his race in Turkey, 'Perhaps I had already convinced Ron to give me the seat before that, but, if not, that would have done it for sure.'

Hamilton was confirmed as McLaren's second driver on 23 September 2006, before the final three races of the season. When Anthony learned from a television news service that his son would be part of the McLaren 2007 team, he jumped for joy but he pulled a muscle in his leg and had to go to hospital for treatment.

Lewis responded by saying, 'Everyone has lots of different dreams and a dream has been for me to be a Formula One driver … this team is the top team, the best team.'

Recalling the reaction of his long-time supporter Dennis, Lewis said, 'You could see that he was very excited about it and was smiling. He even said to me, "You should be smiling!"

'I said, "I am inside."

'It didn't really kick in, if I'm honest. Inside, you are all excited but you have to put on a professional face.'

Ron Dennis did take a chance by putting Lewis in the car; to trust an untried driver – and, as far as Formula One was concerned, Hamilton was unproven – is not in the character of the man, but Dennis is a complex individual with brilliant vision. He is also passionate about Formula One and he's passionate about Lewis Hamilton. However, he understood that, if it worked, he would be hailed as a genius, but, if (and IF is F1 backwards) Lewis failed, as the person who made the decision, he might stand accused by everyone in motorsport. For all this, Dennis was ardent in his will to protect Lewis as much as he could and worked hard to play down the young man's entry into the top echelon of racing.

According to former World Champion Damon Hill, Ron Dennis made a considered decision. Having assessed Hamilton's abilities in testing, with the team and in the fire GP2 competition, Hill concluded that Dennis had certainly had a good close look at what Lewis could do. Given this, although Ron may have taken a risk on Hamilton, it was a risk that had been calculated over more than a decade, and so giving Lewis a drive was not really a gamble, it was the product of logical analysis worthy of the engineer and scientist that Dennis is.

For Lewis, the feeling of reaching the Formula One standard was 'indescribable'. Growing up, he had always dreamed of racing for McLaren and now he had fulfilled that dream. The thought of racing and working with his team-mates and to be driving a Vodafone McLaren-Mercedes was for him 'literally a surreal feeling'.

One of the first things Lewis did was express his thanks to his family as 'without their unwavering support and hard work I would not be here in this position'. He also expressed his gratitude to Ron Dennis, Martin Whitmarsh and Norbert Haug for the long-term support and guidance they had given him for so many years and for the 'wonderful opportunity'.

Although it was likely that some rigid performance criteria had been included in Hamilton's contract (it certainly has a clause that allows him to be replaced after every Grand Prix if he is not up to speed), and Spaniard de la Rosa would attend all the Grands Prix in 2007 as a reserve, opinion was divided as to the wisdom of Lewis, in his rookie season, being put up against the awesome abilities of Fernando Alonso, who switched from Renault as part of an all-new line-up for the Mercedes-powered McLaren in the 2007 season.

Martin Whitmarsh admitted he had high hopes for Hamilton, but warned against raising expectations too far for what would be the 22-year-old's maiden campaign in the top flight. Well before the start of the season, there were high hopes for Lewis both from within and outside of the team. Whitmarsh explained that the approach Hamilton was taking in the build-up to the start of his debut season was meticulous and without fault as Lewis's dedication to preparation was phenomenal. But the McLaren big shot warned that, while the team were very confident that their number-two driver would have a very strong debut year, a little caution and control of enthusiasm was required, given the very challenging environment Hamilton was entering. Whitmarsh cautioned, 'If we look at the World Champions since 1969, they have on average taken over 28 races before their debut win, but in time we have little doubt that Lewis will be a winning driver in the sport.'

However, in mid-October 2006, the 211 Grand Prix veteran David Coulthard openly told the media that Lewis needed a full season testing before attempting to partner Alonso. According to the Red Bull driver, Hamilton's career could be destroyed before it has a chance to develop. He advised Lewis 'not to rush in, because if it doesn't quite work out then his could be a very short career', and argued that McLaren had given him his break way too soon. For the seasoned Scot, the first person a driver is compared to is their team-mate and, if Lewis struggled alongside Alonso, the young man's confidence could be undermined. For the 2003 Australian Grand Prix winner, although Alonso was new to McLaren, he was a double World Champion and this made comparisons between the two Woking-based drivers unfair and loaded in the Spaniard's favour. Coulthard made it clear he was not expressing any doubt about Lewis's potential, but was making the point that he needed time to develop 'not just as a driver, but also as a man'.

The 'Caledonian Cyclone' went on to explain that he was three years older than Lewis when he made his Formula One debut, having had three years of testing, and even then mistakes were made.

However, Hamilton was adamant there was no pressure on him to win as he embarked on his rookie Formula One season. He told reporters at Barcelona's Circuit de Catalunya that he valued Coulthard's opinion and acknowledged his experience. He told how he had always looked up to the Scottish speedsmith and in some ways thought that the man who had 61 podiums to his credit could be right: 'But at the end of the day I have done all I needed to do coming up to Formula One. I have got plenty of time to do the testing in pre-season and so we will have to wait and see.

While Lewis's response was better than magnanimous, it might have been argued that Hamilton could or would say little different, given that he had nowhere to go but forward; to express a lack of confidence in himself would have been worse than self-defeating in terms of his ambitions. But he was to make his position much more definite: 'There is no pressure on me to win. The pressure will come from myself to succeed. The pressure comes with the sport. It's part of the environment and I will get used to it.'

Hamilton made it clear that he understood that he had reached the 'pinnacle of motorsport' and that, if an individual could go into it and straight to the top, everybody would be able to do it: 'I am still 21, so there is a long way to go and I need to take it step by step. The team know I am young and it will take some time for me to get up to speed and learn.'

Lewis emphasised his freshness, determination to do well in the sport and his will to win. He confirmed that he would be pushing hard to achieve success for himself and the team.

Gil de Ferran, the US CART (Championship Auto Racing Team, now 'Champ Car') Champion in 2000 and 2001 and the current sporting director at Honda, seemed to agree with Hamilton. De Ferran watched Lewis carefully at the opening winter test in Barcelona in November 2006. Similar to most former racers, he enjoys getting around the circuit to look at the drivers, and compare lines taken over the Circuit de Catalunya's sweeping fast corners. A new face never fails to motivate curiosity, and De Ferran quickly picked up on Hamilton's reliability and commitment. He commented, 'He looked ready to me. Very organised, few mistakes ... If Ron had offered me a drive at 21, I'd have taken it.'

For Dennis, the signing of Alonso allowed McLaren to be able to afford any risk involved in including Hamilton, who was in reality and is still a novice driver, in the team. Ron admitted that the organisation had reservations about the decision, Hamilton being 'an unproven product'. But he made the point that McLaren were also fielding a double champion and as such didn't think they were going to 'get lost as a result of not having experience ... We can be less conservative and take the opportunity to give Lewis his chance.'

According to Dennis, if the rookie could bring the same determination that he brought to GP2 to Formula One, then he would satisfy the team and all those who invest in it: 'We will be patient ... I am sure he will get the job done sooner rather than later.'

Lewis had no doubts about the decision and provided a different slant on the prospect, believing he could learn a lot by teaming up with the 2005 and 2006 Formula One Champion. He said he was looking forward to working with Alonso and wasn't worried about it. In fact, he saw it as 'a major advantage ... I think being Alonso's team-mate is a positive and I'm looking forward to working with him

... Going into Formula One is extremely tough, so having the best driver alongside you with all that experience would be the best solution for me. The things I can learn from Alonso are endless ... I just feel I'm in a unique position. Who better to learn from? I don't particularly see it as extra pressure, although in reality it is extra pressure, but you just have to put it in a sack, put it over your shoulder and carry it with you.'

Hamilton said that he thought Alonso was going to do what he always does, which is drive extremely well, and that he was just going to try to do the best job he could, learn from the senior driver as quickly as possible and try to eventually compete against him. This is another example of the way Hamilton has of making an advantage out of what others might deem a disadvantage. It is this underlying optimistic and positive attitude and talent that separates Hamilton from many of his peers.

As far as setting himself targets was concerned, Lewis said that he would 'just play it by ear'. He acknowledged that every driver wants to get into Formula One and that once they achieve that they want to win the World Championship. But he claimed that his priority was to learn from Alonso. However, late in 2006, he told how he was yet to get to know his team-mate: 'I have not had a chance to speak to him but we were in the same hotel in Turkey this year ... I was having dinner with my dad and Fernando was just leaving the restaurant and he came over and introduced himself, which was a pleasant surprise. But we didn't really say too much.'

According to Ron Dennis, Hamilton was 'phenomenally respectful of Fernando and he knows where he is going and knows the challenge'.

But, far from being intimidated by having to play supporting role to a double World Champion, Lewis saw Alonso's experience, talent and the fact that the Spaniard was a few years older than himself as giving a lot to the team of which they were both part. However, he threw in a cleverly veiled comment about his own intentions and perspective on Alonso: 'I'm new, I'm hungry, hungrier than most people ... There's more pressure on him – he has everything to lose, I have everything to gain.'

Listening to Hamilton, you can detect three steps he nearly always makes when considering situations:

1) he takes a seeming disadvantage – he will be playing second fiddle to a double World Champion;

2) he neutralises it – he perceives/portrays this as a learning situation and an invaluable part of his 'apprenticeship';

3) he turns it to an advantage – he says that Alonso has it all to lose and he has it all to win – he takes the pressure off himself and puts it squarely on the shoulders of Alonso.

This shows masterful generalship, way beyond his years. And he pressed home the advantage: 'I am looking forward to the challenge. I am ready for it and looking forward to the first race ... I know Formula One is going to be extremely hard but I am just looking forward to competing against Fernando and trying to do my best alongside him. I don't see it as a pressure, I see it as positive. It's exciting for me. I love the challenge. I like to think I'm one of the most competitive people. I just hope I can do the job.'

But, ever the diplomat, Hamilton pulled the situation back to the opening scenario: 'It's truly an honour for me to be given this opportunity to work alongside Fernando in my first year as a Formula One driver. I have a tremendous amount of respect for what he has achieved. The sheer size of the challenge of working with him and competing against him is what is most exciting.

'All of my former team-mates have been hugely competitive and the challenge and excitement comes from having to find the answers to the most important question: "Just how far do I need to push myself to beat that person and just how far can I go?"

'With Fernando being a two-time World Champion, I know I have to dig deeper than ever before which is what I love about being a racing driver. I'm one of those competitors that want to be the best in whatever I do ... to do that you have to compete against the best. I've got the best guy sitting next to me. He can bring a lot to the team; he's been in Formula One for six years; he's very experienced and very talented, not only on track, but off track he's very smart as well. So I just feel I'm in a unique position here, who better to learn from?'

But there is no hiding Hamilton's competitive streak: 'I'm not going out to finish behind him, am I?' He laughs. 'If I was, I shouldn't really be where I am … It's all about living for the moment and making the best use of the time you have. I'm not here to finish second place or to finish sixth or anywhere below first.'

Talking to reporters on the Friday following the announcement of his recruitment to Formula One, Lewis recognised that he faced a steep learning curve: 'I think it's important to understand how tough the challenge is going to be, which I do. You have to make mistakes to learn and to become a better driver. I know I'm going to be making certain mistakes but that's just the way it is in this sport. Obviously, I'm going to prepare the best I can mentally and physically to try and minimise the amount of mistakes that I make. The biggest pressure is going to be the pressure that I put on myself. Making your debut in Formula One is a big thing; there are always going to be pressures there. The way I manage them is going to be important, to determine how well I cope in the first year.'

Those who doubted Lewis's readiness for Formula One competition might not have fully understood his commitment to the same. He has imagined himself on the Grand Prix starting grid ever since he first slid behind the wheel at a kart track. For Hamilton, weeks before the opening day of the 2007 season, he had no qualms about getting into a McLaren car on the Melbourne track. He claimed he was not nervous, just very keen to get to the first race, and that in the seven or eight weeks before his debut he intended to make sure he enjoyed what time he had left as a 'normal individual': being with friends, going out, 'doing all the normal things'.

But it was obvious to anyone who had any connection with Hamilton that his mind would not stray far from what was to come:

'The first corner of the race is going to be cool – I just hope I'm into the first corner first.'

Hamilton was the fourth British driver on the grid when the 2007 Grand Prix season started in Melbourne in March. Jenson Button was a Honda driver and David Coulthard was with Red Bull, while Anthony Davidson had just joined Super Aguri. Britain had not had a World Champion since Damon Hill in 1996 and any success Hamilton or any British racer might have would be a major boost for the sport's popularity in a country that is home to a number of teams.

Despite the evident potential of his protégé, Ron Dennis continued to counsel in favour of patience and realistic expectations. Dennis reminded the world that since 1998 Lewis had formed an important part of McLaren's long-term strategy. He went on to say that the organisation was pleased to be able to help him take another step and achieve his dream of becoming a Formula One racing driver. This was obviously going to be the biggest test of Hamilton's career, but Dennis confirmed that McLaren were sure Lewis would be able to meet that challenge. However, he cautioned that Lewis was still in his very early twenties and had at least 15 years' competitive motor racing ahead of him: 'He has always listened and taken our advice, and the result of him going down this path is that he will be a very competitive Grand Prix driver but he has to take the approach we recommend.'

Martin Whitmarsh stated that it was highly unlikely that Hamilton's first Grand Prix drive would be for McLaren, and that Lewis understood that, but also knew that the organisation would be supportive 'all the way through' and would not obstruct his career.

'He was half as tall as he is today.'

Lewis's graduation had been made public in November 2006 as it had been thought expedient to wait until the World Championship had been decided and allow the commotion surrounding Michael

Schumacher's retirement to die down. Lewis had found it hard to keep the news a secret: 'There have been so many people I wanted to call but just couldn't.'

However, he did tell those closest to him – his father and half-brother Nicholas.

Ron Dennis revealed that the decision to give Hamilton a chance was in part fuelled by a shortage of talent among the established drivers who were competing at that point. He did not feel any racers other than Formula One's 'big three' – Alonso, Schumacher and Räikkönen – were sufficiently impressive. In fact, Dennis admitted to being distinctly unimpressed with the majority of drivers involved in Formula One at that time. He told how McLaren had reviewed the whole grid and, apart from that 'divine trio', concluded that no one really shone. It was reckoned that most of the field had reached a performance plateau and as such it was felt that Lewis was well equipped to deal with those same drivers.

On Lewis being named as McLaren's second driver, veteran Pedro de la Rosa, who stood in during 2006 when Juan Pablo Montoya left the team for NASCAR in July, reverted to his former test-driver status. Pedro had been racing for Team McLaren-Mercedes since the 2006 French Grand Prix and achieved a number of points-scoring performances as well as a podium finish at the Hungarian Grand Prix. He remarked, 'I have really enjoyed the opportunity to race for Team McLaren-Mercedes for the last eight races of the 2006 season. However, I have always been aware that the team might decide to give another driver the same opportunity, so the fact that Lewis will be in the car comes as no surprise. Obviously, I would have preferred to race myself but also understand why the team has decided to put Lewis in the car. I wish him all the best and look forward to continue working with him.'

For Ron Dennis, Pedro had done an outstanding job for McLaren during the 2006 season, 'but we felt it was the right time to provide Lewis with this opportunity.'

Briton Gary Paffett also continued in his role with the team working on the testing and engineering programme alongside Lewis, Fernando and Pedro. On the release of the news about Hamilton, he said, 'I am delighted to be remaining with the team, it is a fantastic racing organisation and I'm looking forward to working with my fellow team-mates on our 2007 Championship challenge. As with any driver, there is always a desire to be racing in Formula One; however, this was not possible. We had a number of other opportunities available and have decided that this was the strongest option. I would like to congratulate Lewis.'

For Lewis, the events of late September/early November 2006 amounted to 'a dream come true ... To be racing in Formula One with McLaren has been the ultimate goal since I was very young and this opportunity is a fantastic way to end what has been the best year for me. I have grown up with McLaren and Mercedes and wouldn't be where I am today without their support and guidance. However, I'm aware that this will be a challenge and I know there will be a lot of attention on me. But the team have told me to relax, do the best I can and enjoy the opportunity. I'll work hard to get results.'

The Vice President of Mercedes-Benz Motorsport, Norbert Haug saw Lewis as 'a gifted driver who proved his talent with two consecutive title wins – 2005 in the F3 Euroseries in a Dallara Mercedes and this year in the GP2 series. McLaren and Mercedes-Benz have supported Lewis already for nine years. He was half as tall as he is today when he started in karting. It's clear that Lewis has less experience in comparison to the other 21 Formula One drivers in Grand Prix cars. However, extensive tests during the coming months will prepare him for his first season – I am very glad that a guy like him gets his deserved chance.'

Dennis (who had up to this point spent around £5 million of McLaren's money on Hamilton) had faith in his protégé: 'For so many drivers, the hardest thing is getting the budget. No other driver has had what he has had. But what's the problem with that if you end up with a very well-rounded individual and talented racing driver? He is coming into the paddock for the first time as a Formula One racing driver and will have to familiarise himself with the pressures of a Grand Prix weekend. However, the confidence we have in Lewis's abilities and talent is clear from our decision to give him the chance. [Hamilton] has been in the family for a long time and he deserves the opportunity we're giving him. It is a little bit of a *My Fair Lady* story. From a background outside the sport and with money in tight supply – a rags-to-riches musical of George Bernard Shaw's play *Pygmalion*.'

Lewis said he hadn't seen the film but agreed that his was also a nice tale. But for Hamilton the move into Formula One was a new beginning: 'I have known Ron for 11 years and it is a great story and a great end to the chapter. But it's also the beginning of a new era, a new chapter.'

Preparation

For Lewis coming from GP2, Formula One was a lot more intense in terms of physical training and mental preparation but also the winter testing had been relatively frenzied. He had needed to squeeze in as many miles through the winter as possible. As such, he was testing three days a week as well as fitting in a much more demanding physical training regime than he had previously experienced. At the same time, he had to become acclimatised to the longer races, which was perhaps his biggest test. On the technical side, there was so much more to learn relative to a GP2 car, which doesn't have all the system controls in the car, so there is a lot less to focus on outside of the pure racing activity. To start with, the Formula One steering wheel has 20 buttons which he had not had to contend with before and of course he needed to faultlessly memorise their functions and look to optimise their usage – this was another big challenge for the rookie.

Hamilton's deal with McLaren was rumoured to be worth in the region of £2 million. He was expected to earn between £350,000 and £500,000 in his first Formula One season, plus bonuses that could total close to £200,000 per race. Although it had been whispered that his team-mate Fernando Alonso would earn 20 times as much, Dominic Curran, a director of Karen Earl Sponsorship, has forecast that Hamilton has the capacity to generate a personal fortune in the hundreds of millions of pounds bracket: 'He has arrived with about as big a bang as possible ... He's got something different; he's the first black Formula One driver, which opens up a whole new market for him. Plus, he has charisma and star quality; he's a good-looking guy who speaks well, which is attractive to sponsors. And he's clean-cut.'

But Lewis does not see himself heading for the high life. Already looking to the time when he turns his back on racing, he says, 'I'd just like to go back to living a normal life and have a family and no worries ... Just enjoy doing things with my brother. There's a lot of experiences in life which I haven't had yet, and doing that with him and doing that with my friends and not having the worries, just enjoying. It's such an important thing.'

For all this, the investment that has been made in Hamilton goes deeper than money. In Lewis, McLaren are in the process of creating a new type of racer.

Sir Jackie Stewart has made the point that Hamilton's extensive work with Dr Kerry Spackman, 'a mind-management guy', is a telling factor in the young man's preparation. Not many people in Formula One were familiar with the New Zealand-born neuroscientist who is also an amateur motorbike racer. His professional focus is on how a driver's brain receives information from a variety of sensory stimuli, for example the vestibular, visual and somatosensory pathways. He uses his research findings to assist Grand Prix teams, such as McLaren and Red Bull, to design cars that 'fit' the 'sense performance' of particular drivers.

Spackman also advises racers, deploying training programmes devised to replicate race conditions. He describes his methods under the banner of 'knowledge of the neuro-computational processes', which is used to instruct the best drivers how to develop their performance further than the point that might be achieved by straightforward practice, sports psychology and feedback. For Spackman, understanding how the brain constructs reality is critical when it comes to tricking the mind into working in a virtual-reality situation.

In the mid-1990s, Spackman's research relating to 'human interaction with vehicle dynamics' motivated a partnership between himself and a physics lecturer from Auckland University, Sze Tan. They worked on cornering speeds and techniques, developing computer simulations. For over two decades, computer programs have guided the design of Formula One cars, so it seems a natural progression that they are now playing a part in driver development. That Lewis is in the forefront of this innovation makes him one of the first of a new strain of racers.

Black Lightning

Lewis made his debut at the opening round of the 2007 Formula One World Championship in Australia. He knew it would be an emotional moment for him, his family and those like Ron Dennis within the McLaren set-up; a seminal point in his development; the most important instant of his career, perhaps his life so far.

People from different nations, races, classes, cultures and backgrounds have many more commonalities than differences; we all need the basics of food, water, shelter, warmth and love. But, as unique individuals, while each of us is representative of the whole, we have facets that mark us out as different from the next person. But, whether he wanted it or not, as Lewis sat on the grid in Australia, he was an ambassador for the future of black drivers in the heady world of Formula One.

So far, Lewis has never had the chance to race against another black driver. Even his friends are more interested in football and basketball. But he believes it's not only a matter of likes and dislikes, it's primarily a question of money. He recalled that, on the day Senna died, there had been another black family at the track: 'But they weren't doing anything big because they didn't have the money.'

Hamilton knows that his example has the potential to demonstrate that, with the right backing and encouragement, people from a much wider sphere of life than was thought possible in the past can achieve in the world of Grand Prix racing. His ethnicity has been and will continue to be a focus of interest as he forges his way into the Formula One scene, but it cannot be said that it is central to the position he finds himself in. Anyone who witnessed his remarkable skill and speed at the Nürburgring, Silverstone and Istanbul in the GP2 series of 2006 will know that he tore his opponents to shreds.

Despite the interest in Lewis being a pioneer in Formula One as a black driver, according to Ron Dennis, the fact that he is black is 'just immaterial ... I have consistently said to him, "The moment that you exploit your blackness, you are going to have a problem with me." Basically, you've got to develop your career on your ability to drive a racing car.'

For Lewis himself, his skin colour is not central in terms of his aims in racing, but consciousness of his identity has had its benefits, although he claims that he doesn't take much notice of the idea of being a groundbreaker. He has said that, when he is at a race, he doesn't think, 'Oh, man, I'm the only black guy here!' This was something he actually noticed more in karting, 'because some of the kids were immature, the odd racist thing would pop up'. But he has told how he chose to channel his aggression into his racing and how that has become 'one of my greatest strengths. I was also taught that the best way to beat them is out on the track.'

For Hamilton, the issue of his race is 'more a thing for the media to talk about. The way I see it, my colour is an advantage in that it's something people talk about. But the bottom line is that it's clearly not why I'm in this position. Being the first black man doesn't matter much to me personally, but for the sport itself it probably means quite a lot.'

Hamilton has said that he doesn't feel different to the other drivers apart from having a certain level of confidence in what he can do: 'I've got an ambition and that's to get to Formula One.'

It is true, in terms of results, the colour of a driver's skin is not the thing that matters and there is no doubt that Hamilton will be judged on his performance. But it is his fate to be seen as a pioneer and he could do for motor racing what Tiger Woods has done for professional golf with regard to expanding the horizons which govern the sport's perception. He could also be instrumental in creating a wider audience for Formula One and not just black Britons, Europeans or Americans. Like Woods and Ali before him, Hamilton could turn the eyes of Africa towards his sport. It would indeed be surprising if sponsors are not especially hoping for some kind of 'Tiger Woods effect'. Golf's 12-time major winner has said of Hamilton, 'Without a doubt, Lewis is one of the most exciting talents to hit the sporting scene in recent years ... Any time a rookie comes through and wins big, it is a story that captures the imagination ... But it's not just his results that I've been impressed by, it's the way he has handled himself off the race track. I think he has the potential to be a terrific role model.'

These were prophetic words. Early in his Formula One career, kart tracks were reporting up to a 60 per cent rise in participation, but how much of this was made up of young black racers has not been established.

As Hamilton has made his impact on Formula One, the Tiger Woods references have proliferated. But Lewis remains philosophical: 'It's going to be a pain, the whole fame thing, but I'm strong enough to handle it.'

However, if Lewis disappears into the realm of the also-rans, even if this is later rather than sooner, the effect could have the opposite effect. His career trajectory will have a huge influence on many lives. Whether Hamilton, Dennis or McLaren like it or not, Lewis is now a role model and the object of hope. But the Hertfordshire Hurricane is clear about his own position: 'I am proud of who I am and where I come from. I don't see it as any extra weight on my shoulders. Getting here, and other ethnic groups seeing it, will open up doors for other cultures. I remember when I was growing up, it was difficult to find someone to relate to. There will be a lot more people able to relate to me, to take what I have experienced, then make sacrifices and become dedicated.'

At a press conference following the news of his move into

McLaren's Formula One team, Hamilton was asked if he saw himself as a trail-blazer for Afro-Caribbean drivers.

'The only time I ever really think about it is when people bring it up. I feel like any of the other drivers that are out there; that it is a dream for me to get to Formula One. But what comes with it is that hopefully it can be of some influence, it can encourage other ethnic groups to get involved in the sport.'

For all this, Hamilton doesn't see himself as an exemplar for any particular group of people: 'It doesn't have to be just for one group of people, it can be for everyone. People that can relate to the path that I've taken will see that it's possible and will try also to get into the sport. I'm doing this for myself because I want to win in Formula One and because I think I'm good enough to get there. I feel more and more ready for the job ahead.'

What is certain is that Hamilton's talent makes him special and his ethnicity is unique in Formula One. Never in the 56-year history of the Formula One World Championship has there been an Afro-Caribbean presence, a discouraging feature for a sport that works to emphasise its cosmopolitan profile.

But perhaps the whole issue was best put in perspective by Lewis when talking about his younger half-brother Nicholas who he sees most weekends when he isn't totally taken up with preparation and racing. The two spend much of their time playing PlayStation and racing remote-controlled cars. 'He can only do half the things I can, but despite that he's still a happy guy. There's a strong message there, and it's certainly had a big influence on the way I look at things. For sure, having him as a brother has had a major effect on the way I think. I think he's just an amazing lad and I really love to do things for him. This weekend we're going racing remote-control cars. We bought him a new one, then I bought one so we can race together. I've been a couple of times and I get hassled a little bit now, but I had my dad to take me and he doesn't have time, so when I do have time I love to just take my brother down to the track. He loves a challenge and he's got a lot of steeper challenges.'

Failure Not an Option

The McLaren enterprise is a rapacious creature that provides employment for more than 1,000 people, and their culture precludes the concept of failure. The organisation was mortified by their incapability to win a race in 2006 following the success of 2005, when they won more races than any other manufacturer, including World Champions Renault. There was a lot of faith, hope and concrete investment in their 2007 'knights of the grid', but Hamilton is prepared to start the process of payback: 'I'm absolutely ready ... I've had a fantastic season winning the GP2 series against some very experienced drivers ... I must put some miles under my belt and the sooner the better. I have nothing left to prove.'

Alonso was McLaren's insurance against Hamilton's inexperience, but this did not translate to a lack of confidence in Lewis and what he might achieve, but it potentially bought time for the Hertfordshire man, providing him with the space of a few races to acclimatise. However, Hamilton was as prepared as a rookie could be to meet the challenge of Formula One combat. His performances in GP2, principally his wins at the Nürburgring, Monaco and Silverstone, had demonstrated his gifts. Lewis is a born racer and he knows it: 'I know how to become the best, I just need time.'

At the start of the 2007 season, bookmakers made Lewis a 25–1 shot to become the World Champion in his rookie season, something which has never been done but for those of us who have followed his career it was certainly worth a bet. Hamilton's own assurance and belief are overt, without being boastful. When asked if his becoming World Champion was a safe gamble, he smiled and said, 'I would have to say yes.'

It was hard to question the young man's conclusion after he beat Alonso on the only day they tested together, leading the time sheet in Jerez, being three-tenths of a second faster than his senior partner, who, although he was also driving the McLaren for the very first time, must have gasped as his supposed understudy bettered him.

But, despite this promise, Hamilton remained focused on his strategy, understanding that he had to be realistic and take the rough with the smooth: 'I know how to lose and turn things into positives ... I have to prepare mentally. I need to start with a good foundation. A nice strong finish would be a great start. Then we can work towards a podium or a win.'

Alonso was well placed to offer an opinion on the astuteness of Hamilton's promotion to the highest echelon of world racing, having started his own Formula One career with the modest Minardi organisation.

The Spaniard stated that he was unsure whether it is best to start Formula One competition with a smaller team, to gain confidence and experience with no pressure, but he was sure that in a bigger team a driver can be up at the front and that can help a racer's development. Regarding Lewis's situation, Alonso believed that, as Lewis was coming into Formula One for the first time, he would naturally bring new ideas and a fresh mentality and he admitted that sometimes this can help change the traditional philosophy of a team: 'He has to be calm with everything. It's fine when you are in the car, but it will be the rest of the time when it can get stressful. He needs to be very focused and that's how he will be. He's really clever and will have no problems.'

During the second week of January, Damon Hill voiced in the press how Hamilton needed to establish himself. The 1996 World Champion was confident that Lewis would make his mark in Formula One, but warned that he would have to assert himself right from the beginning of this part of his career.

McLaren had not scored a single win in 2006 and that hadn't happened since Hill had won his title, but Damon was confident that Hamilton had made the right move, saying, 'It's plausible that he will get a win during the season.'

But the former Williams and Arrows star cautioned, 'You've got a season's grace, maybe even half a season.'

Hill speculated that Hamilton might get some leeway and the benefit of the doubt for the first six months of his Formula One career but if he failed to outpace Alonso at some point the question 'Where is it, where's the spark?' would be asked.

For Hill, 'Drivers who have gone on to become great, like Michael Schumacher, Alain Prost and Ayrton Senna, arrived and went bang. They were outpacing their team-mate right from the word go ... [Lewis] has a window of opportunity to learn, but it's going to be a short one.'

With Hill predicting that Hamilton might have as little as half a season to show something before being potentially perceived as a failure, one might have expected Lewis to defend himself with his record, but with typical integrity he took the former Champion's point as 'fair comment ... Of course, if you go in and don't do well, what are you doing there?'

After six months, Lewis said that he would expect to have learned a lot from his experience of racing at Formula One level, but also realised that he needed to be 'quick and on the pace ... I need to produce the goods. That's what I've been doing for the last 10 years, so this doesn't feel any different. If Fernando has some problems and we have a competitive car, then that could be an opportunity for me to beat him. But I'd prefer it if he doesn't have a problem that I'd be quicker than him, at the front and win.'

For all his rather dour insight, Hill saw Hamilton as having definite advantages. Having made his Formula One debut with the struggling Brabham team in 1992, Hill joined Williams in 1993, partnering three-time World Champion Alain Prost. This encouraged Hill to judge that partnering Alonso would motivate Hamilton: 'It's a wonderful gift for Lewis to be put in a team with a guy like Fernando. All he has to do is beat Fernando and by definition he's a potential two-time World Champion.'

But Lewis's strength lay in his innate genius for racing and the magical motivation of seeing a time come when he might fulfil his dreams. He views his meteoric rise with a sense of gentle incredulity, but this is backed with iron self-assurance: 'Like most kids, I am sure I dreamed of one day racing with Ayrton Senna and Alain Prost. Now my dream has literally turned into a reality and I am driving not only in Formula One but also for the same team as Ayrton and Alain did. I worked hard to make it to Formula One but never imagined it would actually be with a team such as McLaren and in my first year!'

Lewis believes that, if an individual wants to be the best at whatever career they choose in life, they must compete at the very top. Of course, Hamilton sees Formula One as the Everest of motorsport, so he is in effect living out his own philosophy. From the time he started his racing career in cadet karts, right the way through to Formula Renault, F3 and GP2, he has dedicated his life to achieving his goal of becoming a Formula One World Champion, and, as he entered the arena of Formula One, he saw this as another huge step closer to reaching his ultimate dream.

Hamilton made his debut alongside Renault's Heikki Kovalainen and Adrian Sutil. He also faced Robert Kubica of BMW-Sauber and Super Aguri's Anthony Davidson who have only had a handful of races between them. And of course there was Lewis's former karting team-mate Nico Rosberg, who was in his second year at Williams. These were the young men against whom Hamilton would be measured, and he had to take their scalps.

Before his first Formula One race in Melbourne, Lewis said, 'I can't wait to the first race. I really can't.'

This was the first Formula One judgement day for Hamilton. What was worrying for those who would rank against him in future races was the fact he was relishing the competition.

On Friday, 16 March, just half a dozen minutes after 10am, Lewis Hamilton, in his now traditional yellow helmet, which shone like a little sun through the light rain, took his place on the starting grid for the initial formalities of his first Formula One Grand Prix. A couple of long minutes later, his silver McLaren-Mercedes, spraying up the rain water, retreated to the Albert Park pits following an installation lap meant to corroborate that the car's myriad mechanical organisms were performing perfectly. As a public debut it wasn't dramatic but for Lewis it was a 16-year aspiration fulfilled.

After his first drive over the Melbourne circuit, Hamilton told of his excitement coming out of the garage for the first time that morning. He confessed to feeling 'incredible', despite the fact that he found Formula One 'a lot more intense' physically and mentally than any other level of racing he had experienced. This, alongside there being so much technical knowledge to assimilate and so many more 'toys to play with', meant his preparation had been more demanding.

Halfway through the afternoon, at the conclusion of the second of the day's two 90-minute sessions, Lewis was third in the list of fastest times, right behind the two Ferraris and four places in front of his team-mate, the reigning World Champion; not a soul in Albert Park would have disputed that Lewis Hamilton was now an official Formula One driver.

Just a couple of hours later, Lewis was quick to say that these were just test sessions and it was the next day's Grand Prix that really mattered, but his eyes sparkled with excitement as he made his point. This said, all day long Lewis had driven at a commanding speed with wisdom beyond his years, while being observed in the finest detail. On a track that was entirely new to him he made not one mistake and demonstrated that he was able to challenge and better the best in the Formula One field.

During those initial performances his elegance at the wheel, coupled with a calm approach when faced with the media, dispelled any uncertainties about his capability to manage the pressures of his newly found status. For Lewis this ability to remain balanced under pressure is something he picked up from his home life and 'being taught to appreciate things. I was like every kid … You get in trouble … I liked living life on the edge but I was always taught to appreciate things and say "thank you". I got that from my dad but also from my mum.'

The first steps had been impressive. Over 43 laps of the circuit, Hamilton managed the transition from the initially wet conditions of the first session to the dry and windy circumstances of the afternoon; he was placed fourth or better in the timing charts throughout. Those of us who watched couldn't help but note how slick and assured he appeared at the controls of his car that looked more than rapid enough to be among the season's leaders.

Like Hamilton, Sir Jackie Stewart had been a rookie brought straight into a successful team as a potential title-winner, when he joined BRM in 1965, having graduated, again like Lewis, through the lower levels of racing. Stewart stated that he could recall few drivers who had come into Formula One via that route in the contemporary era. On the day of Hamilton's first official Formula One run-out in Melbourne, Stewart said that he thought Lewis was likely to have been better primed than any new recruit to Formula One has ever been, having been looked after by McLaren from his karting career onwards, and gaining a huge amount of support both financially and technically.

As such, Stewart believed Hamilton would be totally at home with the telemetry apparatus that measures and monitors the car's performance and would have a good understanding of the rules of racing, which in itself was something of an achievement, even for a driver with far more experience than Lewis. But Hamilton understood the situation; he declared that his team knew it was a steep learning curve for him and that they had taken a step back to let him get on with his job, to learn as swiftly as possible. He believed that he was realistic and knew what he had to do, but, for Lewis, none of this meant taking a back seat. For those who hadn't heard it before, he reiterated his aim: 'I'm not here to finish sixth, seventh or eighth. Or even second. I'm here to win.'

As Jackie Stewart has pointed out, all young drivers have potential, but it is transforming that into success that separates the winner from the others. However, in and out of the car, everything about Hamilton's showing on his first few days as a Formula One racer had the look and feel of a high achiever. As the laps of the new season went by, the chances of Formula One gaining its first black Champion grew. It was becoming increasingly apparent that it would be only a matter of time, and time is on the side of the 22-year-old.

TESTING TIMES

But in spite of all temptations
To belong to other nations,
He remains an Englishman!
He remains an Englishman!

H.M.S. Pinafore, Gilbert and Sullivan

The Last Days of Magny-Cours

The 2007 Grand Prix de France, held at Circuit de Nevers Magny-Cours, Magny-Cours on 1 July, started with Lewis just behind polesitter Felipe Massa (Hamilton had missed pole by 0.7 of a second). But the McLaren racer was confident that he would be able to get round the Brazilian and give himself a good chance of claiming three consecutive Grand Prix victories.

The race, over 70 laps of the 4.411km (2.75-mile) circuit, boasts one of the smoothest surfaces of all the great Formula One tracks. Michael Schumacher won the race for Ferrari in 2006 and still holds the lap record of 1:15.377, set in 2004. The high-speed Imola chicane is probably one of the most notable aspects of the course. Drivers would approach this at around 170mph and go into it close to 120mph. After commitment to the corner, the sight-line of a racer is restricted to the apex kerb directly in front of them. It is not hard to make mistakes at that stage and that is exactly what Fernando Alonso had done in practice; after losing his back end, he dragged across the grass and sand beside the track.

Late in March 2007, the Fédération Française du Sport (FFSA), the race promoter, let it be known that the 2008 French Grand Prix had been put on an 'indefinite pause' and at the end of May Bernie Ecclestone told the world that the 2007 French Grand Prix would not be held at Magny-Cours again.

Grand Prix racing started in France and the French race is the oldest of them all, going back to 26 June 1906, when it was organised by the Automobile Club de France in Sarthe – 32 cars started in that first race.

The first World Championships were organised in 1925 and the French Grand Prix was one of the original venues (Italy, Belgium and Indianapolis provided the other locations). The French Grand Prix has been part of the Formula One Championship since it began in 1950.

The race has been held at a number of circuits, but, since 1991, it had a home at Magny-Cours (it was situated there, in the heart of France, to stimulate the economy of the district) but the venue has been seen as being relatively inaccessible by many of those involved in Formula One. The 2004 and 2005 races had been threatened due to financial difficulties and the addition of new circuits to the Formula One schedule.

In the 21st century, Ferrari had won at Magny-Cours five times. McLaren hadn't tasted victory in France since David Coulthard won it for them in 2000.

All over the weekend, there was a great deal of speculation about the role the weather might play in the outcome of the race. However, late on the Sunday morning, the rain stopped and, although the skies were cloudy, it was warm and bright as the field lined up for the start. It seemed that the chances of the rain holding off were good.

McLaren opted for a three-stop tactic for Lewis. This relied on him getting off to a good start but, as he was to admit post-race, he got away poorly: 'I don't really know what happened ... I definitely need to look at the data with my engineers, but it didn't go very well and I lost a place to Kimi, who made an exceptional start. Whatever it was, we weren't quick enough off the grid and I lost a bit of pace behind him.'

The first couple of seconds after the five lights had been extinguished had indeed been crucial. Hamilton, on the right, had moved across the track trying to cover Räikkönen (who was sitting behind Massa). But the Finn used that split second to go beyond Lewis. There was no room between the two Ferrari drivers and the Brit was lucky in the end to find some space behind them, having committed to his opening gambit as the front of the pack started to bunch on the left. Reviewing the start over and over again seems to reveal that Massa and Räikkönen had worked as a team, as if they had expected Hamilton's move. In retrospect, it might have been better for Lewis if he had gone more forward than sideways so early on.

The prospect of another Hamilton win looked unlikely after the initial corner. Räikkönen, having effectively elbowed Lewis out as if he wasn't there, seemingly set his sights on Massa. In the opening stint, Hamilton managed to hold on; however, it was obvious that his fuel load was very low and when he came into the pits after 16 laps it was clear that, unless something went disastrously wrong for the Italian team, he was going to be fighting for a podium place at best. The Ferraris had much improved since Indianapolis, bettering Hamilton's car by as much as nine-tenths of a second over a lap. The McLarens just didn't seem to have the speed to match the front two. Massa came in three laps after Lewis while Räikkönen carried on for three more than Massa.

Hamilton rejoined the race in seventh and on his new tyres was almost caught out by Nico Rosberg's lack of pace in the Williams-Toyota.

When all the front runners were on their second stint, Lewis was effectively out of touch in third place, as the Ferraris battled it out for the win. However, Hamilton needed to make sure he maximised the points he would take from the race and minimise the damage to his own and McLaren's Championship ambitions. But he emerged from his second stop behind Robert Kubica. At this point, there was a real danger that he would get stuck behind the BMW and be denied by his rival from their karting days. The Pole thought he had covered the line, but Hamilton saw a path through. On the Adelaide hairpin, Hamilton had the grippy line on the inside but Kubica tried to double back and come underneath the Brit. The pair drag-raced down to the Nürburgring chicane. But Lewis thought and acted swiftly and came out in front. Shortly after that, Hamilton produced the fastest lap of the stint. From then on, he looked pretty secure.

Massa came in for his second pit 29.5 seconds ahead of the leading McLaren. With 27 laps to go, the French Grand Prix was to be a continuance of celebration of the Italian's 60th anniversary as a constructor from the previous week. The Ferrari drivers were separated by Massa's inability to deal with traffic and the grim-faced Finn's better pit tactics. The crucial point had been the second pit stops. The instructable Räikkönen had stayed out longer and took advantage of few slow laps by Massa. On top of this, Kimi the Shimmy's out-laps were better than the Brazilian could match, almost eight-tenths of a second on occasion. Together, this gave the laughing boy of Formula One his first victory since Melbourne.

The last race at Magny-Cours was not a memorable one, especially for Fernando Alonso who had driven well. In the second stint, he had put in a series of laps that had bettered his team-mate's pace. He had dragged himself up from 10th on the grid, and overtaken like a lion on several occasions, but could do no better than seventh (the position he had attained by the end of the first lap) due to a poor qualifying experience thanks to a stuttering gearbox that seemed unresolved by the Sunday; at one point, it looked possible that Jenson Button would overcome the Spaniard in his Honda, but in the end the pride of Frome was satisfied to grab his first point of the season.

In the third stint, Hamilton had been just six seconds behind the leader but his shoddy start, together with the flawed three-pit-stop strategy, had not helped him. He just couldn't match the speed he had found in qualifying and in the end had played the percentages. In his own words, 'I didn't get a good start.' He smiled. 'But, even when you don't win, you finish with a podium, it's still a great weekend.'

British supporters were disappointed as their great hope struggled to stay with the Ferraris but Hamilton did increase his World Championship lead to 14 points, while Massa and Räikkönen both closed on the seemingly vulnerable Alonso. Taking the positives from the weekend, a faint hint of a smile was briefly detectable on the face of the 'Goul from Espoo', as he attempted to look as if he was celebrating his victory; it was also better for Hamilton that Räikkönen (who before the race was 26 points behind the Englishman) came home before the Brazilian, who was looking more like a young Del Boy Trotter as the season continued. In some of the early laps, Lewis had outpaced the Finn and, before the halfway mark, had gone through a phase of out-running both Ferraris. Indeed, Lewis was cutting down space between himself and the Italian cars. But, long before the last part of the race, he had lost touch with the front runners, lost down-force and concluded that there was little point chasing a lost cause. Not for the first time in 2007, he put getting over the line before his instinct to fling his McLaren at the advancing double act in front of him.

Räikkönen's resurgence, and the new lease of life that Ferrari had found, was ominous for both Hamilton and McLaren. With Silverstone next on the schedule, there seemed an equal chance of British thunder being stolen as there was of a home win. Although the season had a long way to go and both Hamilton and McLaren held commanding leads in the respective Championship tables (McLaren 114, Ferrari 89, BMW 48; Hamilton 64, Alonso 50, Massa 47, Räikkönen 42), it really felt as if the next encounter would almost restart the season for Ferrari. A repeat of the Magny-Cours result, while not quite being a hammer blow to British and McLaren morale, given Lewis's achievements thus far, would feel like a reversal.

I got back from France early on the Monday morning after the race and, not being up for much else, decided to watch a recording I'd made of the Grand Prix. It was certainly not a classic from any angle. Räikkönen, who found himself in the best car in the field on the day, had done what he had to do, but no one had made it too hard for him to do that. He had moved up from third on the grid and, as such, had broken a sequence of polesitter wins in 2007 that had only been interrupted by his team-mate in Malaysia.

The cameras followed the three podium men as they picked up their towels and water before the presentation. Räikkönen snatched his cloth and drink from the middle-aged woman who passed them to him, without even a hint that he had noticed her existence. Massa wasn't quite as dismissive, and there was just a flicker of a smile of recognition. Lewis, having gained his eighth podium in as many races, was last into the room. He immediately smiled at the woman as she passed him his towel and, as he took the water, he looked straight at her and said 'thank you'.

Up to that point, I had watched Lewis advance with a certain level of detachment (he is, after all, an Arsenal supporter!). This doesn't mean I didn't want him to succeed (us West Ham fans are not really that bad ... mostly!); since his karting days, I have always wanted him to do well. He is an example to so many young people of what hard work and commitment can do and I have known, along with many others who have followed his progress for more than a decade, that he would reach the top. But, as far as I was concerned, it didn't have to be 2007; a McLaren victory seemed more important to British racing. But, from that moment, from that smile, that simple acknowledgement of another's humanity which cost nothing, my 2007 season would be about wanting him to win beyond any other consideration. His would be a victory for respect and civility as much as anything else. This would make him a rarity in Formula One that had little to do with his black or British identity; he would be the sport's first 'people's champion', a fanfare for the common man and the innate decency we all share but sometimes fail to express.

'Don't do anything. I quite like the car as it is.'

'Everything you need to get that relaxed driving that brings consistency only comes with practice.'

That John Surtees 'remix' of the old adage that 'practice makes perfect' is confirmed by the view of the three-time World Champion gold medallist professional road bicycle racer Greg LeMond: 'Perhaps the single most important element in mastering the techniques and tactics of racing is experience. But, once you have the fundamentals, acquiring the experience is a matter of time.'

This 'time' is located in practice or, in Formula One terms, 'testing'. But testing must be done in the manner that Alain Prost approached it if it is to be a useful means of gaining the experience that LeMond refers to and not just a means of achieving a list of impressive lap times: 'When I test I never go right to the limit. Only because when you are below the limit you can go at the same speed all day, and that's the only way you can be absolutely sure about what you are testing.'

It is certainly the case that things like dealing with working to deliver 1,500lbs per square inch pressure into the braking system to pull five times the force of gravity to get a car moving at 210mph down to 70mph in a few metres takes a little getting used to. Just the right amount of 'foot power' needs to be applied in the right places at the right time if you are going to avoid actually being killed by a car or whatever gets in the way of it.

For all this, Hamilton has said he is doubtful how much testing makes a racer a better driver. For him that 'crafting' is set in place by time spent prior to taking to the great circuits of the world. According to Lewis, the basics are set in karting: the furious, wheel-to-wheel contests on small tracks have provided Formula One with some of its best drivers. Lewis has argued that the more a driver actually races the more they learn. He sees himself as a natural racer and believes this is a primary consideration in terms of his success in the race environment. His philosophy is that the racing is all about achieving consistency, and to get that you need to learn about the car.

That, from his perspective, is what comes from testing. But the test is mainly about building 'awareness of what is around you' and enabling a driver to understand the car, to fine tune it and himself. He has said that he sometimes doesn't 'make any changes to the car and I find half a second in myself. Some people find it really difficult, like the engineers, they say, "What can we do?" and I say, "Don't do anything. I quite like the car as it is, I just need to improve myself."'

Between the end of the 2006 season and the start of the 2007 Formula One campaign, Hamilton was focused on the approaching challenge, but the anticipation must have seemed never-ending as his dream became reality: 'I believe the first time I will get my hands on the new car will be at the launch on the 15th [January] but to drive it will be 24 January when we start our on-track test programme.'

He had been able to watch the development and progress of the new car in the wind tunnel and told how he was 'extremely impressed' by how hard everybody had been working to get the vehicle ready to challenge for the Championship in 2007.

Barça

Leaning against the wall of the McLaren garage, an overcoat between him and the morning chill, with his ear guards on, Anthony Hamilton, one of Formula One's most committed dads, watched as his son gently coasted his Silver Arrow into the pit lane at Barcelona. I was among a tiny band of shivering enthusiasts who shared those few seconds, lost in the yawning grandstand opposite.

It was 9.01 on the first day of winter testing, a time when racers put in the miles, producing data that when analysed might enable them to extinguish another tiny fragment of a second from their time when the real competition began in Australia on 18 March 2007.

The majority of people involved in that initial test day were more than familiar with the routine to the point of monotony. However, for Anthony and Lewis Hamilton, it was the golden gate at the conclusion of a long hard road that was about to open to a future that had been something between a hope and an ambition.

For close to 15 years, Anthony had devoted most of his time, energy and emotional strength to making his son the first black driver to take part in Formula One. At times, he had even washed dishes to raise the funds to keep Lewis's dream alive. But, as Lewis hit the accelerator of the McLaren at the Circuit de Catalunya's first corner, he was, in actuality, speeding inescapably out of reach of his father's influence. At that point, he became a McLaren man, expected to deliver success … and fast.

It was, of course, a proud day for Anthony. He described Lewis getting the nod to move into Formula One as the best early Christmas present he could have had and said he just wanted to be there to see his son start out towards the summit of his career. He would be there the next day too, but, not being one for hanging around, he would then leave, understanding there was little he could do for the boy who had now become a man, saying, 'He's the one driving the car.'

The day started ominously. A mechanical difficulty with the car necessitated an intermission in the test. Lewis came to a standstill in the home straight, provoking a red flag, but he managed to restart and finished 22 laps prior to lunch. However, that was just 50 per cent of what McLaren's test driver Pedro de la Rosa achieved, to top the first time sheets, having got a lap under his belt that bettered Hamilton's best by a second.

As it turned out, times were not important that day. As Lewis had been chosen before de la Rosa, it gave him rank and the kudos that had been missing the previous month when he tested for the first time alongside the Spaniard at Silverstone and Jerez.

With his confidence enhanced, Lewis had gained a new physical and mental prowess that was evident as he met the media corps in the afternoon. Reporters from all over Europe packed the McLaren motor home to take in Lewis's impressions and comments.

Having completed four test days with McLaren, Lewis admitted that, before it was decided who was going to get the drive, there had been a lot of weight on his shoulders and some tension between himself and de la Rosa, but he insisted that, now that it was known who would be on the grid in Australia, they were friends and could get on with developing the car. He saw his day as being a positive one, saying that he enjoyed every moment of it.

Barcelona was the first of three pre-Christmas tests. When the cars returned in the New Year, the double World Champion Fernando Alonso would partner Hamilton. There was wide public and media consensus that McLaren had created an ambitious pairing, seemingly in reaction to their relative failure in 2006. But it was also a partnership that had the potential to falter on a number of fronts. Did the Spaniard want or even have time to be a teacher? What if the young man messed up the team factor? For all this, Alonso's appointment demanded an improvement. Lewis's challenge had two connected aspects: to work for the team and to compete with Alonso.

Early in January 2007, Hamilton told of how he was in the McLaren Technology Centre every day, having relocated to Woking to be close to the team and the facilities offered to drivers. Another part of his daily schedule was his gym work, looking to ensure that he would develop the strength and stamina to cope with the rigours of racing a Formula One car for up to two hours in extreme heat.

There were also plenty of opportunities to meet team members for training and development sessions. Looking at his preparation regime, Hamilton told how exciting his new life was, but also said that there were points where the work became painfully repetitious. However, things would be changed to reinvigorate his concentration when there seemed any threat of him becoming mentally overawed by his routine.

That early part of 2007 also gave Hamilton time to generally get to know people and closely watch the progress of the new McLaren-Mercedes car. Lewis began to work alongside the engineers assigned to his vehicle, to get to know them and allow them to know him.

Lewis said that his aim had always been to win, but, because it was his debut season, he would be trying hard to learn as much as possible from Alonso and the whole Vodafone McLaren-Mercedes team, giving himself the objective to 'do a steady job for the team and help them progress towards both Constructors' and Drivers' Championships.

But Hamilton also made it very clear that he had no intention of being a spear carrier for Fernando Alonso at McLaren – although he had recently been learning how to throw the javelin, as part of one of several team-bonding activities at an intensive fitness camp in Finland just before the launch of the new McLaren car in Spain. He said, 'We all had to do it. We did lots of different things; a lot of things we had to do as a team, to really work together.'

Alonso did not attend the camp but Lewis expected he would work well with the 25-year-old double Champion: 'I think he's [Alonso] going to bring a huge amount to the team. I'm such a strong competitor; whatever I do I want to be up against the best and to beat the best. And I am sitting next to the best driver, so I am able to compare myself to him, to learn from everything that he does and eventually try to beat him.'

When asked if he assumed Alonso would be quicker, the young Brit responded, 'I'm just very realistic. He is a two-time World Champion; he knows all of the tracks and what a Formula One car is like. He knows the ins and outs of it because he has been there for a few years, whereas I am still learning and have a lot to learn. It's better to sit back and say, "OK, he's going to be number one – he's my benchmark, that's where I have to work to and I have to close that gap." Who knows, we might get to the first race and it might be a lot closer than people expect.'

Unlike fellow 2007 'rookies' Heikki Kovalainen and Anthony Davidson, Hamilton had scarcely tested a Formula One car before he was made Fernando Alonso's team-mate. Aware of his young driver's inexperience, Ron Dennis pledged to make sure that Hamilton received the most exhaustive accelerated induction into the art and craft of being a Formula One driver. In fact, he warned that it would be the most intensive it was possible to devise and added that during the winter McLaren were trying to buy Lewis the only thing he lacked – time.

Hamilton started his second full test for McLaren on Wednesday, 11 October 2006. At that time, the organisation had still to decide their line-up for the season-ending Brazilian Grand Prix, which was to take place just 11 days later. There were strong rumours that Lewis might be drafted in for the Interlagos finale, although Dennis sounded unconvinced by the merits of such a debut when he asked, 'Why throw anybody in at the deep end just to satisfy people who would like to see how well he would do? This is a hero-to-zero sport and why put anything at risk? The guy's had a brilliant career so far. His commitment and attitude don't just relate to driving a racing car. He's a very complete, rounded individual. All sorts of pressures will come to bear on him and I'd like to see him as equipped as he could be.'

Dennis told reporters at the previous weekend's Japanese Grand Prix that he did not know who would race with McLaren's Finnish star Kimi Räikkönen in Brazil and no decision would be taken until after the tests in southern Spain. He stressed that Hamilton was not going to Jerez to demonstrate that he had the ability to race but to 'learn things that are important with regard to doing an event': changing the settings on the car without dropping pace, functioning behind the safety car and managing a fuel stop and generally to get more mileage at a different type of circuit.

Dennis insisted that Lewis was not going to be pushed or obliged to run on light fuel and that Hamilton was not being assessed for the Interlagos Grand Prix. But he did hint that Brazil was not out of the question for Lewis: 'Whether anything comes out of that to change our current thinking about the Brazilian Grand Prix, time will tell. We'll discuss it and think it through, but there is no massive upside to him racing in Brazil.'

However, he stated that he could say that, if Lewis were to race in Brazil, he would almost definitely produce a better performance at the start of 2007, if given the opportunity in Melbourne, 'not because of driving, just through having put in test mileage and having come to terms with many parameters of a Grand Prix car that go beyond simply driving it … You have to change the settings without thinking about it. You have to make sure in and out laps are completely on the pace; you need to be able to identify problems and recognise default settings that interrupt the smooth running of the car but aren't going to affect it in any way.'

Pedro de la Rosa had started the last seven races following Colombian Juan Pablo Montoya's departure for NASCAR and was also in Jerez. McLaren were assured of third place in the Championship, with Ferrari and Renault out of reach in a private battle for the Constructors' title. Dennis and his team were desperate to win in Brazil, failure to do so would mean that McLaren would be condemned to their first season in a decade without a victory. This situation led to hot gossip that Jerez was about Hamilton and de la Rosa running through set-up and tyre evaluation programmes for Brazil as well as 2007 development issues.

In the end, Lewis was no more than a spectator in Brazil, where, although Räikkönen finished second in qualifying at the Autódromo José Carlos Pace, São Paulo, he couldn't do better than fifth in the race (de la Rosa was three places behind his team-mate).

At the end of November 2006, Lewis completed his first official Formula One test for Team McLaren-Mercedes at Circuit de Catalunya, Barcelona, and enjoyed every moment of it, having a huge smile on his face each time he pulled out of the garage. He commented, 'To come here knowing that I am the driver for next year meant I could really knuckle down on bonding with the team and my engineer and get on top of the car and up to pace.'

Humour columnist Dave Barry has claimed, 'Auto racing is boring except when a car is going at least 172 miles per hour upside down.'

In December, in Jerez, Hamilton tried this theory out in part when he lost valuable track time having gone out of control heading into the first corner. He careered across the gravel, spun and hit the tyre barriers at high speed.

But, in the three test sessions after his appointment, Hamilton had posted times progressively quicker than Pedro de la Rosa. The spotlight was on Hamilton until the arrival of Alonso on the last day of testing, thus providing Lewis with his first big challenge in a Formula One car. The two had barely met before and many wondered how they would approach each other.

Alonso, running in an unmarked car and carrying just the Spanish flag on plain overalls, banged out 95 near-perfect laps, setting the third fastest time of the day – a superb effort in a situation that was a long way from being ideal.

Hamilton could have chosen the passive path, letting Alonso take his 'rightful place' while he knocked out 'significant' but basically anonymous laps in the shadow of the great man. But Lewis hit the track for all he was worth, achieving the fastest time of any driver that day. The meaning of this behaviour lay not in the time but in the message sent. Lewis was happy to respect the older man but was not prepared to revere him; the rookie would be appreciative but not acquiescent.

Lewis understood his place in the hierarchy; Alonso was the senior driver, an experienced combatant brought into the McLaren fold to win the World Championship for them for the first time in the 21st century. Hamilton's was a support part; it was his task to keep his errors to a minimum and develop his mental strength, to keep his powder dry for a later date. But Lewis has never been a person to stick to a script. Of course he would do what he had to do, he would never do any less, but he would also do *more* than he had to, given even a sniff of a chance. Who really could have expected anything different given his history? Nothing in his past showed him to be anything other than a consummate competitor and a ruthless predator.

The evidence indicated that the world would not have to wait for long before Hamilton made his mark. The only other significant black person he saw, as he took one hurdle after another, was his father. Lewis was fully aware of what it meant to struggle against the odds;

managing Alonso was a huge challenge, but Lewis had already overcome the most challenging obstacles to his success.

According to motorcycle champion Valentino Rossi, 'The work that we do during the winter is very important; we have a new bike and it's important to develop it during this time.'

For Rossi, if he was able to test for a year, he felt he could be 'quite competitive the next season'.

But Hamilton had not had that luxury. With just a few more scheduled tests remaining before the 18 March start of the new Formula One season in Melbourne, time was running out for Lewis but also for McLaren. The organisation had risked so much on fast-tracking his development on the basis of his proven racing talent.

Dennis was evidently conscious of the threat of his protégé starting the season under-prepared; he knew that just one setback could scupper any chance Hamilton had of making an immediate impact on Formula One, and that significant blockages in his preparation could also make him a danger to himself and others.

Fellow Briton Jenson Button warned Hamilton to avoid the mistakes he made when entering Formula One as a youngster seven years previously. The Honda driver said, 'It's difficult to get respect at that age and you need that. I came in thinking it was all going to be sweet and easy – it's not.'

Valencia

McLaren's hopes for their new MP4-22 car were built around a will to banish the reliability issues that haunted them in 2006. The machine they brought to the grids in 2007 was 95 per cent redesigned and hand-built, tailored and specifically set up for each driver. Seven were produced, each one costing several million pounds. The question that was being asked throughout British motorsport prior to the new season and within the realm of Formula One was: 'Will this car be the making of a triple World Champion and put a rookie on the podium?'

On 15 January 2007, McLaren presented their new car to the

world amidst the strikingly innovative and futuristic buildings at the heart of the Spanish city of Valencia. It was the perfect backdrop for the launch of the new 'Woking Wizard's' team, with their new cars, a new sponsor and new drivers. The show closed the roads for a night and created a 4km racetrack to show off both drivers and their cars.

The evening before the launch, Lewis said the ambience was 'just, very surreal – knowing that I'm here not just as a guest, I'm here as a race driver; the whole atmosphere already, this evening is looking quite impressive and I can imagine tomorrow … it's just getting better and better. The biggest part of it is the media. The attention, the amount of money that's put into it is unreal.'

McLaren had brought their entire pit crew to Valencia just as they would for a Grand Prix. Ron Dennis told his team, 'I appreciate and am very respectful of the fact that your primary purpose is to drive cars in our racing team but that's not the priority of the next 24 hours. You will have to sense the speed; we've lit the circuit.'

Dennis smiled as he told his troops, 'We have an expression in England; it says you should never bite off more than you can chew.'

He might well have come close to that point in Valencia.

The press call was just a taste of what was in store for Hamilton in the coming months. He commented, 'For me it's really exciting … it's my first time at a launch and to be standing next to this guy [Alonso] as a driver is quite a special thing.'

With the aristocracy of motorsport watching, and more people lining the streets than attend a Grand Prix, the cars had to be prepared to full race specification to get them round the circuit. Nothing on the night could go wrong.

The McLaren drivers took to the streets in their race cars that sported fresh livery. Inside the main venue, 1,000 guests were invited to watch a Formula One spectacular with the drivers playing central roles. But the real high point of the evening took place outside, on the streets of Valencia. National hero Fernando Alonso was back in front of a quarter of a million of his fellow Spaniards who had turned out to watch. The double World Champion addressed the throng: 'Welcome to Spain, my home country. I brought a few friends with me, to introduce you and to celebrate this fantastic evening. I present my new car, and the Vodafone McLaren-Mercedes team. Please enjoy the evening.'

Anthony Hamilton was agog at the whole affair: 'It's bloody amazing, the whole thing … but it is the fumes and the noise that you like, isn't it, really.'

Lewis dealt with the media with the same skill he had demonstrated in connection with all his McLaren duties thus far. At the city's Restaurante Submarino, he addressed guests before moving from table to table to respond to journalists' questions. In the process, he repeated the objective he shared with Dennis a dozen years before and told how he was 'very relaxed but extremely excited. To have come off such a fantastic season in 2006, the icing on the cake was getting the drive alongside Fernando. In terms of my life, nothing has changed … but now I have to start on my next chapter of life, which is becoming a World Champion.'

During the evening, Alonso pointedly noted that Lewis had 'no experience' of Formula One, but conceded that the young Englishman brought 'fresh ideas' to the McLaren team.

Lewis told how he was looking to make a podium within 'one or two years'. But there were not a few of us in the motor-racing public that were predicting this would happen much sooner, and, of course, come Melbourne in March 2007, we would be proved right.

As the invited guests took their seats, there was standing room only around the improvised circuit as the time came for the McLaren racers to hit the streets in their 230mph supercars that, if need be, had the capacity to move from 0 to 60 in 2.3 seconds. Lewis looked composed as he was introduced to the thousands of Spanish fans. He waved to them from the back of an open-topped Mercedes before transferring to his Formula One car to demonstrate his ability, showing that the hype wasn't just all torque, cruising the tight little route that had been constructed around the Ciudad de las Artes y de las Ciencias, the centre of Valencia. For Lewis that was 'something incredibly special ... Starting the New Year as a Vodafone McLaren-Mercedes Formula One driver is extremely exciting. I am very excited about the launch of the new MP4-22 and just being there as a Formula One driver. Sounds strange every time I say that, but I am going to enjoy myself just as much if not more than the fans! I think that the team's car has been by far the most elegant car on the grid for years and, in 2006, the MP4-21 took beauty to another level. The new 2007 Vodafone McLaren-Mercedes MP4-22 is off the hook! Just wait and see; this car will blow the socks of anyone who even looks at it!'

When he looked back on the preliminaries to the evening and the tour around the course in Mercedes S Class Saloons Hamilton recalled, 'We sat on the back of the SL55s and went round waving for 4km, and it seemed to last forever but it was just an unreal feeling. I've never had that feeling before. Really just proud to be there and proud finally to be a driver for McLaren.

After his excursion around the crowded Valencia streets in his MP4-22 Lewis was typically pragmatic as he headed back to the festivities: 'It was quite tough actually, there was no grip out there, absolutely no grip, so I went out on new tyres and came back on new tyres.'

The day culminated with fireworks, an outdoor performance by the Cirque du Soleil and an extravagant dinner at the City of Arts and Sciences, a futuristic 'city within the city', which is made up of some of Europe's most fantastic architecture. The complex, designed to celebrate the coming of the 21st century, gives the impression that one has just been transported to some advanced civilisation in another universe.

As Lewis continued to chat confidently to the media in the underwater restaurant Submarino, Arun Sarin, Vodafone's chief executive, took to the stage to repeat his organisation's alliterative, but not entirely inspirational, maxim: 'Red! Rock-solid! Restless!'

Thereafter, Lewis returned to the platform to meet Redmond Carter, the lad who would play him in the massive advertising campaign that was about to be started in the UK. Lewis smiled as he said of the handsome young lad who would represent his childhood self, 'I wish I'd been as mature at that age.'

Living the Dream

Early in January 2007, Ron Dennis made the decision to limit the media's access to Lewis, not wanting him to be 'distracted' during his initial season in Formula One. Dennis was conscious of the growing hype worldwide that was being generated around Hamilton and revealed that McLaren would deploy a policy of 'controlled exposure' of Lewis during 2007. He made no secret that he was determined to avoid any advertising campaigns that aimed to use Lewis as an 'ethnic type', being conscious of the dangers of giving Lewis too much media coverage. He commented on the threat of over-exposing Hamilton, 'the idea to put up the whole Lewis story' was 'a global issue' and all that could be done was to look to follow a 'path of quality-controlled exposure, with fair rules of engagement'. He told how McLaren would make the driver available to the media but would 'certainly limit' exclusive interviews, as they are 'massively time-consuming and can be very intrusive and distracting for a young driver. In some instances, it's like the young driver being thrown to the wolves and that certainly isn't going to happen.'

However, this statement was contradicted to some extent by Hamilton's involvement in the huge nationwide advertising campaign that started in the first part of 2007 with the potential to become a global project. With Lewis already the poster boy for Tag Heuer, the luxury-watch manufacturer and a long-time McLaren partner, and Steinmetz, one of the world's most exclusive diamond houses, providing the glitter of a diamond earring to Lewis's accessories, this was always going to happen despite the best intentions to the contrary. Lewis is a talented, handsome, clean-cut, well-behaved, polite and articulate winner, a sponsor's dream. American singer, rapper and producer Pharrell Williams is among many who have plans to work with Hamilton in the future. One of the first to get a leg up on the Hamilton bandwagon, Williams said Lewis was 'a good kid and represents a lot of humility. He thinks everything is achievable when he puts his mind to it ... It's not about the money either, it's about the heart and the mind.'

A predictable variation on the sound bites that had started to surround Hamilton in 2007, the statement attempts to depict Williams – who, when interviewed in the pits at the 2007 United States Grand Prix, talked of being involved in the Hamilton 'brand' – as being uninterested in the financial potential of such a venture. Whether Williams was motivated by money or heart and mind remains to be seen, but what is clear is that he certainly wants to be associated with what Lewis is and represents – or a piece of the Hamilton action.

Another new Hamilton admirer is P.Diddy, who some newspapers have reported as being a 'hero' to Lewis, and, it was said, the music of the formerly named Puff Daddy (whose nearest and dearest know him as Sean Combs) was heard five years ago coming from the stereo of Lewis's first car.

Combs and Lewis met at the Concert for Diana at Wembley in the summer of 2007 where Combs told the racer that, if he won at Silverstone, he would throw a party for him. Lewis said he couldn't believe that the rapper wanted to talk to him. It seems the Diddy man (from Harlem, rather than Knotty Ash) wished the racer luck and told him that he 'wanted to share my victories'. Lewis described this as a 'big motivation' for him.

One might be forgiven for thinking that the vultures are gathering about Lewis, but it's likely that, as on the track, Hamilton knows all the moves. His support of young drivers, his attitude to fans and the way he stands respectfully under the Union Jack as 'God Save the Queen' becomes the background theme to another victory all demonstrate that he understands the percentages. But he has openly declared that he only has a few real friends, despite inevitably being courted by a grid-load of wannabes and transparent hangers-on. He has vowed that he will never ditch old friends for those attracted to his fame and has admitted that he finds it difficult to trust people, believing that trust, like respect, needs to be earned: 'I can count my friends on one hand and I keep them close to me … It's easy to see the people who are trying to cling on.'

Naturally, family is Lewis's first priory. In this, he is wise and one hopes that, if he loses anything as a result of his success, it won't be this.

'If you can drive, you can drive' is an often-heard mantra in the motor-racing world. But being able to drive well is *not* a passport to finding a place in among the elite of motorsport. Many fall by the wayside on the way up, and there are even those who have to some extent made it, but find themselves outcasts if not immediately successful.

There are those who say that car racing is the last 'true' sport in that it remains faithful to the code that dictates that the first to take the chequered flag is the winner. It has to be agreed that in a unique sense the sport it is a great equaliser. Theoretically, people from every and any background can get in a car and race against each other competitively. Drivers come from many nations and in many sizes, cover a relatively wide age range of backgrounds and there are both male and female racers (although they rarely race against each other for reasons that are not altogether convincing). People with mental and physical handicaps race cars, and there are gay and heterosexual drivers. In fact, you can find professional racers that fit into one or more of any number of categories

So, variety seems to be ingrained in motorsports. However, historically, there have been noticeable limitations on diversity within Formula One. It is not an altogether straightforward task to discover why there are not more black drivers in the category, even in marketing terms alone. Putting talent to one side – where it has often been put for too long – there is a vast virtually untapped demographic that just needs a role model to open it.

However, to successfully compete in Formula One, you need finance and plenty of it. Without generous sponsorship, it is hard to break into the professional ranks without a contact 'on the inside', unless you are born into a family with a background in the sport, as many Formula

One drivers are. This makes it difficult for whole groups of people to find representation on the automobile-racing circuits of the world.

Hamilton turned 22 in 2007 but, with his slight build and clear skin, he continues to look like a teenager. However, that wasn't quite young enough for advertising agency Bartle Bogle Hegarty (BBH), who portrayed him as a child (played by nine-year-old Londoner Redmond Carter) in a television campaign for Vodafone that was launched in Britain during March 2007, in time for the new Formula One season. The young Lewis is seen racing a toy rocket ship around the galaxy, as a voiceover tells the viewer, 'When we are young, we all have dreams of speed and excitement and adrenaline. Some have those dreams and they don't quite happen.'

The implication of the advert was that, with the right mobile phone, an individual can achieve anything they wish and Hamilton is the example of a young man living his dreams, which people of all colours and classes can relate to.

Handsome, polite, courageous, self-effacing and devoted to his family, at the start of 2007, Lewis looked nearly too good to be true and was a world away from the ubiquitous stereotype of young black men that is continually presented in the media. Little wonder the hounds of advertising grabbed him. They clearly believe that his marketing potential is huge.

Hamilton is the diametrical opposite of the 'bad (sad) arse' rapper, backward baseball cap perched jester-like atop a hooded head or the droopy-drawers gangster/clown, shoelaces trailing, a false limp, grasping his crotch like a pilgrim might hold a relic before a shrine. These are the caricatures, some sucking dummies, that so many young black men have been seduced into depicting themselves as by the (mostly white) media vultures of the music industry. This sick parody of 'fashion' makes them look like they are literally falling apart, having nothing to hold them together. They roam around the urban wastelands, seemingly to the uneducated eye as doubly incontinent, carrying the burden of facial expressions that mimic the mock anger and vacancy of those who manufacture the pap noise they are 'medicated' by; repetitious dirges of drab, joyless doggerel. Unknowingly, they sacrificed their potential dignity on the altar of a heatless and thus impotent rebellion; there is nothing more conformist than mass non-conformity.

As he entered Formula One, Hamilton had the style that comes of a personal integrity that demanded that the world moved to his resolve and not the other way round. He seemed every inch a person that leads from the front, finding no attraction in being part of a following pack.

But, perhaps most interestingly, the Vodafone campaign shows Lewis to a mass audience as a black person 'making it' in what is taken to be a traditionally middle-class and very white sport and as such he has become a powerful indication that black people in Britain are moving up into the middle class. This is a huge compensatory force to the British media's seemingly constant insistence that most of Britain's youth population, and particularly black youth, are locked in a crime- and drug-infested underclass.

Lewis, portrayed as a successful motor racer, helps open doors for a sport that's looking to win over new markets and audiences while being painfully aware that ethnic diversity is not its strong point. At the same time, the image Hamilton represents also challenges the ill-defined notion that black people only do well in track and field because they are built physically differently from white people. There is, of course, some truth in this, but we are *all* built differently, and, taken to extremes, this position humiliates black athletes because it misses the fact that physiological advantages do not of themselves produce talent, which is only generated through focused and disciplined hard work. The most powerful lesson I have been taught in a lifetime in sport in general and athletics in particular (close to 20 years as a participant and around the same amount of time as a practising, qualified club coach) is that the greatest gift a sportsperson has is their ability to train regularly and hard. This, together with the confidence this brings and a will to win, will nearly always defeat the genetically endowed but indolent crowd who may shine as an 11-year-old but be off the map by the time they are 18.

It certainly can't be said that Lewis Hamilton has succeeded in motor racing because of a biological lucky dip. He has reached the acme of his sport in the same way that all black sportspeople (all *people*) excel: graft, commitment and a determination to prevail and be first. As such, the Vodafone campaign might well have more important and lasting outcomes than just selling telephones or Formula One.

But Hamilton, who inside Formula One is already known simply as 'Lewis', would be good box office in any circumstances and for those who do not pay too much attention to motor racing, despite all the resistance to the analogy, he could be as groundbreaking as Tiger Woods ('the most gifted of Thai sportsmen ever', as I recently heard him referred to!) was in golf.

But, as Hamilton took his first steps into the Formula One arena, the only race issue for most knowledgeable fans was whether or not he would be on the podium after the next race. In the last analysis, it is that which makes him interesting. Without that, he is little more than a nice young bloke with a winning smile ... but let's not underestimate those qualities; they too should be appreciated for the rarity they are.

Lewis played a crucial role in the marketing of Vodafone. The mobile-phone company were looking for him to produce similar levels of publicity to those generated by David Beckham in the former England soccer captain's Vodafone-branded time with Manchester United – although, it has to be said, Lewis makes ol' Goldenballs look a bit like Slowpoke Rodriguez (cousin of Speedy).

Ron Dennis renamed the 2007 season as 'Vodafone McLaren-Mercedes' (VMM), but expressed concern that market research carried out the previous year indicated that McLaren was viewed by the public as 'cold, grey and unemotional'. The ideal answer to that was believed to be Lewis. Dennis believed that, through Lewis, McLaren would demonstrate that 'we are full of emotion and we are going to facilitate people realising their dreams'.

However, when you listen to Dennis speaking to Lewis over the in-car communications after a Grand Prix, even when he's won, whatever he says sounds about as emotional as 'I'll get the kettle on then'.

Vodafone's global director of brand, David Wheldon, was equally keen to create a dynamic image: 'This is a wonderful young man, inspirational to all sorts of people. It's probably the same kind of empathy and success we had in the early days of Beckham. We were very lucky when we first started sponsoring Manchester United – that was on the upswing of Beckham. I hope this is going to engage the British public with Formula One in a way they haven't before.'

In terms of marketing, Lewis is gold standard. His rise to fame and fortune is the stuff of fairy tales and feel-good movies. Growing up in Stevenage, in a household dominated by hard work and breaching the problems associated with restricted finances, he competed on the kart tracks with the children of wealthier families and left them far behind. But, while Hamilton's track skills provide the main conduit for sponsor interest, he has an engaging personality to go with all his other qualities; he is rarely seen without his warm and attractive smile and is at ease with the media. His dual English/Afro-Caribbean background can appeal to a broader demographic than previous British motor-racing idols; the likes of James Hunt and Damon Hill did not have his 'street cred' or his taste for R&B, funky house and hip-hop, in particular, Kanye West and Pharrell Williams. (Although it must be said Nigel Mansell probably had *Coronation Street* cred!)

The original concept for the BBH campaign featuring Lewis was premised on the image of a young lad standing on a chair, looking into a mirror and seeing a motor-racing driver in the reflection. The 'Where you finish is up to you – make the most of now' theme identifies the significance of time to the phone company sponsors and the motor-racing team.

One poster, which was scheduled to be seen all over the UK, included Lewis's own words of appreciation at having risen to a status where he partnered Fernando Alonso in the 2007 VMM line-up: 'Every time I start the car, I smile. When I pull down my visor, I smile. When I pull out of the garage, I smile. I'm just living my dream.'

Vodafone looked to exploit the fresh image that Lewis has with the aim of producing exclusive video content for the company's phone subscribers. A documentary about the new VMM team was made including a video diary by Hamilton. The phone company had previously been involved in the sponsorship of Michael Schumacher's Ferrari team, which won them business in Italy and Germany, critical new markets. However, by backing Ferrari, the British phone company was something of an appendage in an aristocratic Italian court.

The bottom line was that Vodafone's David Wheldon appeared pleased with the new representation of his company's product. This was just as well, as the advertising campaign cost millions of pounds. This huge investment in Hamilton occurred before he had even driven in competition for his new team, which demonstrated the power of the belief that Lewis would become a sporting icon. This was not just because he was young and good-looking, as youthful and attractive racing drivers are not exactly scarce. It was blatantly tapping into and attempting to replicate the 'Tiger Woods effect' in the Formula One milieu; Lewis is seen as having the potential to do for motor racing what Tiger did for the image of golf. This is happening regardless of what Ron Dennis or McLaren might desire.

Crash

The Valencia launch night over, the team decamped down the road to the Ricardo Tormo race circuit to begin the real work of testing the new cars with their new drivers on board, and it was there that the reality of Formula One racing awaited the apprentice racer. On the afternoon of Thursday, 25 January 2007, during a closed test session, an ominous silence fell over the track like a huge dark, damp blanket. The McLaren pit crew realised there was something wrong. News came in that Lewis's car had left the track. It was only 10 days after the unveiling of new MP4-22 in Valencia. A fire engine followed by an ambulance was despatched to the scene of the accident. The test session was immediately suspended as the McLaren crew waited anxiously at the other end of the circuit. Only moments before, Lewis had been travelling at 185mph.

In Formula One, it's not so much a question of *if* a driver will have an accident as *when* they will crash the car; hurtling around, feet first, at 220mph, almost day in and day out, in many ways sets up the impetus for an accident waiting to happen. From time to time even the best of racers will make a mistake or somebody else will; cars fail, or the track conditions catch drivers out. The day of any crash is a bad day; no team will be pleased about it. But there was something of an over-reaction by the media about Lewis's mishap in Valencia.

Although immediately after the accident happened a freak gust of wind was cited as a possible cause, in the first instance it was not possible to say whether mechanical failure or driver error was the cause of the shunt, but a McLaren spokesperson confirmed, 'Lewis had an accident at the circuit in Valencia this afternoon, the cause of which is being investigated. Lewis is uninjured; however, the MP4-22 is badly damaged and will not be repairable in Valencia to allow him to continue his test programme tomorrow.'

In fact, Hamilton had merely dropped a wheel over the kerb and crashed into the barrier; it was the sort of incident that can occur two or three times a day at any winter test. Teams clear the bits up and, if they can, repair the car and get back on the track a day or two later. However, because it was Hamilton who had the accident, the focus of so much interest and hope in British motorsport, his crash was made to look like a disaster, which it patently wasn't: Lewis walked away with a bruised knee! But his car did need shipping back to the Woking factory to be rebuilt.

This first notable accident in Formula One for Lewis left him a spectator on the final day of the three-day test session. Fernando Alonso continued the team's testing programme alone.

Although Lewis was said to have been eagerly anticipating the following week's testing, again in Valencia, the crash was a considerable setback to driver and team. At that point, McLaren had only two versions of their new charger available, and the team faced a race against time to fix the car for the next test, scheduled to start on the following Tuesday.

The crash was all the more unwelcome for Hamilton because of McLaren's target, motivated by necessity, to give Lewis a concentrated education in Formula One racing during winter testing. This was only Hamilton's fourth test session, and the first with the MP4-22. To make matters worse, Lewis's running had been curtailed in each of those four tests. In November, there were two separate mechanical failures during a test in Barcelona.

After an exasperating week of waiting, Lewis was back out on the Valencia track. He got 120 laps under his belt and concluded with the fastest time ahead of the other eight drivers testing that day.

Lewis reflected on the crucial moments of his January experience in Valencia: 'I went into the first corner a little bit faster than usual just trying to find the limit of the car and lost the back end and went flying backwards into the wall. You know when you're flying backwards at 170mph it's actually quite exciting. But then you're like "Shoot! It's coming" and then you hit the wall.'

Indy Lall, the test team manager for McLaren Racing, commenting on the episode, poured some oil on the turbulent water: 'He's young. He's at the early stages of his top-level career ... he's doing his job. It's one of those things; it's gonna happen. In many ways, you can say that it's good that it's happened earlier rather than later.'

Considering the incident, Anthony Hamilton told how, other than Lewis's health, he always worries about the car: 'It's a multi-million-pound car we're driving. I feel sorry not just for the car but for everybody, the team, the investors, the sponsors, because it's expensive crashing a Formula One car. He smiled. 'And we like to pay for the things that we break, but we just can't afford that one.'

Reflecting on Lewis's crash, Damon Hill commented, 'Some drivers cope by getting back into a car, if they've got a car to get back into, and they just carry on and forget about it. You go from being completely in control of what you're doing to being just a passenger watching the bits just fall off the car.'

But Lewis seems to have got better as he has gained horsepower and that is what is really important. Faced with the 750bhp packed by a modern Formula One car, Lewis shows a calm confidence, even though he's crashed the monsters.

A few days after Lewis's unfortunate event in Spain, the former McLaren driver David Coulthard – who, at 35, would be the oldest man on the 2007 starting grids following Michael Schumacher's retirement – tried to ease the commotion surrounding the rookie's setback, amid media speculation that it was a driver error at turn one. The Alba Ariel declared that he expected his fellow Briton to surface from his first significant Formula One crash as fast and as brave as before. During the unveiling of the new Red Bull at the Circuit de Catalunya, the Barcelona track where he made his race debut in 1994, Coulthard told the media that that the shunt didn't matter: 'It is what it is. You drive cars quickly and occasionally you drop them ... It's not a problem. I destroyed a Williams on the day that Frank [Williams] came to Jerez to tell me I'd got the drive for this Grand Prix. I had never damaged a Williams in the two years that I had driven there ... I still don't know today whether I dropped it or something broke. But it was a moment that passed, and I knew I would be racing again that weekend because it's what I love to do.'

Coulthard stated that he had never been worried by accidents, apart from a plane crash in 2000. Even then, he was back racing in qualifying for the Spanish Grand Prix three days later.

After surviving that disaster in which the pilot sadly died, Coulthard had to disconnect himself from what had happened, although probably not in any conscious way. This doesn't mean that he had walked away from the wreckage feeling nothing. He may possibly have caught sight of the dead pilot, but, for him to have returned to dicing with death so soon, he had to have a means to quickly detach himself from the trauma he must have felt. This exemplifies how drivers who inhabit the 'altitude of danger', wherein Coulthard has not only survived but thrived, develop a means of dealing with extreme circumstances while avoiding the type of emotional ordeal that those of us who exist on a 'normal' plain might experience in the same circumstances.

Coulthard would have reacted in a similar way on the track; the plane crash was another accident, something not to be analysed, intellectualised, certainly not something to dwell on. He survived and then went back to work, back in the race – literally.

Referring to Lewis, he added, 'If he's sore, I'm sorry for him. But I don't doubt for one moment that he'll get back in the car and do the same thing because that's what racing drivers do. We don't have an imagination for the injury; otherwise we'd never get into the car in the first place. Of course, if something happens you are going to hurt yourself, and at worst kill yourself. But, if we turn that thought into a known fear, then we'd be doing something else.'

Coulthard said his initial response to the episode, which made headlines in the British press, was to fault the McLaren team rather than Hamilton: 'I crashed McLaren cars, I have to say, more often than not because of car failure ... McLaren have had their fair share of testing-car failures. So, when I see that he's crashed the car, the first thing that I think is "Has the car broken?" rather than "Has he run out of talent?"'

The Twynholm-born driver took the opportunity to defend himself following his apparent criticism of McLaren for recruiting Hamilton to Formula One in 2007, despite his lack of experience. The Scottish racer, who was entering his 14th season in Formula One (in 2007, only three drivers in the history of Formula One, Riccardo Patrese, Michael Schumacher and Rubens Barrichello, had driven in more races), was attacked by a range of people within the sport for his seeming censure of Ron Dennis and his team. Coulthard, who insisted that he had simply pointed out Hamilton's inexperience, asked, 'Why would I want to say anything negative about someone I believe is a clear talent and deserves to be in Formula One?'

He said that he wanted to be quite clear about what he had said about the matter as he felt as if he'd been used, and represented as saying McLaren's decision was wrong, but, according to Coulthard, 'I never said that at all.'

Having known Hamilton since the McLaren man's childhood, Coulthard claimed to consider him a friend and that there had been times throughout his teenage years when Lewis had come and asked Coulthard for advice. DC claimed he had always 'given him my opinion. So it's very disappointing when I see headlines saying, "Coulthard slams McLaren's decision".'

For Coulthard, Lewis was good enough, so therefore his age was not an issue, but he admitted he 'had made the mistake of trying to give a ... slightly more detailed answer. That was to say he would be a more complete driver, because he would be a more complete person, with the benefit of time.'

But the Scot stuck by his assertion that, if Hamilton had taken a year of testing, like Fernando Alonso and Heikki Kovalainen had, 'there is no question that would make him a better driver. Not necessarily quicker, but more able to deal with what he is going to deal with this year.'

For Coulthard that was not 'slamming', it was an observation and an opinion. He concluded, 'So is there any link between me "slamming" their decision to rush the first black kid into racing with him crashing the car? None whatsoever!'

However, before this, in December 2006, Lewis seemed to have taken the hint and, probably in an attempt to lower the general expectations about his chances on the circuit, he speculated in *El Mundo Deportivo*, the Spanish nationwide daily sports newspaper, that it was possible he might not win a Grand Prix in his first campaign for McLaren, despite the probability that he would drive potentially one of the best cars of the season during his debut year. He told how he understood that it was going to be difficult, but that, like all the drivers, his objective was to win. However, he did not consider winning an immediate necessity and that his priority for

2007 was to continue to grow as a driver. He said that he would be lying if he said he wanted to finish 10th and perhaps the opportunity to win would come during 2007 but that it might not happen until 2008. However, he claimed that he was also realistic and knew that his team-mate was going to be Fernando Alonso: 'The team knows that I am young and that I will need some time ... I think I can do a good job. I believe that I have qualities that are similar to Alonso but I am going to have to work really hard, also on my fitness, because, although I feel comfortable in the car, my neck muscles still need work.'

When reflecting on the winter testing that is part of the vital preparation of Formula One drivers, Damon Hill has argued that it 'is essential but there comes a point where you have had enough of all the rehearsals and the pretend racing. You just want to get down to the real action.'

There's little doubt that Hamilton, waiting for the season to start, would have agreed with the former World Champion. Lewis told how, with his potential trip to Australia getting ever closer, the thought of lining up on the starting grid in Melbourne on 18 March was giving him 'goosebumps': 'There's not a day that goes by that I don't think about it. I'm just on a unique roller-coaster ride right now and loving every minute of it. I can't wait until the first race. I really can't wait.'

SILVERSTONE

Bring me my Bow of burning gold:
Bring me my Arrows of desire:
Bring me my Spear: O clouds unfold!
Bring me my Chariot of fire!

'Jerusalem', William Blake

Thursday

On the Thursday before the British Grand Prix, Hamilton had paid
a visit to the Daytona track in Milton Keynes to watch the top 10
racers in the 'Stars of Tomorrow' series. He spent his time at the
circuit cheering on the young drivers and signing autographs. He
commented that he had not seen a kart race for a long time and that
the experience had been 'good fun' and it had 'really brought me
home'. He told the racers that, if they had ambitions to make
Formula One, they needed to work hard at school as well as at their
racing in order to be able to deal with the technical demands of the
sport and the media. He concluded by telling them, 'Never give up –
Keep fighting.'

Later, Lewis told how he had noticed one lad who was barely able
to see over the wheel and thought to himself, 'That was me.' He
recalled how as a boy he had met David Coulthard, who had

encouraged him, but that in the main most drivers didn't give him much time. 'So I always said to myself that it would be important to give youngsters as much time as my schedule would allow. Give them positive advice.'

Caroline Hoy of the BRDC has pointed out the tremendous job Lewis has done working with young karters and how, in the Mini Max class, he sponsors the 'Lewis Hamilton True Grit Award' that is given to the young driver who achieves the most overtakes in a race.

Friday

Looking at Hamilton's prospects for the British Grand Prix, Sir Jackie Stewart talked of how Lewis claiming a podium place in each of his first eight Grands Prix was spectacular and unprecedented, but warned that Ferrari and Alonso remained serious threats and that, 'whether you're a champion boxer, a racehorse or a football team, you can't go on winning seamlessly. In sport, there is always a glitch.'

The tartan-trousered Knight of the track cautioned that, sooner or later, Lewis's run had to come to an end, whether because of 'mechanical failure, an incident on the first corner, a fuel leak or bad weather'. Although the Scottish triple Champion hoped that wouldn't happen at 'Silverstone of all places', with a dollop of Dunbartonshire pragmatism, he pointed out, 'Lewis is going to have a nation's hopes on his shoulders this weekend and we've got to be fair to the boy. It's asking an awful lot for this run of podium finishes to continue unabated.'

David Coulthard, the last British driver to win a Formula One Grand Prix at Silverstone when he drove for McLaren in 2000, pointed out that, even though expectations were high, Lewis had to be one of the favourites to win in Northamptonshire, and, given the rich history of motor sport in Britain, it was 'fair and reasonable to expect' a homegrown driver to win the event. He said, 'It would be fantastic if Lewis did do it. He certainly has the best opportunity to do so, and it would be the icing on the cake of a very short career.'

BBC columnist and Renault driver Heikki Kovalainen thought that, although Lewis had shown that he was able to manage pressure, he believed that being in front of his home crowd could negatively affect Hamilton's driving, but conversely it would provide him with 'an extra boost' seeing the massive crowd that would come to support him.

Sir Sterling Moss, winner of the British Grand Prix in 1955 and 1957, remarked, 'Silverstone is a tough circuit but Lewis Hamilton is a tough guy.'

However, Damon Hill, the 1994 winner and last home driver to achieve pole at the British Grand Prix in 1996, cautioned, 'This is motor racing – nothing is certain.'

Nigel Mansell, victorious in 1986, 1987, 1991 and 1994, thought that McLaren and Lewis's talent, alongside the will of the Silverstone crowd, was a winning combination.

According to Martin Whitmarsh, 'Since I joined McLaren in 1989, I've worked with a lot of great drivers, including [Alain] Prost, [Ayrton] Senna, Mika Häkkinen and now Fernando Alonso. It's pretty clear that Lewis ticks all the necessary boxes. It's too early to analyse, but if the trend continues there is no reason why he could not become the greatest driver ever.'

For Ron Dennis, Lewis had 'enough Brownie points to avoid criticism if something goes wrong – which it will. It's inevitable for any driver. But you have the feeling that Lewis will be able to cope with that too.'

Saturday

It was decent weather for the qualifying day alongside the A43, clear and dry. But the wind, the speed of which registered 2.5 m/s, was blustery and unpredictable as it blew across the old airfield circuit. Stowe and Club corners were going to be places where the drivers would really feel the gusts as they came in at 150–160mph, but Copse (turn one) would be the place where everyone would suffer. It is one of the fastest corners in Formula One; drivers can take it at 170mph as it has plenty of grip and the camber falls away. It can make a racer feel they can have a go at it, but the threat of missing the line and losing time is a constant. Silverstone's 3.2-mile (5.141km) route provides a relatively open track with the biggest infield of any Formula One circuit. So, as the cars tear around, the race can be dominated by the direction and strength of the wind.

Although it needs updating, Silverstone is one of the most demanding of Formula One tracks and is still among one of the great high-speed tracks in motor racing with 60 laps, for which Schumacher holds the record (1:18.739 set in 2005). The British Grand Prix asks a lot of racers but gives a great deal to the watching public. In 2006, Alonso was first home for Renault.

Drivers love the circuit – a racer can be almost halfway round, down to Stowe, before a thought has to be given to hitting the brakes hard. The track has a lot of grip and some challenging corners, while, at the same time, it demands a lot of physical effort from racers.

The best crowd Silverstone had seen for a good while came to witness the qualifying competition. Indeed, the turnout for the qualifying on the Saturday beat the 2006 race-day attendance. For British drivers, the fans at Silverstone have always been worth at least a couple of tenths of a second, although famously Nigel Mansell claimed they could motivate him to the tune of a 'second or two' a lap. For him, the fans at Silverstone made his job easier, giving him more commitment and more power.

Hamilton emerged from McLaren's futuristic motor home waving to the crowd and smiling.

As the drivers went out, a tail wind blew down Hangar straight to the turn through into Stowe corner, just one of the likely nasty surprises the qualification could throw at the racers.

The Ferraris had looked powerful in practice. The McLarens were just about able to stay with them on a single lap. Räikkönen had been the quickest, and the Ferrari looked faster on the long runs. It was pretty plain to most seasoned observers that the Woking drivers would have to control the race from the front of the grid and look to spoil Ferrari's race, so the competition for pole seemed crucial.

At the start of qualifying, Hamilton's car was looking completely animated. Lewis's loose driving style, which sometimes gives the impression that he's going to lose it at any moment, was causing his vehicle to scrabble around like an animal.

He was ragged in the first session of qualifying, but Lewis, the last driver to cross the line that Saturday, produced a 'Fifth Cavalry' crescendo to that final lap of qualifying that made him the first British polesitter at Silverstone for 11 years; it was a run of pure genius belying once more the number two emblazoned on his car.

Anthony was jumping around in front of the crowd. He told the watching TV cameras that Lewis could never be ruled out and that his son was loving his time in the car. Not for the first time he made the point 'that's what it's all about'.

But Alonso, Räikkönen and Massa (in that order) were going to be behind him on the grid the next day and everyone concerned knew Hamilton would still have to produce a marvellous performance on race day to capitalise on his hard-won pole.

At the press conference after his fine show in qualifying Lewis told how the day had been tense but that he had done 'a sweet job', although he gave a lot of credit to his team who had made sure he had got out quickly. He said how he could still hear everyone outside and that he felt the support he got was 'unreal … it was an extra buzz'. But having got carried away with his own celebrations he had nearly lost his voice screaming as hard as the fans were. Hamilton confessed that he liked to 'make people happy' and seeing the sea of flags bearing his name gave him 'a lot of energy'.

Winding down in the McLaren motor home after qualifying, Lewis said, 'I don't know what to expect. All Grands Prix are intense but this is intensity multiplied by five.'

He told how he was 'blown away' by achieving pole position and said that it felt better than winning a race because in a race gaining the glory is 'lengthened out' while qualifying is one big hit. He reflected, 'I make it harder for myself, positive or negative.' He conceded that the Ferraris were quick but that he was picking up 'a lot of positive vibes from the fans, a lot of energy'.

During the season, Lewis made the top names challenge him rather than the other way round, and, in a little more than 100 days, he was now the youngest British driver on pole in the history of the British Grand Prix.

Sunday

As the Royal Marine band entertained the vast crowd, the wind speed at Silverstone had dropped to 0.7m/s. The track temperature was 35°C, some 15°C below the air temperature. Humidity stood at 44 per cent.

Hamilton had won three times in four races on this circuit, once in F3 and twice in the GP2 event of 2006. Before his first Formula One race at Silverstone, Lewis had a quiet breakfast and composed himself in his dressing room. He has said, 'I'm not into all those lucky charms or voodoo routines before a race. I just talk to my family and get into the dressing room, focus and get out there. I'm lucky to have such a tight family supporting me.'

However, since Melbourne, the Hamilton father and son team had been doing the same things in the same order and fashion, creating a sort of 'custom and practice' in preparation. According to Anthony, he and his son never talk just before a race: 'We just laugh at the unreal world we're living in.'

The grid and garages at Silverstone looked like they had developed a magnetic pull on British entertainment and sporting celebrities. The likes of the Beckhams rubbed shoulders with Prince Michael of Kent, who would present the podium drivers with their trophies at the conclusion of the Grand Prix, but before the start he was in deep conversation with Anthony.

Ferrari chose to start the race on soft tyres (Lewis had chosen to start with the hard option). This would give the Italians a potential three metres from the off.

The Englishman went through his warm-up slowly to take in the energy of the spectators. Following the warm-up lap, Massa stalled on the grid and, as such, was obliged to get himself into the pit lane where he would start while the pack were sent round again.

At Silverstone, both sides of the grid have plenty of grip and as such offer a good start. That's just what Hamilton got, good but not great, and moved to the middle of the track. Räikkönen, having found ample traction, went to the left, but had to take avoiding action as Lewis, showing a 'Senna attitude', aggressively defended his pole placing on the run down to Copse. Alonso found third place. The ferociousness shown by the Brit was beginning to be something of a characteristic of his and seemed to indicate he was developing something like the uncompromising start style that had been associated with Michael Schumacher.

However, Lewis wasn't able to get totally away from the Finn, who, feeding off of the Herts man's slipstream, hung in the 22-year-old's mirrors like a spectre, showing that he clearly had the faster car.

By lap 10, there was just 2.5 seconds between the leading trio. Three laps on, Hamilton was struggling. Räikkönen attacked him at Brookland but didn't get by. However, it would not have escaped Räikkönen's notice that Hamilton's tyres were not giving him grip and the subsequent lock-ups would have given the Ferrari man encouragement.

Of the leading three, Hamilton was the first into the pits on lap 16 and this demonstrated that he had won pole position probably, at least in part, because he had been driving the lighter car. Attempting to get away before his crew had finished refuelling cost Lewis time. He later said that he had selected first gear, was ready to go and thought he saw the lollipop move, so he let the clutch out too early. For many, it was his first big mistake in a Grand Prix but Hamilton confessed that this wasn't his first mistake of the season but 'the first one that people have seen'.

Räikkönen came out ahead of the homeboy from his first stop (two laps after Hamilton). After the race, he reflected on his tactics against the Championship leader: 'Once we knew we had enough fuel, I was able to close on Lewis and try to overtake him. But we knew he was coming in so didn't take too much of a risk.'

However, Alonso was still out on the track, and leaped to a close to four-second lead after his first stop two laps later, pushing Hamilton into third. When Alonso darted into the pits, Massa pushed into sixth. The Brazilian was only 20 seconds behind him.

The race became a straight fight between the Spaniard and Räikkönen, as Lewis fell further behind seemingly every lap. The leading pair looked well matched.

Between laps 30 and 31, Hamilton had an awful time in the traffic having lost two seconds per lap in the previous three laps. He was 21 seconds behind Alonso.

Congestion caused the extent of the lead to fluctuate, but, with less than half the race to run, Alonso pitted. He came out to find his way blocked by traffic while Räikkönen was left with a clear path.

Hamilton took on soft tyres during his second pits but the stop was not as quick as Alonso's.

If Räikkönen had been packing no more than a couple of laps' worth of fuel, the Spaniard would have had a chance of holding on to the lead, but finishing on hard tyres, well ahead, he had stayed out and in a light car had registered some quick laps. Ferrari's Red Baron went on until the 43rd lap and roared out of pits holding a 3.2-second lead.

Emphasising the consciousness that had been lurking all weekend around Silverstone that Räikkönen and Ferrari had been the most powerful combination at the event, the Finn extended his lead as the race came to a close.

Hamilton seemed to be in free fall at points, but, never in any danger from Kubica in fourth place, he managed to hold on to what he had. But the BMW man did well to fend off Massa's charge in the closing laps.

Räikkönen claimed back-to-back wins, became the first driver in the 2007 season to triumph in three Grands Prix and notched up his 12th Grand Prix victory almost uncontested in the latter stages of the race in a time of 1:21.43.074 (222.629km/h).

Alonso and Lewis took up the other podium places.

In the last analysis, the front of the field was relatively spread out. Massa did well enough to finish 54 seconds off the lead, but would have done better had Kubica been less adept at getting in his way. Alonso was 36 seconds in front of Hamilton.

Hamilton got a standing ovation from the Silverstone crowd going down into the garage and it was hard to disagree with Anthony when he declared they were 'the best fans in the world'.

With the European Grand Prix just two weeks away, McLaren promised Lewis a swifter car for the encounter at the Nürburgring and he vowed to raise his own game. Unfortunately, he would not be allowed this luxury. Having started from pole in Canada and America, Silverstone was the first time he had lost a Formula One race from the front of the grid.

He had been dogged by handling problems but it was his ninth consecutive podium of his nine-race career, something the likes of Juan Manuel Fangio, Jackie Stewart, Alain Prost and Ayrton Senna had never achieved. The only Briton to have matched Lewis was Scotland's Jim Clark in the process of winning the 1963 World Championship, but he didn't do it in his initial nine Grands Prix.

While acknowledging his achievement, Lewis was clearly not satisfied with his Silverstone result and conceded after the race that Ferrari had the edge and the greater power on the day. While he doesn't take a great deal of instruction from anybody and largely makes his own decisions, at the same time Hamilton deals with the consequences of his own actions. Reviewing his performance post-race, he said, apart from qualifying, he had struggled the whole weekend to find some balance and could not match the pace of the Ferraris. He took responsibility for making the wrong choice of tyres, which he saw as also being a significant element in his team's failure to overcome the Italians – Lewis went two stints on hard tyres and might have been better to have started out on soft tyres like Räikkönen: 'I think I made a wrong decision with the set-up. I chose a different rear end to Fernando and I think it really caused me problems during the race and even in qualifying.'

Hamilton said he had chosen to start with the soft option but hadn't wanted to take the gamble of the tyres 'going off too quick'. He told how the last stint was better in terms of stability of the car.

Although it had not occurred to him to give up in any way and he 'kept pushing, because you never know what might happen', the team had given him instructions 'to wind the engine down' but he continued to 'keep pushing' himself to compensate for that.

Although Lewis declared that without his team's support it would have been a harder race, he assessed that he and the team needed to 'push even more … I am still learning, there is still time to find in myself. Knowing the tracks should make it easier, but I have been here [Silverstone] before and I struggled all weekend in terms of pace.'

Hamilton conceded that, having been on pole, he felt he could have achieved a better result. He admitted he had made mistakes and, while he thought the race had been 'interesting' and that he had started well, towards the end of his stint the tyres were falling away. He reflected, 'It wasn't the best result for us.'

He also rued his error during his first pit stop. But Lewis was still able to draw the positives from his weekend: 'To come into your first home Grand Prix and still end up on the podium after having trouble is good.'

And Anthony spoke wisely when he said, 'You can't be disappointed, it's about having a mature head: take the best out of a bad situation; bring the car home; collect the points.'

As is his habit, Hamilton made the most of his situation, but he had not judged his tactics well and Ferrari got the overall strategy right. In truth, Lewis, as the race wore on, dropped pace. At points, he was one second per lap slower than Räikkönen and Alonso. His pit stops had been poor and he knew the car wasn't going to get him a win, so he had played safe and looked to get home for a podium place. While this had been sensible, his choice had been limited by circumstance, but some of that had been of his own doing and his inexperience had been exposed for the first time in Formula One.

For those of us who were at Silverstone on that Sunday, it was hard to escape the fact that Massa, although only finding fifth place, had been the most impressive racer in the field. Having started behind the pack, he and his car had looked in another class until he was shut out by the Pole in the BMW at the end of the race. Up to that point, he had cut through his opponents like a Brazilian dagger scything through soft Northamptonshire cheese (if there was such a thing). Hamilton did not miss the quality of the little man's charge and was convinced he would have probably not made the podium if Massa had not stalled on the grid and started the race from the pits.

This said, Ron Dennis cited team tactics as the root of Räikkönen's success at Silverstone. He argued that McLaren had made the wrong choice of tyre and had asked both the drivers to turn their engines down with Germany in mind (McLaren had to use the same engines they deployed at Silverstone in the European Grand Prix), but this fails to really explain lack of speed. Dennis judged that his team didn't have the pace of the Ferrari cars but claimed that both his drivers did a great job and had gained valuable points despite the problems.

It was true that things still looked healthy on paper for both Lewis and McLaren. Hamilton had 70 points and Alonso 58. Räikkönen's score climbed to 52 and Massa was on 51. McLaren, with 128 points in the Constructor's Championship, were a long way ahead of the 103 Ferrari had gathered. But, with both the Italian team and their Finn fully functioning and in the ascendant, Ron Dennis and his team were probably looking towards Germany with some justified concern. The European Grand Prix was going to be favourable for Ferrari. The prancing horse is always strong at the Nürburgring; it's a smooth circuit and that would suit the Italians. But it is of course McLaren's partner Mercedes' home territory so maybe the German air made a difference, at least for Alonso.

While Bernie Ecclestone said he would have liked to see Hamilton win the British Grand Prix in his rookie year, he argued that the result at Silverstone was good for Formula One in general, as it opened out the season, showing it to be a much more competitive affair than might have been the case had McLaren and Hamilton prevailed.

Straight after the British Grand Prix, McLaren headed for testing at Spa-Francorchamps in Belgium to begin preparations with their engine partner Mercedes-Benz's home race at the Nürburgring on 22 July, the European Grand Prix.

Martin Whitmarsh told how his team had new aerodynamic components and a variety of other parts to put on the car. He predicted that the Surrey men would come out of testing with a faster vehicle. But he acknowledged that Ferrari were also likely to do some work on their car. 'So it's down to who improves their car the most.'

For all this, Whitmarsh believed that fortune would swing both ways in what was shaping up to be a classic and exciting season. With nine races run, McLaren had put a car on the podium 16 times, but for Whitmarsh things were so close in terms of performance and reliability that either manufacturer could trip up. He declared, 'If just one of your cars doesn't score points, then the pendulum swings very quickly.' A prophetic statement as it turned out in terms of the next race.

Considering Lewis's conviction that he would improve his performance, Whitmarsh said that he had 'done a fantastic job' and that the whole team had to raise their game, as the challenge to win the World Championship was tougher than ever. But he emphasised that McLaren had to get some speed from somewhere. However, for Whitmarsh, it was 'extraordinary that Lewis feels like that, but that's one of his great strengths. He knows the team's working very hard; he knows that we expect to have a quicker car at every successive race.'

After his British Grand Prix debut. Lewis had a takeaway Chinese with his family. One wonders what the fortune cookies had to say.

CONCLUSION

I will not cease from Mental Fight,
Nor shall my Sword sleep in my hand,
Till we have built Jerusalem
In England's green & pleasant Land.

'Jerusalem', William Blake

In the summer of 2007, Sir Stirling Moss declared that Hamilton was the best racer he had ever seen. Sir Jackie Stewart, who tasted 27 victories and 43 podium appearances during his 99 Grand Prix career, agreed that the young man from Hertfordshire was on the way to becoming a legend of the track, perhaps even having the potential to better Michael Schumacher's seven world titles. However, Sir Jackie believed Lewis should avoid cultivating the kind of strategic callousness characteristic of the German's style and urged him not to replace his clean-cut image with the ruthlessness of winning at all costs.

At the Royal Bank of Scotland Grand Prix Challenge, the 68-year-old flying Scotsman stated, 'Great drivers don't need to be ruthless or to resort to things which are morally or physically inappropriate ... Invariably, the great names in Formula One, like

Juan Manuel Fangio, Stirling Moss and Jim Clark, were clean and well mannered. Michael's seven world titles was incredible, but a couple of actions he took on the track affected the kind of respect he might have been afforded.

'More than being a World Champion, I'd love to see Lewis Hamilton become a *great* Champion ... And, yes, I think he can do it. Of the millions who hold a driving licence, thousands make a living out of motoring but only 22 of those become Grand Prix drivers in any single year. Among those 22, there may be six who are special, two or three who are extraordinary, and, in a lifetime, maybe one genius ... and I think Lewis has the look of a genius.'

Stewart sees Hamilton as one of the first of 'a new generation of what I call properly prepared, professional racing drivers. I'm talking about fully rounded; Schumacher became that, but even Schumacher wasn't as good as he should have been, not in terms of the driving but the total package.'

But, almost as the former triple World Champion spoke, the environment was impinging on the dream world that the realm of Formula One can sometimes be.

Ferrari-Gate

On 6 July 2007, Telegraph.co.uk told the world that, the previous evening, the FIA had announced that they were to initiate a 'major investigation' that would constitute 'one of the most important probes in Grand Prix history'. This followed an internal investigation by McLaren concerning allegations that the team might have an involvement in 'spying and espionage' after a 700-page file detailing the technical background of Ferrari cars had been placed in the hands of McLaren's chief designer, Mike Coughlan. Coughlan was suspended while Nigel Stepney, Ferrari's technical manager, was sacked.

The internal investigation had exonerated McLaren employees of incorporating Ferrari intellectual property into McLaren cars and the organisation invited the FIA to conduct a full review of the cars.

Ron Dennis, commenting at Silverstone in July, said that nothing had occurred inside McLaren that would compromise the team's integrity and saw the whole affair as a 'silly sequence of events that's going to damage people's careers but won't damage McLaren [as there was] no intellectual property of any other Grand Prix teams in our cars and there never will be'. He concluded by saying that McLaren would be 'transparent and co-operative with the FAI investigation'.

Honda had met with Stepney and Coughlan about possible employment, but, according to Honda, they had been talking to a lot of people about jobs, but nothing confidential had come into it. People often move around within Formula One and intellectual property in effect moves with them. Teams have employed photographers to take pictures of cars for years, but what was beginning to be called 'Ferrari-Gate' had been made public.

But none of this seemed to overly concern Hamilton who, speaking at the TAG Heuer pre-Grand Prix lunch on the eve of the British Grand Prix, declared that he wanted to spend the rest of his career with McLaren. His seeming lack of apprehension appeared to be well founded as, on 26 July, the FIA ruled there was insufficient evidence to show any wrongdoing by McLaren. But the whole affair – alongside the accusations about McLaren's performance at Monaco and Alonso's alleged remarks about the team favouring Hamilton – was making the season feel like a long and complex one.

Watching Lewis

McLaren have been massively protective of their number-two (officially) driver. But the media of the world is now hungry for stories about Hamilton and have been shown to pounce on the slightest morsel. For example, at the Spanish Grand Prix in 2007, Lewis speculated, almost light-heartedly, that he might one day have to move to Switzerland for tax reasons. Although his father quickly countered this potential 'bombshell', the story would have been taken by many as showing Hamilton to be a selfish, money-grabbing individual, who, although quite prepared to stand under the flag, was not prepared to honour his roots and stick with the country that nurtured his talent. Although such an interpretation might be shallow and not reflect Hamilton's nature, it would be a bone that a press which makes a sport of building up heroes and then destroying them would be only too happy to throw to a disappointed but newspaper-buying public. However, Hamilton is not only generally careful about what he says; he is also circumspect about his reading habits. He claims he has never read about what he says because he knows what he has said. Even if his family ask if he wants to read something in praise of his efforts, he refuses just in case he begins to say to himself, 'Wow, it's great.' Lewis has told how he wants to keep his feet on the ground and avoid feeling himself 'floating'. He claims not to 'feel like a superstar' and doesn't 'understand people who do have that mentality'. For Hamilton, at the moment, what he does is 'just a job [but] a fantastic job'. He sees himself as 'just Lewis. I've always been Lewis, and it's important to me to stay like that.'

Hamilton's impact is already going way beyond Formula One. Michael Eboda, of *New Nation*, has seen his influence on Britain's black communities and tells how Lewis is 'incredibly popular' and 'a fantastic role model'. For Eboda, this is as true of Anthony as it is of his son as 'he sends out a message to people that that is the way to bring up a kid'.

Damon Hill has remarked that he has 'never seen a rookie as good as him ... Nobody has. He's coped with everything he's faced. He's been superb.'

Even the imperturbable Bernie Ecclestone has expressed his excitement about Hamilton, saying in 2007, 'He's got a lot of talent ... The guy's a winner. It became clear pretty quickly that he will win the Championship ... but I don't think this year. It would be asking a bit much and be a lot of pressure to expect that. It would be fantastic if he did, but I don't think we should talk about that at this stage.'

The Price of Fame

Hamilton's success provides him with another big challenge: in the space of a few months, he went from being virtually unknown to becoming one of the most recognised faces in the world. Since Silverstone 2007, Hamilton has been mobbed by fans everywhere he goes, but he says that his fans mean a lot to him and that he is always happy to chat and sign autographs: 'Teenage girls come up to me with their mums and their brothers ... Everyone wants autographs and photos ... it is flattering. I like it when people – girls and boys – come up to me and say well done ... My life has totally flipped upside down and I'm on a different planet ... All this popularity is something new to me. From being someone virtually unknown, I've become someone everyone recognises. I've had lots of letters from kids who say that they want to be a driver like me.'

This life must take its toll and it has to be said the signs of it happening were there from the middle of the 2007 season: 'Being away from your family, not seeing your friends, doing media and marketing appearances, it all builds up more and more. It is extremely tiring.'

Favourite Son?

Lewis has little truck with fear and has shown that he has the ability to get at his rivals mentally. However, the dividing line between confidence and arrogance is fine and some drivers have had their fill of 'Hamilton Fever'.

Four-time World Champion and former McLaren driver Alain Prost has remarked, 'Ron Dennis fell in love with him ... To the point where everyone thought he was his nephew. He has helped him, advised him and, above all, financed him, without knowing that he would get to this level.'

This in itself can look like favouritism even if it isn't, and given this closeness it can be hardly surprising, as he pushes all before him, that Lewis might be seen by the likes of Alonso and others, to be getting preferential treatment.

It also seemed that Hamilton was never absent from national television screens. From early summer 2007, Abbey was using him to publicise its takeover by Santander, and Lewis was the central figure in the massive Vodafone campaign of that year. Added to this, the youngster did not endear himself to some of his rivals when he described backmarkers in the Canadian Grand Prix as 'monkeys'.

Bigger Battles

After the 2007 British Grand Prix, Lewis was the major player in two of the most intriguing team battles Formula One had seen for a long time. His ongoing spats with Alonso took fans back to the late 1980s and early 1990s, when the then McLaren racers Ayrton Senna and Alain Prost had mutual enmity. Although this was not what was going on between Hamilton and the Spaniard, who were more awkward with each other than hateful, Lewis had said, 'We are both fighters…We both want to win, simple as that.'

At the same time, the war between McLaren and Ferrari for both the Constructors' and the Drivers' Championships was the best for many a season

However, Frédéric Vasseur, who knows Hamilton better than many, sees his mental strength and determination as his main weapon and this may well be crucial to him as he faces the challenges to come: 'His determination is at the basis of everything. If he has to spend two hours on something, then move on to the next thing, he can engage with it 100 per cent but then afterwards knows how to relax and enjoy himself. He still comes to eat here, for example, with us in the F3 paddock. He spent three hours here on the Friday night of the French Grand Prix weekend among us. He has the ability to put barriers between different aspects of his life. When something goes wrong, he tries to solve it rather than complain about it.'

And, of course, the foundation is always there: 'When I'm away from the track, I try to just live my normal life, playing golf with my dad and playing video games with my brother.'

Whatever the pressures, overall, Lewis gives every sign he is enjoying the experience and, as Frédéric Vasseur has said, 'There are millions of people who want to be in Formula One and yet a lot of Formula One drivers don't smile. Lewis is different.'

BIBLIOGRAPHY

Our Grands Prix now are ended. These our drivers,
As I foretold you, were all racers and
Are sped into air, into thin air:
And, like the baseless fabric of television,
The McLaren Technology Centre, the gorgeous Circuit de
    Nevers,
The Brickyard, the great FIA itself,
Ye all which it inherit, shall dissolve
And, like this track faded,
Leave not a car behind. We are such stuff
As dreams are made on …

Adapted from *The Tempest*, Act IV, Scene i, Shakespeare

Belton, B. (2006) *Fay Taylour: Queen of Speedway*, Panther
Publishing Ltd

Complete Encyclopaedia Formula 1 (2006), Parragon
Book Service Ltd

Daley, R. (2005) *The Cruel Sport: Grand Prix Racing 1959–1967*, Motorbooks International

Donaldson, G. (2002), *Formula 1: The Autobiography*, Weidenfeld Nicolson Illustrated

Hayhoe, D. Holland, D. (2006) *Grand Prix Data Book: A Complete Statistical Record of the Formula 1 World Championship Since 1950*, H Haynes & Co Ltd

Higham, P. (2003) *International Motor Racing Guide: From Formula 1 to Nascar*, David Bull Publishing

Jones, B. (Ed) (2006) *ITV Sport: The Complete Encyclopaedia of Formula One*, Carlton Books Ltd

Lang, M. (1983) *Grand Prix: Race by Race Account of Formula 1 World Championship Motor Racing: 1977–80*, G T Foulis & Co Ltd

Legate, T. (2006) *100 Years of Grand Prix: Celebrating a Century of Grand Prix Racing 1906–2006*, Touchstone Books Ltd

Pritchard, A. (1991) *Grand Prix Racing: The Enthusiast's Companion*, Aston Publications Ltd

Pritchard, A. (1990) *Marlboro McLaren*, Aston Publications Ltd

Prost, A. (Foreword), Kapadia, B. (Ed) (2006) *Formula One: The Story of Grand Prix Motor Racing*, New Holland Publishers Ltd

Menard, P. Cahier, B. Roebuck, N. (2006) *The Great Encyclopaedia of Formula 1*, Chronosports

Turner, B. (2004) *The Pits: The Real World of Formula 1*, Atlantic Books

Journals, Newspapers, Magazines, Websites
Auto Motor und Sport
Auto Racing1
Auto Racing Daily
Autosport
AutoWeek
Barnet Times
BBC Top Gear
Bishops Stortford Citizen
Borehamwood and Elstree Times
El Mundo Deportivo
eMercedesBenz
Express
Formula One News International
Formula One Racing
F1Racing.net
Fast Car
Ferrari: http://www.ferrari.com
Formula Magazine
Formula One Online
Formula Renault 2000
Guardian
Harlow Star
Hemel Hempstead Gazette
Hertfordshire Mercury
Herts & Essex Observer
Hoddesdon and Broxbourne Mercury
Independent
Independent on Sunday
ITV Sport – Formula One

Justin Wilson: http://www.justinwilson.co.uk

Karting Magazine

McLaren International Ltd: http://www.mclaren.co.uk

Mallory Park (Motorsport) Ltd

Mail

Mail On Sunday

Metro

Mirror

MotorSport

Motorsports Almanac

Motorsport.com

Motorsport Today

National Speed Sport News

New Nation

News of the World

Observer

Planet-Formula One.com

Racecar

Racer Magazine

Racing Press

Racingline – The McLaren Group Magazine

Racingweb

St Albans Observer

Star

Stars & Cars – Powered by Mercedes-Benz

Sun

Sunday Express

Sunday Mirror

Sunday People

Sunday Telegraph

Sunday Times

Telegraph

The Comet

The Morning Star

The Times
Times Magazine
This is Hertfordshire
Watford Observer
Welwyn & Hatfield Times
Who Won